The Theatre of Naomi Wallace

The Theatre of Naomi Wallace

Embodied Dialogues

Edited by

Scott T. Cummings and Erica Stevens Abbitt

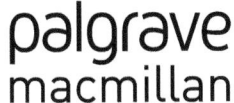

THE THEATRE OF NAOMI WALLACE
Copyright © Scott T. Cummings and Erica Stevens Abbitt, 2013.

All rights reserved.

First published in 2013 by
PALGRAVE MACMILLAN®
in the United States—a division of St. Martin's Press LLC,
175 Fifth Avenue, New York, NY 10010.

Where this book is distributed in the UK, Europe and the rest of the world, this is by Palgrave Macmillan, a division of Macmillan Publishers Limited, registered in England, company number 785998, of Houndmills, Basingstoke, Hampshire RG21 6XS.

Palgrave Macmillan is the global academic imprint of the above companies and has companies and representatives throughout the world.

Palgrave® and Macmillan® are registered trademarks in the United States, the United Kingdom, Europe and other countries.

ISBN: 978–1–137–01791–8

Library of Congress Cataloging-in-Publication Data is available from the Library of Congress.

A catalogue record of the book is available from the British Library.

Design by Newgen Knowledge Works (P) Ltd., Chennai, India.

First edition: December 2013

10 9 8 7 6 5 4 3 2 1

For Leon Katz, my teacher.
—Scott T. Cummings

For Jerry W. Abbitt, Renée Felice Paley Stevens, and C. F. B. Stevens (*fons et origo*).
—Erica Stevens Abbitt

Contents

List of Illustrations	xi
Preface: Embodied Dialogues Erica Stevens Abbitt	xiii
Acknowledgments	xv
Introduction: The Discourse of the Body *Scott T. Cummings*	1

Part I Writings on Wallace

1. Death and Desire, Apocalypse, and Utopia: Feminist *Gestus* and the Utopian Performative in the Plays of Naomi Wallace
   Shannon Baley 19

2. Love in a Wound
   Scott T. Cummings 35

3. Messianic Marxism in Naomi Wallace's *Slaughter City* and *Things of Dry Hours*
   Buell Wisner 45

4. An American Exile in America
   Vivian Gornick 57

5. The City that Embraced Naomi Wallace
   Walter Bilderback 65

6. Naomi Wallace and the Dramaturgy of Rehearsal
   Lindsay B. Cummings 71

7. Naomi Wallace and the Politics of Desire
   Josephine Machon 89

8	Crucial Unspeakables, or Pedagogies of the Repressed: Directing Sex in the Plays of Naomi Wallace *Beth Cleary*	103
9	Mapping *The Inland Sea*: Naomi Wallace's British Epic Drama *Art Borreca*	117
10	Slip's Bluff *Neil Chudgar*	127
11	Journeys into the Heart of Whiteness: A Labor Historian Looks at the Work of Naomi Wallace *Peter Rachleff*	135
12	Unbearable Intimacies: Occupation, Utopia, and Creative Destruction in *The Fever Chart* *Adam John Waterman*	155
13	To Girl or Not to Girl *Erica Stevens Abbitt*	169

Part II Collaborators

Dominic Dromgoole, Standing on Your Head	191
Ron Daniels, Naomi Is Inside My Head	195
Riccardo Hernandez, Designing Wallace	199
Jessica Dromgoole, In the Fields of Naomi Wallace	203
David Gothard, Radical Poetry	207
Ismail Khalidi, Being the "Other": Naomi Wallace and The Middle East	211
Dominique Hollier, Translating Wallace	215
Raz Shaw, Betting on Naomi and The Boss	219
Erin B. Mee, Mindscapes of Palestine	223
Jo Bonney, Directing Wallace	227
Abdelfattah Abusrour, Beautiful Resistance	231
Robin D. G. Kelley, The Facts of Love	235
Bruce McLeod, Nettle Soup	241

Part III Wallace in Her Own Words

Strange Times	247
Seven Poems	251
Let the Right One In: On Resistance, Hospitality and New Writing for the American Stage	257
Manifesto	265
We Are Also Each Other	267
The Fish Story	271
The Tal Pidae Lehrstücke	275
On Writing as Transgression	281
Appendix A: Naomi Wallace Selected Production History	287
Appendix B: Naomi Wallace Play Titles and Their Sources	297
Bibliography	301
List of Contributors	313
Index	317

Illustrations

I.1 Naomi Wallace in Ashland, Oregon, 2013. Photo: Jenny Graham. Courtesy of Oregon Shakespeare Festival — 2
1.1 Richard Thompson (Bunce) and William McNulty (Snelgrave) in the 1996 Actors Theatre of Louisville production of *One Flea Spare*. Director: Dominic Dromgoole. Photo: Richard C. Trigg. Courtesy of Actors Theatre of Louisville — 25
1.2 Tami Dixon (Pace) and Michael Linstroth (Dalton) in the 1998 Actors Theatre of Louisville production of *The Trestle at Pope Lick Creek*. Director: Adrian Hall. Photo: Richard C. Trigg. Courtesy of Actors Theatre of Louisville — 29
2.1 Dianne Wiest (Darcy Snelgrave) and Bill Camp (Bunce) in the 1997 Public Theater production of *One Flea Spare*. Director: Ron Daniels. Photo © Michal Daniel, 2007 — 40
3.1 Phoebe Jonas (The Textile Worker) and Sharon Scruggs (Cod) in the 1996 American Repertory Theatre production of *Slaughter City*. Director: Ron Daniels. Photo: Richard Feldman. Courtesy of American Repertory Theatre — 50
3.2 Roslyn Ruff (Cali Hogan) and Delroy Lindo (Tice Hogan) in the 2009 New York Theater Workshop production of *Things of Dry Hours*. Director: Ruben Santiago-Hudson. Photo: Joan Marcus — 54
4.1 Bill Camp (Bunce), Jon De Vries (William Snelgrave), Mischa Barton (Morse), Paul Kandel (Kabe), and Dianne Wiest (Darcy Snelgrave) in the 1997 Public Theater production of *One Flea Spare*. Director: Ron Daniels. Scenic design: Riccardo Hernandez. Costume design: Paul Tazewell. Lighting Design: Scott Zielinski. Photo © Michal Daniel, 2007 — 62

Illustrations

6.1 Zubin Varla (Remzi) and Richard Dormer (Craver) in the 1994 Bush Theatre production of *In the Heart of America*. Director: Dominic Dromgoole. Photo © Mark Douet/ArenaPal.com — 78

6.2 Robert Glenister (Boxler) and Toshie Ogura (Lue Ming) in the 1994 Bush Theatre production of *In the Heart of America*. Director: Dominic Dromgoole. Photo © Mark Douet/ArenaPal.com — 83

7.1 Sally Oliver (Dee) and Cat Simmons (Jaime) in the 2011 Finborough Theatre production of *And I And Silence*. Director: Caitlin McLeod. Photo: Andrew Reed. Courtesy: Caitlin McLeod — 97

11.1 Sharon Scruggs (Cod), Judith Hawking (Maggot), and Starla Benford (Roach) in the 1996 American Repertory Theatre production of *Slaughter City*. Director: Ron Daniels. Photo: Richard Feldman. Courtesy of American Repertory Theatre — 140

11.2 Michael Cullen (Staddon Vance, kneeling) Jesse L. Perez (Lex), Kevin Jackson (Coyle, with gun) in the 2009 Actors Theatre of Louisville production of *The Hard Weather Boating Party*. Directors: Jo Bonney. Photo: Harlan Taylor. Courtesy of Actors Theatre of Louisville — 150

12.1 Lisa Caruccio Came (Um Hisham Qishta) in the 2010 Pilot Theatre (UK) production of *A State of Innocence*, the first play in *The Fever Chart: Three Visions of the Middle East*. Directors: Katie Posner and Marcus Romer. Photo: Toby Farrow. Courtesy of Pilot Theatre — 158

12.2 Sidney Kean (Mourid) and Daniel Rabin (Sami) in the 2010 Pilot Theatre (UK) production of *Between This Breath and You*, the second play in *The Fever Chart: Three Visions of the Middle East*. Directors: Katie Posner and Marcus Romer. Photo: Toby Farrow. Courtesy of Pilot Theatre — 162

13.1 Lauren Shannon (Pace) and Ben McGinley (Dalton) in the 2011 Rogoff Theatre Company production of *The Trestle at Pope Lick Creek*. Director: Braden LuBell. Photo: Elizabeth Cocco. Courtesy of Braden LuBell — 177

13.2 Jon De Vries (William Snelgrave) and Mischa Barton (Morse) in rehearsal with director Ron Daniels for the 1997 Public Theater production of *One Flea Spare*. Photo © Michal Daniel, 2007 — 179

Preface: Embodied Dialogues

Erica Stevens Abbitt

This book came out of a series of conversations between Scott and me that began in 2008 at the Association for Theatre in Higher Education conference in Denver. We shared a fascination for Naomi Wallace's drama and a desire to create a book that takes full account of the scope and importance of her work. We both agreed that the first book-length publication on the theatre of Naomi Wallace should reflect a wide range of perspectives and approaches. We imagined what we called "a symposium on paper" and set to work.

We came to the project with different orientations and backgrounds. Scott has a particular interest in Wallace's work in the context of contemporary American playwriting. I am interested in the way her plays advance feminist theatre in the twenty-first century and excited about their use as a powerful (even transformational) force for intercultural exchange and progressive theatre pedagogy. Our original exchange expanded into a dialogue with colleagues from a range of countries and disciplines, which has finally resulted in this book, designed to be accessible as well as collaborative: a joint venture providing resources for those producing Wallace's work, teaching her plays, and exploring their significance in contemporary performance.

We have divided the anthology into three sections:

- Writings on Wallace. The first section is a collection of essays on Wallace's plays. Many of these are new, but a few key articles and reprints of important publications have been included. These writings examine aspects of race, class, gender, and sexuality, as well as aesthetic innovations in the plays and their practical application to the classroom and rehearsal studio.

- Collaborators. The second section is a collection of statements by theatre practitioners from North America, Europe, and the Middle East who have worked with Naomi Wallace in some way to bring her work from the page to the stage. The focus here is on praxis as well as vision: the challenges and opportunities of producing Wallace's work from the perspective of those engaged in it.
- Wallace in Her Own Words. The third section includes a sampling of Wallace's writing over the past two decades: poems, polemics, essays on theatre, and occasional scripts, which illuminate both her process and her agenda as artist and activist.

At the end of the book, we have provided a selected production history and a selected bibliography, which includes all works cited in the various essays.

We hope that this volume encourages further dialogue between those who have been exploring Wallace's work—and embodying it in performance—and emerging scholars and practitioners who are just discovering the richness of her innovative, provocative, and inspiring theatre.

Acknowledgments

A book of this nature, drawing on a wide range of perspectives and based in large part on performance research, would not be possible without the work, ideas, and support of many others.

First, we thank our many contributors for taking precious time away from their busy professional and academic careers to join the project. Some of them led us to others, and the book is the richer for their suggestions. For the gift of their knowledge, insight, and experience—and for their patience with the vagaries of the editing process—we are grateful.

At Palgrave, Associate Editor Robyn Curtis and her assistant Erica Buchman have been steadfast, painstaking, and cheerful at every step of their work with us. We appreciate their concerted and professional effort to make our vision for this book a reality.

Gathering illustrations and seeking reprint permissions are challenging tasks that depend on the kindness of others. We want to acknowledge the courtesy and aid of (among many others) Zach Chotzen-Freund, Michal Daniel, Julie Danni, Meg Dobson, Kirsty Gaukel, Vivian Gornick, Biddy Hayward, Siobhan Juniku, Braden LuBell, Doug MacLellan, Caitlin McLeod, Neil McPherson, Katalin Mitchell, Rebekah Paine, Amy Richard, Amanda Smith, and Nicole Estvanik Taylor.

At the University of Windsor, Erica received a sabbatical grant and a Research Grant for Women in support of this project. For their help in this regard, she thanks Pierre Boulos, Bruce Tucker, Diane Awram, Lionel Walsh, and Lori Buchanan. She is also extremely grateful for ongoing support from the School of Dramatic Art and its Director, Tina Pugliese, as well as colleagues in the department and across the university, including Brian Rintoul, Kathryn Brennan, Valerie Newell, Simon du Toit, Johanna Frank, Anne Forrest, and Charlene Senn. At Windsor, Erica was ably assisted by a trio of dedicated, detail-oriented research assistants, Adrianne Clipperton, William Chandler, and Olivia Steven.

Erica also expresses thanks to a wide network of friends and colleagues: for facilitating the research, Kate Harper, Philippa King, and Kate Lushington; for encouragement, Heinrich Falk, Ah-jeong Kim, Sara Warner, and Rose Malague; for their insights on Wallace and other subjects, Gwendolyn Hale, Charles Haugland, Batool Khattab, Sarah Bay Cheng, Claudia Barnett, Kim Solga, Dorothy Chansky, Tracy Davis, and Ric Knowles; and for friendship and guidance that goes back a long way, Sue-Ellen Case.

At Boston College, Scott benefitted from a series of Undergraduate Research Fellowships that made it possible for Cara Harrington to assist on the project: kudos to her for her meticulous care and steady commitment. At an earlier stage, Han Cho also provided valuable research assistance. Scott also wishes to acknowledge the continued support of David Quigley, Dean of the College of Arts and Sciences. And a special nod goes out to Libby McKnight for taking the bait and to Sean P. Murphy for being a rock.

We thank our families for encouragement, particularly our spouses, Jerry Abbitt and Janet Morrison, who provided boundless hospitality and support throughout years of working sessions in Boston and Windsor. To Jerry, thanks for true partnership, vision, *caritas*, love, and support. To Janet, I love you.

Finally, to Naomi Wallace, we feel a gratitude that defies articulation. For your generosity, trust, and unstinting cooperation in the face of one request after another for a script, a contact, a clarification. For permission to include your writing in this book. And most of all, for a body of work that inspires and challenges us with its integrity, tenacity, and creativity.

Introduction: The Discourse of the Body

Scott T. Cummings

Over the past 25 years, Naomi Wallace has established herself as a major contemporary dramatist whose work combines political engagement, stylistic innovation, and erotically charged lyricism in a unique and compelling manner. She has garnered international attention, won prestigious awards, and received numerous commissions from major theatres. Her plays have been produced by the Royal Shakespeare Company and the Royal National Theatre, the Public Theater and New York Theatre Workshop, the Comédie-Française and the Festival d'Avignon, and by regional and provincial theatres on three continents. They have also found favor with fringe theatre groups looking to make their mark and university theatre departments interested in challenging their students with work that examines the relationship between identity and power. Her plays are taught in college drama courses and analyzed from a variety of theoretical perspectives by theatre scholars. She is an original and provocative voice in the theatre of our time.

The Theatre of Naomi Wallace: Embodied Dialogues seeks to advance the examination of her work by presenting a collection of scholarship, criticism, and commentary that constitutes a thorough analysis and a prospectus for further investigation. By way of introduction to Wallace's drama and the essays in this book, this overview falls into two parts: a biographical overview that traces in brief the arc of her career to date and a critical overview that outlines some of the basic elements of her playwriting.

Biographical Overview

Born in 1960, Naomi Wallace learned about the contradictions of life from an early age. She is the fourth of six children born to

Sonja de Vries, a Dutch journalist and activist from a working-class background, and Henry F. Wallace (1915–2006), an international-correspondent-turned-gentleman-farmer and member of the wealthy newspaper family associated with the *Louisville Times*. Legendary in Louisville for his outspoken editorials, Henry was a lifelong activist vocal in his support of Castro's Cuba, the civil rights movement, and gay rights and his opposition to the arms race and the Vietnam War. Naomi grew up with her four sisters and one brother outside of Louisville on a 600-acre farm in Prospect, Kentucky, which remains the family homestead today, protected from development by a conservation agreement. As a child, she attended left-wing demonstrations with family members and went to progressive schools, where her position of relative privilege was highlighted by her friendships with children whose parents earned a living doing manual labor in local factories and farms. As a teenager, she learned to negotiate between languages and countries, as she alternated between Holland and the United States, before and after the divorce of her parents.

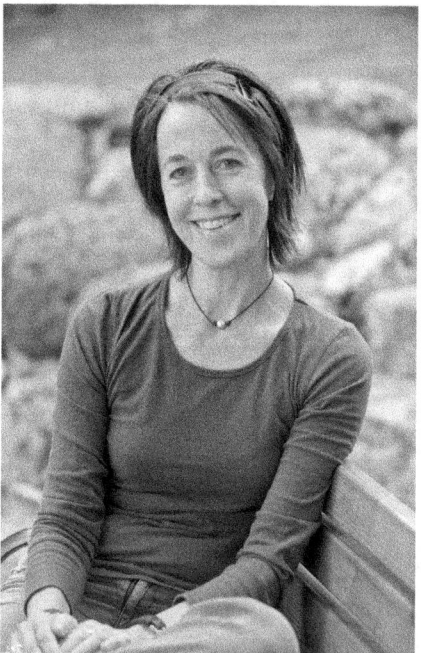

Figure I.1 Naomi Wallace in Ashland, Oregon, 2013. Photo: Jenny Graham. Courtesy of Oregon Shakespeare Festival.

During undergraduate and graduate school, Wallace developed a highly individualistic poetic vision and an ongoing commitment to social and political activism. She received a BA in Women's Literature at progressive Hampshire College in Western Massachusetts and entered the MFA program in poetry at the University of Iowa. As she completed this degree, her writing interests gravitated towards playwriting as a less solitary, less isolating form, and so she took an MFA in playwriting at Iowa as well. Her involvement in theatre up to that point had been minimal. As a graduate student, Wallace came into contact with two teaching artists who supported her professional development. The first was playwright Tony Kushner, who encouraged her to keep writing explicitly political theatre and recommended her to his agent in New York. The second was British director and producer David Gothard, one-time artistic director of Riverside Studios, who provided Wallace with valuable links to the professional theatre community in London. At Iowa, she also met a Scottish-born PhD candidate in English Literature named Bruce McLeod, who became her life partner and collaborator on many plays, screenplays, and other projects. Together, they moved to England in 1997, where they settled in rural North Yorkshire and raised three daughters. The Yorkshire Dales remains her home base today, although she spends time back home in Kentucky on a regular basis.

In the 1990s, Wallace came to enjoy a measure of recognition and success in Britain—rare for an American playwright. Her professional debut came in 1993 when the Finborough Theatre produced *The War Boys*, an exploration of violence and homophobia on the Mexican–US border. That same year, the London New Play Festival produced *In the Fields of Aceldama*, which uses flashbacks and jump cuts to tell the story of a Kentucky farm family defined by poverty, abuse, xenophobia, and despair. Dominic Dromgoole staged two Wallace premieres during his tenure as artistic director of London's Bush Theatre, another venue noted for supporting new plays. First, in 1994, came Wallace's hard-hitting Gulf War drama *In the Heart of America*, with its sharp critique of American foreign policy and its unexpected erotic encounter between two young soldiers. Then, in 1995, came *One Flea Spare*, inspired by the recent Los Angeles riots over the Rodney King verdict as well as the seventeenth-century plague writings of Daniel Defoe. Each play went on to receive the Susan Smith Blackburn Prize for women writing plays of "outstanding quality in the English-speaking world." Also in 1995, Peterloo Press in Cornwall published *To Dance a Stony Field*, a collection of her poems.

Wallace soon found her way onto major London stages. In 1996, Ron Daniels directed the Royal Shakespeare Company production of *Slaughter City*, a neo-Brechtian historical drama about labor, sexuality, and social exploitation set in an American meatpacking plant. Around that time, Wallace was tapped to write a stage version of *Birdy*, the 1979 William Wharton novel about a young American soldier who thinks he can fly, already adapted into a popular 1984 film directed by Alan Parker and starring Matthew Modine. Wallace's adaptation of *Birdy* first played at the Lyric Hammersmith in 1996 and then in the West End at the Comedy Theatre in 1997. That same year, her play for young people, *In the Sweat* (co-authored with McLeod), received a workshop production at the Royal National Theatre. Within just a few years, Wallace was established as a writer of interest and merit.

The American theatre was slower and more ambivalent in its embrace of Wallace's heightened, sensual, and frank political work. Tony Kushner introduced *In the Heart of America* to US audiences by directing a 1994 workshop production at Long Wharf Theatre. The Actors Theatre of Louisville began an effort to repatriate Wallace when it brought Dominic Dromgoole from London to direct *One Flea Spare* at the 1996 Humana Festival of New American Plays. Three Humana world-premiere commissions followed: *The Trestle at Pope Lick Creek* (1998), a Depression-era drama about two Kentucky teens flirting with danger by trying to outrun a train; *Standard Time* (2000), a monologue about a working-class teen who shot his girlfriend because he wanted her car and she threw the keys in the river; and *The Hard Weather Boating Party* (2009), a play about three men who meet in a Motel 6 in Louisville's industrial Rubbertown district to plan a vengeful murder.

From early on, mainstream New York critics were hostile to Wallace's work. When *One Flea Spare* opened at New York's Public Theatre in 1996 in a production featuring Dianne Wiest and child-star Mischa Barton, Ben Brantley, the influential critic of the *New York Times*, described the writing as "stiff, schematic and surprisingly unaffecting" and derided the play as "carved in stone" (1997, 11). All the same, the play received an Obie for Best Play from the *Village Voice*, and Wallace began to receive grants and other awards, including the Fellowship of Southern Writers Drama Award, the Joseph Kesselring Prize for up-and-coming playwrights, and an NEA poetry grant. Vivian Gornick, in a sympathetic 1997 profile for the *New York Times* Sunday magazine (included in this volume), described Wallace as "An American Exile in America." Then, in 1999, her status in the United States received a major boost when at age 38 she was awarded a prestigious MacArthur Fellowship (the so-called genius grant in the amount of $285,000) for a growing body of work described as "provocative and full of haunting images, startling metaphors, and rich language used to comment on issues of class, gender, age, sensuality, and desire." In the fall of 2001, most of that work—including plays for children, poetry, her prize-winning dramas, scripts in progress, and the quirky 1997 independent film *Lawn Dogs*, for which she wrote the screenplay—was showcased in Atlanta, Georgia as part of a city-wide Naomi Wallace Festival spearheaded by Vincent Murphy, artistic director of Theatre Emory.

With widening acceptance in America and continued attention in Britain, Wallace turned her focus more and more to the geopolitical issues of the Middle East. In 2001, at Cooper Union in New York, she produced "Imagine: Iraq" (an evening of staged readings of related plays) with the Artists Network of Refuse & Resist! Wallace's contribution to the program was *The Retreating World*, a monologue commissioned by McCarter Theatre and inspired by a March 2000 article by John Pilger in *The Guardian* ("Squeezed to Death") about the debilitating impact on ordinary Iraqi citizens of economic sanctions. In 2002, she organized a goodwill visit to Palestine by a group of US playwrights, including Robert O'Hara, Kia Corthron, Betty Shamieh, Lisa Schlesinger, and Tony Kushner, to meet with Palestinian theatre artists, including Abdelfattah Abusrour of the Al-Rowwad Center in the Aida Camp. (Their trip is described in the July/August 2003 edition of *American Theatre* magazine.) Wallace used a commission from the Guthrie Theatre to recruit Schlesinger and Abusrour to collaborate with her in writing *Twenty-One Positions: A Cartographic Dream of the Middle East*, a theatrical response to the 430-mile security wall dividing Israel and the Palestinian West Bank that Wallace described in 2006 as "a play with songs, sort of *West Side Story* meets *Mother Courage*" (MacDonald 2006, 100).

Wallace went on by herself to write two short plays set in Palestine. *A State of Innocence* takes place in a ruined zoo in Rafah, where an Arab woman confronts a dying Israeli soldier over the death of her daughter. *Between This Breath and You* presents a surreal encounter between a Palestinian man and an Israeli nurse whose life has been saved by his son's transplanted lung. Developed and workshopped independently, these two plays were eventually bundled with *The Retreating World* to comprise *The Fever Chart: Three Visions of the Middle East*, which premiered in the United States at the Public Theater in New York in 2008 under the direction of Jo Bonney. By then, Wallace had written two more short pieces rooted in the region: *One Short Sleepe*, a monologue for a Lebanese university student with a fondness for spiders who turns out to be already dead from an Israeli air raid; and *No Such Cold Thing*, a one-act about two teenage Afghan sisters and their encounter on the edge of the desert near Kabul with a young Chicano solider in the US army. Wallace has returned to Palestine numerous times since her first visit to promote solidarity with theatre artists there; in 2011, she visited the Freedom Theater in the Jenin refugee camp just weeks before co-founder and director Juliano Mer Khamis was gunned down by an unknown assassin. In an obituary tribute, she called him "a radical's radical" who "believed in active, continual resistance, through a 'cultural intifada'" (Mee 2011, 15). In a broader context, Wallace's mission might be described in similar terms.

Wallace's writings set in the Middle East tend to be occasional pieces, monologues, or short plays written for inclusion in an anthology project or a new play festival. As her career advanced into the twenty first century, she continued to write full-length plays deeply rooted in other historical contexts and events. In 2002, for the Oxford Stage Company, Dominic Dromgoole directed the world premiere in London of *The Inland Sea*, an epic drama inspired by the eighteenth-century landscape architect Lancelot "Capability" Brown and his movement to redesign the English countryside. In 2004, Pittsburgh Public Theatre premiered *Things of Dry Hours*, a taut three-character drama based on Robin D. G. Kelley's *Hammer and Hoe: Alabama Communists During the Great Depression*. The play went on to notable productions at Baltimore's Center Stage, directed by Kwame Kwei-Armah; the Royal Exchange Manchester and the Gate Theatre in London, directed by Raz Shaw; and New York Theatre Workshop, directed by Ruben Santiago-Hudson. One Wallace history play without a track record is *To Perish Twice* (originally titled *Rawalpindi*), a play that takes place in the British War Graves Memorial in Rawalpindi, Pakistan and that lambastes many of the pieties of the British Empire. Commissioned by the Royal National Theatre, the play received a reading there staged by Raz Shaw in 2005, not long after the July 7 terrorist bombings in London. The National declined to pursue the play, and it has yet to be fully produced elsewhere.

Wallace's most recent history play is *The Liquid Plain*, written for the Oregon Shakespeare Festival and its ambitious ten-year commissioning program, "American Revolutions: The United States History Cycle." *The Liquid Plain* takes place in 1791 (Act 1) and 1836 (Act 2) on and around the docks of Bristol, Rhode Island, where two runaway slaves awaiting passage to Africa rescue and revive a drowned white man. They share a troubled past linked to the historical figure of James De Woolf, sea captain, slave trader, and eventual US Senator from Rhode Island. Drawing inspiration and information from Marcus Rediker's *The Slave Ship: A Human History*, the play joins the broader effort to give an identity and even a name to otherwise anonymous figures once bought and sold as property and thereby write them into cultural memory. The mystery at the heart of the play is inscribed in a water-soaked copy of William Blake's *Songs of Innocence*; in a fantastic sequence in Act 2, the spirit of Blake appears to Bristol Waters, "an educated free black woman" come from England to America looking for De Woolf and seeking justice. Speaking of his poem "The Chimney Sweeper," Wallace's Blake says,

> Words are merely what come after love, to placate the emptiness. *(Beat.)* I never was happy with that last line either. Irony is a cheap ejaculation. I prefer its whorish neighbors: polemic, expostulation, mockery, hyperbole, provocation, abuse, which polite society so often misreads in my verse. I'll change that line.[1]

As the writing of this introduction was in process, lines were still being changed during rehearsals for the world premiere of *The Liquid Plain* in July 2013. Even before its opening, the play was awarded the 2012 Horton Foote Prize for Promising New American Play, just one of several accolades in recent years that have reinforced Wallace's importance as a contemporary playwright. Two decades after launching her career with *The War Boys*, Finborough Theatre produced the 2011 world premiere of *And I and Silence*, a play about two American women in the 1950s, one black and one white, who meet in prison and form a close bond that they find difficult to maintain once they return to society. Also in 2011, two small US theatres—Forum Theatre in Washington DC and Chicago's Eclipse Theatre—presented festivals or seasons of her work.

Then, when *One Flea Spare* opened in Paris in the spring of 2012, Wallace became only the second American playwright (after Tennessee Williams) to have a play enter the permanent repertoire of La Comédie-Française, the national theatre of France. In spring

2013, Katarzyna Klimkiewicz's *Flying Blind*, with a screenplay by Wallace, Bruce McLeod, and Caroline Harrington, was released, a suspense film starring Helen McCrory as an aerospace engineer who designs drones for the military and has a passionate affair with a French-Algerian student. Also in the spring of 2013, Wallace became one of nine writers (including two other playwrights, Stephen Adly Guirgis and Tarell Alvin McCraney) to receive an inaugural Windham Campbell Prize for literary achievement from Yale University. The unrestricted $150,000 award makes it one of the largest literary prizes in the world; the citation credited Wallace with mining "historical situations in plays that are muscular, devastating, and unwavering."[2]

Wallace's widely circulated 2008 *American Theatre* article "On Writing as Transgression" issued an unapologetic mandate for the arts in general—and theatre in particular—to empower young artists to challenge the status quo. She echoed the call in her 2013 *American Theatre* article "Let the Right One In" when she wrote:

> Writing that does not actually violate boundaries, that does not enter into the process of trespass, is often a writing that is safe, consumable and shallow. A theatre that does not challenge its own assumptions, its own ignorance, with curiosity and humility is a contracted theatre, a diminished theatre. (Wallace 2013, 88)

Wallace backs up this rhetoric with her ongoing engagement in activist, educational, and artistic collaborations. With Erin Mee and Ismail Khalidi, she is editing an anthology of plays by Palestinian playwrights to be published by Theatre Communications Group. Her plays continue to attract attention in France, where *The Fever Chart* played at the 2013 Festival d'Avignon and a new play, *Night Is a Room*, is slated to premiere in 2014. And there is a co-commission in the works from Actors Theatre of Louisville and Berkeley Repertory Theatre. While the provocative nature of her work seems to disqualify her for success on Broadway, she is at this moment a celebrated playwright whose work is widely produced in the English-speaking world and beyond and studied more and more by students and scholars of contemporary theatre. She continues to work on projects that combine political critique with poetic humanism, creating plays in which, as she said in an interview with her friend Tony Kushner, "the structure of power suddenly becomes visible" and change becomes possible (Kushner 1998, 258).

Critical Overview

To dissect the body politic, Naomi Wallace writes plays about the politics of the body. "I want to challenge the smug notion that there is political and non-political theater," Wallace said early in her career. "One usually gets called a 'political' writer when one's politics do not coincide with the mainstream. When we think of political theatre, we think of something dry about ideas. I love ideas, but I like trying to put issues of the heart onstage and seeing how those issues are affected by the world around us" (Mootz 1994). While the intersection of the personal and the political has been a focus for two generations of women playwrights (and a number of men, as well), Wallace's approach is unusually penetrating and imaginative.

From the very beginning, she has demonstrated a sustained commitment to examining the relationship between identity and power as it is manifest in the corporal experience and physical well-being of her characters. In this regard, her oeuvre needs to be seen as a series of embodied dialogues in which personal desire is negotiated within the structures of race, class, gender, age, nationality, and sexual preference. As one essay after another in this volume points out, her characters are defined in large part by these basic traits. To those who would criticize this approach to character as materialist or schematic, Wallace might well reply, "Yes! Exactly!" An individual Wallace character needs to be seen as the embodiment of his maleness or her femaleness, his wealth or her poverty, his blackness or her whiteness, and so on. But they are more than this. Wallace also endows her characters with an imagination that goes beyond the confines of social identity and that often reveals itself in lyrical stage gestures that express a world of possibility. She portrays her characters as resistant to demographic determinism by having them figuratively or metaphorically cross the border—or violate the boundary—between one social identity and its opposite. This dialectical crossing can take theatrical form, with a character putting on the clothes/costume of the 'Other' or taking on the role of another and 'acting it out.'

Alternatively, it can take the form of an intimate physical encounter that closes the gap between two social opposites. This contact, often graphic in its violence or its sexuality, foregrounds the corporal presence of the actor in performance and demonstrates how the exercise of power is played out—or resisted—through the human body. The action of a Wallace play often pivots on these moments. Writing in

The Guardian, Lyn Gardner (1996a) described one of them in the production of *Birdy* at the Lyric Hammersmith:

> There is an extraordinary scene in Naomi Wallace's adaptation of William Wharton's novel. Sergeant Al sucks up some porridge, cups his lips over the open, greedy chick-like mouth of his boyhood friend Birdy and feeds him like a mother bird. It is a moment of almost obscene intimacy, so naked and tender that you want to avert your prying eyes. It is like watching someone make love or give birth.

This "almost obscene intimacy" is fundamental to Wallace's dramaturgy. Again and again, she presents characters who come to erotically charged moments when they make themselves vulnerable, risk physical injury, relinquish power, and submit to the will of another. This discourse of the body is the lifeblood of her theatre.

There are other recurring strategies, techniques, and motifs that can be seen to define Wallace's body of work. As further context for the discussions ahead, here are a few of them.

Historical Materialism and Work

Wallace's theatre offers a version of historiography based on the notion that we can—and should—re-examine the assumptions we make about our national and cultural narratives of conflict and triumph. The most obvious reflection of this is its historical settings: 1665 London at the time of the plague (*One Flea Spare*); 1760s England in the middle of the landscape movement (*The Inland Sea*); the late-eighteenth century slave trade in Bristol, Rhode Island (*The Liquid Plain*); the steel industry of 1930s Birmingham, Alabama (*Things of Dry Hours*); the Gulf War of the early 1990s (*In the Heart of America*). But Wallace's plays are more than costume dramas. They are inquiries into history, both how it is made and how it is written. Influenced by Howard Zinn and other radical social historians, they offer a robust corrective to the outworn Great Man theory, focusing instead on everyday men and women caught up in the gears of Capital and War and Empire.

This means that they are always about work and the wear and tear it takes on the body of workers. Her characters are soldiers, sailors, shipbuilders, steelworkers, meatpackers, and factory workers: in short, wage earners whose daily lives are defined by long hours of manual labor, repetitive movement, and threat of physical injury. As Wallace sees it:

> How the body is damaged through labor intimately affects how you function in the rest of your life. Whether you can lift your children, and you can't because your back has gone out from work, or if you have carpal tunnel syndrome and you can't cut out little paper dolls with your grandson...Whether you even feel enough energy to have sex after working fourteen hours, those things affect your personal relations. It's interconnected, what happens in the world, how we labor, and what happens inside us and in our relationships with others. (Julian 2004)

Wallace's populist reworking of history involves a painstaking and focused dramaturgical process. "It is my own ignorance that often leads me to choose to write about a certain era or event in history," she has said. "I do research, interviews; sometimes, if possible, I travel to the area I am writing about. And I attempt to learn" (Svich 2009, 92). Wallace is well-known for the thorough historical research that goes into her plays, often spending years, off and on, reading, gathering materials, making notes on a subject, and then "usually a few weeks before I write I try to forget everything. I read poetry or look at paintings so that I think in a different way" (Istel 1995, 25). Her published scripts often include an extended bibliography of works consulted, and the dialogue of her characters often includes arcane details pulled from her research, such as the technical list of Gulf War bombs recited by Craver in *In the Heart of America*, the architectural elements of the Homa Umigdal (Wall-and-Tower) houses built by Zionist settlers described in *A State of Innocence*, or the anatomy of the common mole included in *The Tal Pidae Lehrstücke*. *A Hard Weather Boating Party* was inspired by a series of interviews that Wallace did with working-class residents of Louisville's industrial Rubbertown area. It is not an oral history or a docu-drama or a history play in the strictest sense—none of her plays is—but it is a work of the imagination steeped in historical research into the lives of the marginalized, the exiled, and the dispossessed.

Over time Wallace has developed relationships with a cadre of progressive historians—Robin D. G. Kelley, Rashid Khalidi, Peter Rachleff, Marcus Rediker, David R. Roediger, among others—whose scholarship has grounded her work and with whom she maintains an active dialogue as she develops a new play. While the scripts that emerge from this process are uniquely her own, the element of collaboration here is essential: in her words, "these writers give me fire" (MacDonald 2006, 98). This spirit of collaboration goes beyond historians to include directors, designers, dramaturgs, actors, and the occasional co-authors who work with her to make a play. Theatre is labor, too, she reminds us, and needs to be seen as choosing to acknowledge its own means of production and its own history or to ignore it.

Danger Zones

Wallace's plays often take place in danger zones, settings that by their very nature pose a threat to the human body. *The War Boys* takes place at a checkpoint on the Mexico–Texas border where three young men gather to help authorities spot and catch illegal aliens sneaking through holes in a barbed-wire fence. *In the Heart of America* is set during Operation Desert Storm in the Persian Gulf and includes an extended dialogue that details the destructive capacity of a number of high-tech weapons. *One Flea Spare* takes place in London during the Great Plague of 1665, which forces a wealthy trader and his wife into quarantine with a debased merchant seaman and a street urchin. *The Inland Sea* centers on the threatened removal of a group of villagers as the English countryside around them is being torn up as part of a massive reconfiguration of the landscape. Inspired by a strike at the Fischer Packing Company in Louisville, Wallace set *Slaughter City* on the assembly line of a meatpacking plant, where workers trim animal carcasses with sharp knives and show off their scars from on-the-job accidents.

In a similar fashion, *The Hard Weather Boating Party* takes place in a motel room in Louisville's Rubbertown, home to nearly a dozen large chemical plants infamous for toxic emissions and related public health issues. The eponymous setting of *The Trestle at Pope Lick Creek* is a place where Depression-era teens race the 7:10 freight train across a bridge for sport. "The engine herself's one hundred and fifty-three tons," says tomboy Pace Creagan. "Just cold, lip-smackin' steel. Imagine a kiss like that. Just imagine it" (Wallace 2001, 285). The places of Wallace's Middle East plays—a bombed-out zoo in Rafah, a hospital clinic in West Jerusalem, Iraq, Lebanon, Afghanistan—bear witness to the uncounted human costs of perpetual conflict there. In one way or another, Wallace situates her characters in places where by definition the body is especially vulnerable to injury or illness and where the workings of capitalism, nationalism, and imperialism are indelibly marked on human flesh. Where they live is life threatening; where they work can kill them.

Ghost Girls, Time Travelers, and the Living Dead

No wonder then that so many Wallace characters are dead. Or somehow already dead and alive all at once. The plays are populated with characters who are not bound by time or mortality, giving them an affinity with Noh plays, traditional fairy tales, and Latin American magic realism. Sometimes they take the form of time-travelers, figures tied to a historical event who slip forward in time to join or haunt the present-tense action of the play. *In the Heart of America* includes two such characters from 1968: Lue Ming, a Vietnamese woman killed in the massacre at My Lai, and Lieutenant Boxler, the ageless soul of Lt. William Calley, the US Army officer found guilty for his role in the atrocity. *Slaughter City* has a similar duo: a young female textile worker who died in the Triangle Shirtwaist Factory fire of 1911 and a spectral figure called the Sausage Man, a nineteenth-century German émigré whose hand-cranked sausage grinder paved the way for the modern-day meatpacking industry. One of the three characters in *A State of Innocence* is the architect Shlomo, an incarnation of Shlomo Gur-Gervosky (1913–2000), inventor of the wall-and-tower concept for Zionist settlements in the British Mandate of Palestine in the late-1930s.

Sometimes the already dead take the form of what Claudia Barnett, Erica Stevens Abbitt, and others have theorized as "ghost girls." This is Wallace's variation on a contemporary archetype of liminality: emblems of female subjectivity between childhood and maturity, between naive vulnerability and determined agency, and by virtue of their ghostly status, between living presence and the absence of the dead. Wallace's ghost girls—including Morse in *One Flea Spare*, Pace in *The Trestle at Pope Lick Creek*, Bliss in *The Inland Sea*, and the Afghan sisters Alya and Meena in *No Such Cold Thing*—are often precocious and alluring, gentle and tough, prescient and forlorn all at once, drawing the audience into a mystery that often reveals itself as tied to a fateful act of violence. Wallace's first play, *In the Fields of Aceldama*, provides a prototype of this figure in the farm girl Annie, thrown by her horse and kicked to death at age 17. Two decades later, *And I and Silence* works a variation on the theme insofar as its action switches back and forth between the present, when Dee and Jamie are 25 and 26, and nine years earlier in the past, when the teens Young Dee and Young Jamie are in prison. By virtue of the murder/suicide that will end the play, Young Dee and Young Jamie are always already ghost girls, whether they know it or not.

There are other examples. As he tends to the abandoned zoo in *A State of Innocence*, the Israeli soldier Yuval has already been struck by a sniper's bullet and has died in the arms of Um Hisham, a Palestinian woman mourning the loss of her daughter. As he digs his own grave in *One Short Sleepe*, the Beirut University student Basheer is already dead from an Israeli bombing raid. And the prologue of *Things of Dry Hours* introduces Tice Hogan as an already dead black man come "from another world" to tell the story of the knock at the door that brought the white man Corbin Teel into his house. "Funny thing about time is, not how it doesn't come back to you. But how it does," he says in the epilogue as he prepares "to return to where he came from" (Wallace 2007a, 91). This is the key to the living dead: they are not ghouls or restless spirits in any conventional sense; they are embodiments of how time comes back. They blur the boundary between past and present in a way that theatricalizes Wallace's contention that history is never over and challenges the audience to embrace a narrative that loops back on itself like a theatrical Möbius strip.

Witnessing and Re-enactment

In *In the Heart of America*, the Palestinian-American Fairouz confronts her brother Remzi over an incident from their childhood when she was attacked by a bunch of kids and he looked on in hiding and did nothing. "There are three kinds of people," she says. "Those who kill. Those who die. And those who watch. Which one are you, Remzi?" (Wallace 2001, 96). Wallace's plays raise the same question for their audiences. The triad of perpetrator, victim, and witness recurs in one form or another in many of them. Sometimes, the encounter at hand is more sexual than violent, as in *One Flea Spare* when the merchant Snelgrave is forced to watch as his wife begins to make love to the sailor Bunce. In either case, the trope of enactment brings a subtle but important metatheatrical dimension to her work, triggering a Brechtian awareness of the contrived nature of the theatrical fiction and raising questions about alternative courses of action and different possible outcomes. The plays abound with instances of acting something out—sometimes with the use of props, make up, costume pieces, puppets, charades, songs, or theatricalized gestures—either as a simple historiographical narrative or as a preparation for an anticipated event. This is another example of ghosting and the slippage of time in Wallace, a means of bringing the past into the present through re-enactment or bringing the future into the present through rehearsal.

As mentioned above, as one type of enactment, Wallace's characters often change clothes in the presence of others, a basic playwriting tool she uses to blur the boundaries of gender, race, class, or ethnicity. In *One Flea Spare*, the aristocratic Snelgrave is so confident of his privilege that he gives "history a wee slap on the buttocks" by inviting his servant to try on his fashionable high-button shoes and learn the proper way to sport a cane. In *Slaughter City*, Brandon strips down, puts on a woman's work dress, plays the role of helpless girl—"I'm just a girl, a waif like a wafer you could snap in two" (Wallace 2001, 255)—and implores Roach to manhandle him. In *No Such Cold Thing*, at different moments, both the burka and the hidden US army boots worn by the Muslim girl Alya are removed; in the end, she uses the burka as a shroud to cover the dead body of the Chicano soldier Sergio. Instances of dressing/undressing such as these reinforce the understanding that identity—rich or poor, male or female, black or white, gay or straight—is a social construct, a role that is historically conditioned and therefore subject to resistance and revision.

The role of the spectator and the act of bearing witness is further emphasized in *The Trestle at Pope Lick Creek* when Pace Creagan forces her reluctant friend Dalton to stand guard as she races across the trestle to beat an oncoming train. "I want you to watch me," she says, "to tell me I'm here" (Wallace 2001, 326). This validation of presence by a willing spectator brings with it a share of responsibility for what has been seen. Wallace's viewers become, in Fairouz's terms, "those who watch," neither victims nor perpetrators but witnesses who are compelled to make a conscious choice to speak up or not.

Other elements of Wallace's playwriting should be mentioned. There is her insistent focus on youth and her belief in the young as agents of transformation, indicated not only by the preponderance of youthful characters in her plays but by two scripts—*The Girl Who Fell Through A Hole in Her Jumper* and *In the Sweat*—written with Bruce McLeod for young audiences and performers. There is her theatrical interest in material objects—shoes, feathers, apples, oranges, knives, books—and their palpable connection to a world of invisible forces and impulses. "An object is not only a physical form," she has said. "It is also the story of the creation of its being" (Macdonald 2006, 96). There is her agile and commanding use of language: the elaborate, vivid metaphors; the polyrhythmic cadences of her extended monologues; the incorporation of ditties, jingles, lullabies, and snippets of folk tunes in her dialogue; and the inter-textuality that comes from references to poets she favors, including those from whom she borrows a phrase as the title for a play. Her plays display a lyricism that contradicts the harsh realities they depict and that delivers an unexpected satisfaction for those who do not turn away. Wallace clearly believes in the pleasures theatre has to offer and the sensual experience to be derived from a stagecraft that is evocative, rich in imagery, magical, visceral, confrontational, zealous, surprising, and virtuosic. There is a recuperative, even hopeful, dimension to her work that is all the more invigorated by the energy of performance and the efficacy of theatrical process itself.

Those who dismiss Wallace as dry and didactic have not found access to these aspects of the work. Her focus on history, social justice, and the dynamics of power beyond the family circle makes her work undeniably political, but she does not exhort or ridicule or proselytize or belittle. Nor does she offer superficial palliative gestures or false promises of redemption. She presents what Erica Stevens Abbitt and I are calling "embodied dialogues," engaged, feisty, performative, violent, explicit, often erotic encounters that pose material reality against a vision of how things could be otherwise. Her bold and unusual aesthetic represents a compelling form of dialectics, combining sensuality and ideology, pragmatism and poetry, and vivid imagery with heightened language. Her theatre encourages spectators to take part in the dialectical process that already defines them and to awaken to the possibilities of change.

Notes

1. Quoted with permission from a unpublished "rehearsal draft" of the play dated April 9, 2013 provided by the playwright.
2. http://windhamcampbell.org/prize-winner/naomi-wallace (accessed June 10, 2013)

Part I

Writings on Wallace

1

Death and Desire, Apocalypse, and Utopia: Feminist *Gestus* and the Utopian Performative in the Plays of Naomi Wallace

Shannon Baley

> *Capitalism plunders the sensuality of the body.*
> —Terry Eagleton (qtd. in Gornick 1997, 31)
>
> *Some labor destroys the body... If your hands are damaged, it doesn't just mean you can no longer work and earn a living, it also means that you will no longer be able to touch someone you love. If your body is destroyed and exhausted, then how can you desire?*
> —Naomi Wallace (qtd. in Gardner 1996b, 5)
>
> *I could touch myself at night and I didn't know if it was her hand or mine. I could touch myself. I could put my hand. I could. Maybe I was asleep. I don't know but sometimes I put my hand. Inside myself.*
> —Dalton Chance (Wallace 2001, 310)

In the final scene of Naomi Wallace's Depression-era play *The Trestle at Pope Lick Creek*, the two youngest characters—Dalton Chance, the 15-year-old protagonist, and Pace Creagan, the 17-year-old young woman whose presence literally and figuratively haunts the play—engage in a highly erotic sex scene without touching. This scene, like the prologue, book-ends the play in a kind of 'no-space,' which is neither the place of memory (the 'when' of the majority of *Trestle*) nor the present moment, as indicated by Wallace's opaque stage direction: "[Dalton] is in a place that is both the past and the present at the same time" (2001, 340). During the course of the scene, Pace completes her arm's-length seduction of Dalton from beyond the grave, commanding him to lie down upon her dress (a material presence that complements—and complicates—her own ghostly presence), and to "touch" her by touching himself. Dalton complies, and audience members watch both characters climax, a charged and complicated "looking" that, for audience and actors alike, balances on the thin edge between radicalism and voyeurism. Pace's last line, and the last line of the play, is particularly lyrical and complicated, apropos of Wallace's writing throughout *Trestle*. After a few "quiet moments," she observes: "There. We're something else now. You see? We're in another place" (342). What they have been transformed into, and what or where that other place exactly is—whether it is apocalyptic or utopian, a place of redemption or a place of loss—are the open questions of the play.

A similar scene takes place in Wallace's *One Flea Spare*, set in plague-ridden seventeenth-century London. Trapped in a quarantined home, Morse, a mad servant girl; Bunce, an escaped conscripted sailor; and William and Darcy Snelgrave, the elderly, wealthy lord and lady of the house, wipe the walls with vinegar and mercilessly enact physical and emotional torture on each other while waiting out the disease. Near the climax of the play, Darcy, who had been horribly scarred in a fire when she was much younger, asks to see Bunce's wound, an unhealed hole in his side. Obliging, he takes her hand and guides her finger into the hole; her reaction echoes Dalton's experience with Pace in *Trestle* as she comments with wonder, "My finger. I've put my finger. Inside. It's warm. (*Beat*) It feels like I'm inside you" (53). Afterwards Wallace's stage direction dictates she, "looks at her hand as though it might have changed" (54). The much younger Bunce then begins slowly, almost scientifically, to explore Darcy's body while relating the horrific details of life as a conscript in the Royal Navy, searching for places where she can feel through the layers of scar tissue. Wallace juxtaposes Darcy's slow sexual reawakening and Bunce's own digital penetration of her with his bleak, jarring narrative of a young man vomiting his "stomach into [his] hands" and gulls whose wings "caught fire, so close did they circle the sinking masts" during a sea battle (55–6). Darcy's sexual climax, like Dalton's, occurs in an odd, liminal "someplace else," a space in which intimacy and physical desire can subsist with war, immolated birds, and bodies literally unmaking themselves, whether it be throwing themselves from a railroad trestle or throwing their internal organs out into the light of day.

These scenes open up fascinating questions about sensuality and trauma, presence and absence, materiality, and the limits of representation in Wallace's work. In both *Trestle* and *One Flea Spare*, Wallace combines an unflinching, distinctly feminist attention to gender and sexuality with unabashed socialist politics.[1] The real tragedy of these plays, Wallace implies, is not only the ravages of the Black Death or of the American Depression, but also of the crushing economic forces and class-based hierarchies attendant to laissez-faire capitalism that not only denies Pace and Dalton, Bunce and Darcy access to material ease, but also cuts them off from themselves and, to paraphrase Terry Eagleton, from their "sensual" capacities (qtd. in Gornick 1997, 31). Each of these plays gestures to apocalypse, whether it be unleashed by the bubonic plague or by junk bonds; however, these apocalypses exist on the edge of utopia, a place where death and desire co-exist, where bodies can be expanded, become fluid, and new horizons can be seen from what is possible, both in the world of the play and on stage in production. Though the men and women, boys and girls of *One Flea Spare* and *The Trestle at Pope Lick Creek* scramble to survive in the most horrendous conditions, through these plays we can glimpse the possibilities of a better world, a radical feminist utopia in which the conundrums, pleasures, and dangers of gender, class, and sexuality are made palpable for audience and artists alike.

In "Performance, Utopia, and the Utopian Performative," Jill Dolan proposes that theatre is an ideal place to glimpse utopia, a place to "enact an ideal future" by moving away from the real and into the realm of the "performative," a *doing* made communal by the presence of the audience that gestures to "better ways to be together as human beings" (2001, 457). The utopian performative, as defined by Dolan, is not only something that happens on stage, propelled forcefully into being by the virtuosity of actors and directors, playwrights and dramaturgs, designers, and technicians, but a collaborative "intersubjective" and affective event occurring among all present at a performance. This co-creation of the utopian performative is a distinctly social, public process that models democracy as a "participatory forum" as much as it models what a more just, equitable world "might *feel* like" (456, my emphasis).[2] Dolan notes that, contained in the collective effort of the utopian performative is a sense of "relief," a respite shared between performer and audience, during which "gestic moments of clarity" can occur (475). I wish to explore this small thread of Dolan's observation further, looking at how *gestus* itself can serve as the point of origin for utopian performatives and, more particularly, how an explicitly feminist *gestus* can help draw the counterpublics of theatrical audiences into a momentary construction of a world in which desires, bodies, and identities are fluid, escapable, anything but fixed.[3] In addition, I am interested in exploring how the utopian potential of *gestus* can help us understand—and perhaps better harness—the staggering but often elusive, affective power of *gestus*, its ability to make us feel, even just for a moment, part of something larger than ourselves. Naomi Wallace's plays, her ongoing engagement with issues of representation, class inequities, and desire are an ideal site to trace this kind of feminist *gestus* and its resulting glimpses of utopian performatives; to that end, I will more closely explore several of the gestic feminist moments that pervade *One Flea Spare* and *Trestle*, looking for clues to how they gesture towards both apocalypse and utopia.

I draw my understanding of *gestus* and its affective power not only from Brecht but also from Elin Diamond's *Unmaking Mimesis*, and her insightful interpretation of how the strangely apt relationship between feminism and Brechtian theory and theatre—more a "fellow-traveling" than a wholesale endorsement—emerged through a shared desire to explode realism's stranglehold on theatre and its subsequent "recontainment of difference", whether those differences be class-based (Brecht's favored critical lens) or gender-based (feminist critics' forte) (1997, 54, 44). Diamond defines Brechtian *gestus* as a "gesture, a word, an action, a tableau, by which, separately or in a series, the social attitudes encoded in the playtext become visible to the spectator"; it is a moment that "explains" the play, but also "exceeds" the play (52–3). Like the utopian performative, *gestus* is elusive, latent in the words of the text but only fully realized when it is embodied by an actor and received by the spectator. *Gestus* becomes feminist when its power to comment upon class or economic inequities is harnessed and expanded to condemn gender and sexual inequities ever-present in patriarchal power structures; it reveals gender as ideology and performative, a "system of beliefs and behavior mapped across the bodies of women and men which reinforces the social status quo" rather than as something fixed or irrevocable (47). Feminist *gestus* and feminist gestic criticism thus assist in the project of "ruin[ing] the scopic regime of the perspectival realist stage," and opening up a "provisional, indeterminate, nonauthorative" space for a distanced, distinctly alive and empowered spectator, and, even more importantly, an actor who is "free" to gaze back at her audience (53–4). Gestic feminist criticism, to paraphrase Diamond, thus allows the reader/spectator to engage dialectically rather than masterfully with the playtext before her, to "see" as a "transformative act of cognition," to witness the, "possibilities emerging of another reality, what is not there, but could be"—to enact, in other words, the utopian performative (145).

For Wallace, this longing to witness, to see possibilities of another reality, a utopia in the midst of chaos and death appears in her writing as just that—a desire: "Desire—that's really what I'm talking about... I don't mean love. I'm not sure I know what that means. Desire serves the need to end one's singular state. It creates the space in which to reimagine oneself. That alone ends loneliness" (Wallace qtd. in Gornick 1997, 31). Desire imbues Wallace's work, an ever-fluctuating configuration upon which the need for communion overlies the unruly sexual desires of her characters whose hunger for each other is equally paced by their hunger for community. Feminist *gestus* like Dalton's unnerving dis-substantiation of himself and Darcy's penetration of Bunce's open wound demonstrate the points where the two axes of physical and communal desire intersect, points at which the body—and all its attendant identity markers—blazes into being with a startling intensity for character, actor, and spectator. Ron Daniels, director of *One Flea Spare* for the Joseph Papp Public Theater in 1997 and Wallace's *Slaughter City* at the Royal Shakespeare Company, notes Wallace's particular gift for hailing, and implicating, bodies into being in her plays:

> In Naomi's work something is always being done to the body... It is always being touched, caressed, burned, perforated, poured on and spat on. It's standing in a river of life-and-death fluids: alive to blood, sweat, snot, running sores and oozing wounds. For Naomi, it has to do with making the body—for which read "class"—burst its bounds. Now here's the catch: it's all in the name of change, hope, possibility (Daniels qtd. in Gornick 1997, 31).

Daniels's connection between the effluence of the live body and "hope" is useful in illuminating how Wallace uses her textual bodies—as well as the physical bodies of the actors who take up the roles of her characters—to dramatize the ongoing history of class struggles. Like Dolan's utopian performative, Wallace's bodies are anything but static: the body, a site of unmaking or remaking, is a place where, Wallace observes, "it's possible to make a new vision" of oneself as well as a "new vision of desire" (Greene 2001, 466).

It is this new vision of desire that is the hope and the heartbeat of *One Flea Spare*. Drawing its title from John Donne's tongue-in-cheek *carpe diem* poem, in which a man asks his lover to "spare" the life of a flea in which his blood comingles with hers ("Where wee almost, yea more than maryed are"), *One Flea Spare* investigates the power of desire under the most extreme circumstances. When two vagabonds—Bunce, the escaped sailor, and Morse, a servant girl masquerading as her dead mistress—sneak into the Snelgrave house looking for shelter, they breach the house's nearly completed quarantine cycle of 28 days, imposed by Kabe, a "guard" hired to keep the quarantine enforced. When confronted, Kabe, a shrewd capitalist, observes merrily that it's not his job to keep people from breaking and entering the Snelgrave home, but to "make sure no one gets out," the prospect of further profit for "guarding" the Snelgrave residence making him positively gleeful. Like Helene Weigel's much-cited purse-snap *gestus* in the Berliner Ensemble's staging of Brecht's *Mother Courage*, Kabe's periodic carnivalesque appearance—only at the window and no further—serves as a reminder of the profits to be made from great suffering caused by war or plague (Wallace 2001, 12).

Under the pressure of enforced quarantine, the Snelgraves initially attempt to maintain the rigid class hierarchies of 1665 London, forcing Bunce to swab down the kitchen repeatedly and attempting to force the amoral, often cryptic Morse to behave like a "Christian" (13). These class distinctions, however, quickly break down under the pressure of impending apocalypse, and desire, both physical and imaginative, erodes the line between master and servant. In one particularly vivid scene, William Snelgrave, whose wealth, Wallace implies, is a result of his work with the Royal Navy, tries to push Bunce into revealing what he did at sea when his "baser instincts" took over (47). William's interest in Bunce's imagined homoerotic activities is salacious and romanticized; his use of multiple euphemisms for how Bunce might have used his "foul and fleshful instrument" is interrupted only by Bunce's blunt observation, "You mean my prick, sir?" (48). Frustrated (one suspects sexually), William commands Bunce to speak; in a stunning display of *gestus*, Bunce instead chooses to *act*:

> Bunce nears Snelgrave, close, too close. He takes Snelgrave's finger, examines it a moment, then forces it through the rind of the orange. Bunce turns the orange on Snelgrave's finger, slowly, sensually. Then he pulls the orange off of Snelgrave's finger. Involuntarily, Snelgrave looks at his wet finger. Bunce raises the orange over his head, squeezes it and drinks from the hole in the rind (48).

Death and Desire, Apocalypse, and Utopia   25

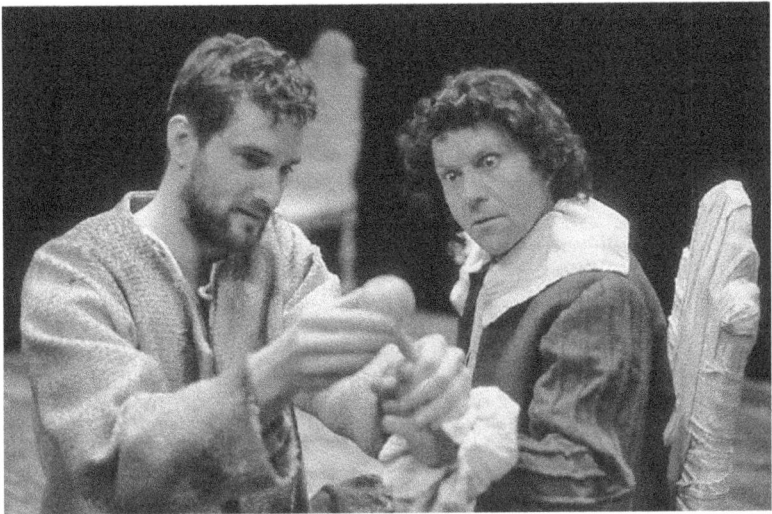

Figure 1.1 Richard Thompson (Bunce) and William McNulty (Snelgrave) in the 1996 Actors Theatre of Louisville production of *One Flea Spare*. Director: Dominic Dromgoole. Photo: Richard C. Trigg. Courtesy of Actors Theatre of Louisville.

In this incredibly rich moment we can witness both feminist *gestus* and the utopian performative at work. Like most *gestus*, Bunce's actions—imagined here through Wallace's stage directions—speak far louder than any words. Bunce's *gestus* of piercing the orange on the wealthy older man's finger is, on one level, defiant and brutal, gesturing to the systems of oppression just outside the action of the scene in which lower-class men like Bunce are "pressed" into the British Navy, the brute force of the seventeenth-century British Empire, and forced to fight without any training or adequate food, clothing, or shelter. On another level, this *gestus* is highly seductive: Bunce using the orange as an erotic teaching tool to show—rather than tell—his "master" what a sailor "does" to quench his desire on the high seas. Although impossible to embody fully in a reading of the text, contained here also are the seeds of the utopian performative: the sensual presence of the orange, its powerful, mouth-watering scent once pierced, and the drip and stick of its juice splashing on the stage floor and actor's shoes. One can imagine that the physical sensations accompanying the orange assault and seduce the audience as much as they assault and seduce William, connecting all present in a highly affective experience of class violence and the redemptive—and subversive—possibilities of desire. Indeed, reviewer John Lahr found this moment "electrifying" in the 1997 Public Theater production, a gesture, like Darcy's later penetration of Bunce, that is "at once proper and rapacious," one that captures a feeling of "thrilling transgression" of class boundaries that also "serves to liberate them" (1997, 87).

The later sensual encounter between Darcy and Bunce contains similar subversive possibilities of desire and a re-coding of class and power dynamics. As with William, Bunce at first succeeds in turning Darcy's half-serious seduction of him on its ear; when asked why she dreams of "ravish[ing]" him in her sleep each night, Bunce, ever candid, replies, "It's nothing to worry over, Mrs. Snelgrave. You people always want to fuck your servants" (54). Bunce's comment lays bare the implicit connection between labor exploitation and sexual exploitation, and a commodification of desire specifically because it lies outside of normative class boundaries. Both Darcy and William find Bunce exciting because he is outside their social class, an exotic other whose imagined "adventures" at sea make him even more sexually attractive; they attempt to use him to service their romantic and sexual needs, much as they use—indeed, expect—his services to swab down their kitchen. However, Bunce quickly pierces and deflates their fantasies as brutally as he does William's orange—the exploited becoming the exploiter. Instead of receiving the wound in his side from a glamorous sea battle as they imagine, he informs them his side was punctured when he attacked his "master" in a coal mine where his younger brother was crushed to death, which makes Bunce's unclosable wound an apt metaphor for the abuses and exploitation of the body under capitalism (20). Darcy's digital penetration of that wound thus balances on the thin edge between further exploitation and genuine sensuality and exchange. Rather than repeating the violence implicit in the interaction between Bunce and her husband, however, this exchange is one of mutual seduction, in which both gain pleasure from the other, a kind of shared intimacy and remaking of the body rather than the destruction of it. Darcy, who has been taught to hate her scarred body by her husband, has become deadened to all physical sensation below her neck; by juxtaposing his narrative about his brutal life at sea with his slow exploration of her body, Bunce remakes her body as effectively as she has just remade his, finding new and unexpected (or long-forgotten) openings and sites of pleasure.[4]

These gestic actions gesture toward a feminist utopia, in which physical boundaries are melted and pierced in a powerful attempt to imagine a world outside of the class-constricted, brutally capitalist, plague-infested London of the play, an imaginative world where bodies, genders, and sexualities are mutable, and, more importantly, free. However, as is the case with most of Wallace's plays, this glimpse of utopia, of the harnessing of the power of desire to transcend reality and powerlessness, is always counterbalanced with apocalypse and death. Darcy and William do not survive to see their reimagined world through, and Bunce disappears without a trace as Morse's final monologue reveals. The entire play, a kind of murder-mystery in reverse, is revealed to be Morse's remembering of events: "Everyone had gone. One way or another" (Wallace 2001, 73). *One Flea Spare* is a ghost story in which the past continually intrudes upon the present, much like the material representations of Bunce, Darcy, and William haunt Morse; indeed, the first line of the play, "What are you doing out of your grave?" ventriloquized from Morse's interrogator, could as easily apply to their absent presences as her own unlikely survival (7). *One Flea Spare*'s bleak conclusion, however, is mitigated by Morse's transformation; no longer a child, she observes that she has been "marked" by Darcy, William, and Bunce, by her "love" for them (74). Witness to—and arguably also the author of—the transformative feminist *gestus* of the play, Morse becomes a force to be reckoned with, tossing an orange, a reminder of the earlier sensuous and juicy utopian performatives, up into the light as the final gestic action of the play.

Memory and the haunting of the present by the past are also central thematic concerns of *The Trestle at Pope Lick Creek*, as Dalton struggles from his jail cell to remember (and speak about) what really happened to Pace (and to him) at the railroad trestle where these two young characters practiced playing chicken with each other and with the speeding, unrelenting steam engines. As Wallace gradually reveals through her nonlinear, episodic structure, Pace dies because Dalton refuses to watch her while she attempts a solo run at an oncoming train; this is the weighty, delayed secret of the text, much like Morse's delayed revelations of Darcy's, Snelgrave's, and Bunce's fates in *One Flea Spare*, leaving Dalton's innocence in Pace's supposed rape and murder in question until almost the final scene. Pace, a ghostly presence, speaks to the importance of shared memory near the end of the play, declaring the need for Dalton to look at her because, "we can't watch ourselves. We can't remember ourselves. Not like we need to"

(Wallace 2001, 337). Pace, however, does not want Dalton simply to watch or remember her—her seduction at the trestle also has a didactic, utopian, and distinctly feminist purpose.

An exchange between Dalton and his mother Gin in the jail cell is one moment when the complicated problems of understanding (and staging) Pace's lessons in memory present themselves in full force. Trying to explain to his mother how Pace changed his world, Dalton begins an odd, poetic duet with Pace's own ghostly voice:

> DALTON: It was something more. Like at school. At school they teach you. To speak. They say it's math—
> PACE: History—
> DALTON: Geometry, whatever. But they're teaching you to speak. Not about the world but about things. Just things: a door, a map,
> PACE: a cup. Just the name of it.
> DALTON: Not what a cup means, who picked it up, who drank from it,
> PACE: who didn't and why;
> DALTON: where a map came from, who fixed in the rivers, who'll take the wrong turn; or a door. Who cut the wood and hung it there? Why that width, that height? And who made that decision? Who agreed to it? Who didn't?
> PACE: And what happened to them because of it? (308–9)

Dalton's obvious frustration at not being able to explain himself clearly to his mother is evident in Wallace's text in his short, clipped sentences, and his continual stopping and starting of new questions and ideas. However, what is most odd about this exchange (other than his being echoed—or ventriloquized—by a ghost) is its subject matter. In trying to explain to his mother Pace's effect (and affect) on him physically and emotionally—her long-distance penetration of his body and his psyche—Dalton turns his description away from the body to questions of history and labor. Instead of directly addressing the traumatic event of Pace's death, and his mother's goading question if it was "easy" for him to hold Pace's dead body after her plunge from the trestle, he asks his mother why he wasn't taught better in school to question the production of the things surrounding him in the jail cell and, more importantly, the history of production (or the production of history). Frustrated by his inability to explain himself, Dalton finally breaks his cup, showing it to his mother: "Look. This was sand and heat. Not long ago. Other things, too. Pieces and bits. And now. It's something else. Glass. Blood. And it's broken. (*Picks up a large piece, nears Gin*) I could cut you open with it" (309).

A lot is hinted at ideologically and discursively in this dangerous moment in the text and in performance, Pace's ghostly memory-lessons become almost malignant as Dalton threatens his mother with the now destroyed cup. *Gestus* is, of course, present here as well: in the destructive and desperate act of breaking his cup, Dalton makes a violent comment upon the social attitudes of the emotionally and physically impoverished world of the play in which material things are so scarce and valuable that the loss of even one cup is shocking. Here Wallace's socialist politics become abundantly clear. Part of Dalton's problem (other than his "bad" memory and Pace's haunting presence) is that he cannot escape the institutions of a destructive, inhumane capitalist system that has conspired to keep him in the dark about the real politics of his world, the "who" of the things surrounding him. His responsibility in Pace's death, therefore, is part of the failure of a capitalist political economy that refuses to 'see' its

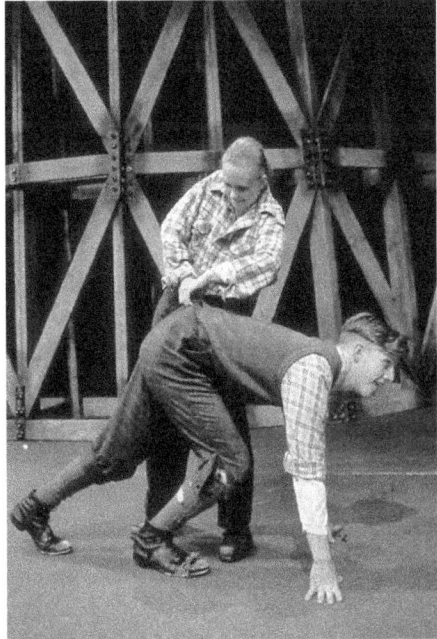

Figure 1.2 Tami Dixon (Pace) and Michael Linstroth (Dalton) in the 1998 Actors Theatre of Louisville production of *The Trestle at Pope Lick Creek*. Director: Adrian Hall. Photo: Richard C. Trigg. Courtesy of Actors Theatre of Louisville.

laborers as human beings. More damningly, Wallace implies Dalton's previous inability to see the cup for what it really is (an amalgamation of organic and inorganic items: "sand and heat," "glass" as well as "blood" as a product of someone's labor) imprisons him as firmly as the "real" jail cell surrounding him on stage. The defamiliarizing, gestic, and utopian act of breaking down a cup to its component parts thus becomes a kind of alternative history-making, a way of revealing and remembering an unofficial 'past' and imagining a previously unimaginable future.

In the moments following Dalton's gestic smashing of his cup, he finally pushes through to his real revelation: that his relationship with Pace, like that of Darcy and Bunce, transcended traditional parameters of gender, desire, sexuality—even the confines of his own body: "I could touch myself at night," he relates, "and I didn't know if it was her hand or mine. I could touch myself. I could put my hand. I could. Maybe I was asleep. I don't know but sometimes I put my hand. Inside myself" (310). The complexities of the sex-gender system become more than just fluid in this moment—they become practically transparent, a gesture towards the final scene in which Dalton allows Pace to finally dissolve his gender and sexuality completely. This final act of release, a feminist *gestus* and utopian performative rolled into one, allows Dalton and Pace to dissolve and escape the hetero-normative, capitalist system that attempts to yoke them irrevocably to singular bodies and a closed, monologic history. In doing so, he finally remembers (and re-members) her as much as she has re-membered him, rearranging their bodies until they flow into each other, a dialectical and potentially utopian exchange.

While attempting to explicate Brecht's theories of "not...but" for the feminist critic, Diamond observes that, "[d]ifference is where we imagine, theorize, while gender is where we live, our social address, although some of us wish (and some of us have the privilege) to leave home" (1997, 48). In Naomi Wallace's *One Flea Spare* and *The Trestle at Pope Lick Creek*, characters like Pace and Dalton, Darcy and Bunce have the unique 'privilege' of leaving the 'home' of their gender and their bodies at the very moment of their worlds' apocalypses. They achieve this escape through a radical, reciprocal looking and remembering, as well as through feminist *gestus*, slipping out of the confines of their crumbling, constrictive worlds with only their desire and their willingness to reimagine themselves as their baggage. In performance, these feminist gestic actions are the breeding ground for the utopian performative, providing the basis for a collaborative experience of their desire, the audience's reception and re-membering of these characters longing for each other as crucial as Wallace's words themselves in glimpsing utopia. Despite these plays' historical removal—or perhaps because of it, historicization being one of Brecht's, and Brechtian feminists' favored alienation effects—the utopian performatives present in *One Flea Spare* and *The Trestle at Pope Lick Creek* seem as urgent and as contemporary in helping audiences and artists envision a more just and equitable common future as a play whose social milieu is closer to home.

Unfortunately, however, not every spectator feels this urgency. Reviewers of the 1999 New York Public Theater production of *Trestle* failed to glean either *gestus* or utopian performatives from Pace's ghostly seduction of Dalton, a problem perhaps endemic to American critical reception of Wallace's work and the reason, along with her socialism, for her continued relative anonymity in American theatre. Anita Gates of the *New York Times* found the dialogue of *Trestle* "self-consciously portentous at times" (1999, 9), while *New York*'s paragon of truculence, John Simon, mounted a full-scale attack at what he perceived as Wallace's "affectively artsy" play (1999, 74). Referring to Wallace's previous work (*One Flea Spare*) as "phony and smart-ass," Simon eviscerated the text of *Trestle* as well as the direction of the production, writing:

> Wallace, too, makes it hard for the spectator. Thus in the last scene, the dead Pace and the doomed Dalton are simultaneously in his cell and at the trestle. As she says in a stage direction, "The Pace Dalton sees we cannot see, and the Pace we see is not the Pace Dalton sees." This is not entirely off the wall: The play the MacArthur people must have seen is not the one we see. Then factor in the further legerdemain of the director, Lisa Peterson, who has penniless people play Frisbee with their plates until they get smashed, shattering a cup for good measure (74).

Simon's skewering of the production and his bewilderment at the Chance family's destruction of property reveals his fundamental inability to see beyond the fetishism of commodity capitalism. For Simon, the plates and cup are only property, their destruction inexplicable and impractical rather than "an act of desperate resistance," as Erica Stevens Abbitt points out (2002, 500). However, Stevens Abbitt is careful to articulate that audience reactions to Wallace's work such as Simon's are not completely unwarranted since the "visceral," *gestic* power of the destruction of things in the play's world of scarcity is often performed "cavalier[ly]" in American productions of Wallace's plays. Because, Stevens Abbitt contends, Americans tend to, "concentrate on psychological motivation over material reality" in the theatre, we are unable to appreciate the, "body's wear and tear" in a world of material overabundance (500). Thus, both cultural conditioning and the constant pull of psychological realism's black hole in American theatre interfere with our ability to pinpoint feminist *gestus,* much less its utopian potential.

Regardless, Wallace continues to pursue her singular vision of desire, hope, and the end of the singular state, both in her writing and in her political work. Recently, she has traveled to occupied Palestine, not once but twice, to talk to and learn from artists attempting to make theatre in a militarized zone, and to write more explicit critiques of American foreign policy—to embrace her label of being a "political playwright" for better or worse.[5] Her most recent short play, a one-man show called *The Retreating World,* written before the current war with Iraq, was originally meant to be a condemnation of the decade-long US-led sanctions against Iraq. Read after September 11, however, and after the American incursion into and subsequent occupation of Baghdad, *The Retreating World* becomes practically prophetic, depicting one man's battle to survive the intense hardships of a city and country under siege. Ali's slow loss of his beloved pet pigeons is only the first layer of this stark play in which pigeons become confused with children, and children become confused with the other, tragic fallout of war, such as Ali's entire family. As in *Trestle,* the play's most devastating *gestus* is reserved for the conclusion. Telling the audience he asks for the bones of his pigeons from his customers after they have been eaten, Ali picks up a steel bucket, commanding the audience to "listen" to the sound of bones rattling. "It is a kind of music," he observes, holding the bucket out to the audience, "These are the bones of those who have died, from the avenue of palms, from the land of dates. I have come here to give them to you for safekeeping. *(Beat)* Catch them. If you can" (40). Wallace's stage directions, however, describe the following: "*He roughly throws the contents of the bucket at the audience. Instead of bones, into the air and across the audience spill hundreds of white feathers*" (Wallace 2003c, 40). I can only imagine the power and grace of Ali"s final *gestus* in performance; first the threat of violence, the flinching tension of the audience readying itself for the recriminating assault of dry, brittle bones, magically transforming into the smooth, gestic clarity of relief and wonder at the hundreds of white feathers slowly falling around them. I also can't imagine a better example of a utopian performative at work, a more devastating or eruptive glimpse into—or sensation of—a future where visions of violence and pain, suffering and loss are replaced with a vision of pleasure and peace, surrender and love.

Notes

1. When pressed by interviewers, Wallace identifies as a socialist, happy to be labeled as a "political writer." She comments in an interview with Alexis Greene: "I write about capitalism, because that is how our society is organized; and how we make our way or don't make our way economically affects all aspects of our lives. That is usually at the base of anything I write" (Greene 2001, 451).
2. Dolan also notes the dangers inherent in writing about or envisioning utopia, that in its forward thinking "something coercive lingers about the term" (2001, 457). Citing political scientist Lyman Sargent, Dolan reminds us that utopian thought is not restricted to just "fiction" but also, "includes visionary...and *apocalyptic* as well as constitutional writings united by their willingness to envision a dramatically different form of society as either a social ideal-type or its negative inversion" (457, my emphasis). Utopia and its dark inverse, apocalypse, thus are never far apart. As Dolan notes, it is "idealism" that continues to draw her to utopian thought despite its whiff of apocalypse, an idealism that I suspect many feminist scholars, including myself, share.
3. I use the term *counterpublic* to describe the kinds of publics that gather at theatrical performance in much the same way Michael Warner does in his discussion of the historical construction of publics, official and unofficial. Counterpublics are not "counter" simply because they are, "subalterns with a reform program," but because they, "supply different ways of imagining stranger sociability and its reflexivity; as publics they remained oriented to stranger circulation in a way that is not just strategic but constitutive of membership and its affects" (2002, 121–22). As in a theatre audience, a congregation of strangers coming together for the pleasures of witnessing performance, counterpublics create the "spaces of circulation" in which the "poesis of scene making" can be "transformative," rather than merely "replicative" (122).Like Dolan, I find Warner's definition of counterpublic quite freeing when contemplating who goes to the theatre and why and how an audience coalesces at the point of performance.
4. In an interview with Heidi Stephenson and Natasha Langridge, Wallace noted that part of her motivation in creating the character of Darcy was to portray "a woman on stage who is complex in her sexuality at a much older age, to show that at sixty-five you can be just as complicated as you are at twenty, if not perhaps more so" (168). Women in particular, she observes in the same interview, are taught by the capitalist system that their "exchange value" decreases with age, that they become "diminishing people" who must

be "dead from the neck down" (168). Darcy's sexual awakening is thus doubly subversive, an awakening of a woman who should otherwise be "dead" emotionally and physically when her physical and sexual usefulness has passed.
5. For more information on Wallace's trip with fellow playwrights Tony Kushner and Kia Corthron (among others), see the July/August 2003 issue of *American Theatre*.

2

Love in a Wound

Scott T. Cummings

Two Sonnets of a Woman Working in a Morgue

I name her Rika. Her skin is a delicate web.
My finger is an insect that could tear the surface.
This little piggy will wear the 'unknown' tag.
She *went to market* but didn't have a dime.
Will I be left like this on the roadside, a pyre
of old twigs that the sun sets on fire?
A whisper is still in her throat: *A dream is a fly
that fell in the water.* I know, I answer. That's why
I don't dream. Him I name Alexis,
a union man who *stayed home*, on strike,
and got a bullet in the neck for his trouble. His face
is flat and beautiful, like a stone rising out
of the water. I put my finger inside his wound.
He is the first man that I have entered.
I name her Matilda. Her hands are black and thin.
She worked for the assembly line, packing *roast beef*
and heart for the dogs and children of wealthy men.
She rests like someone who's been falling like a leaf
from very high up for years. She drowned
because she *had none* and the bailiffs were mad.
Her mouth is covered in lime: What is the sound
of a shout under water? A lily pad
floats in her dream. Near morning I kiss
them goodnight. Their lips are cold and dark
as plums but not as sweet. We're labour and piss
here below. Our prayer is a fly that doesn't mark
the water. The Lord is not their shepherd at minimum
wage; I am. *All the way home.*

—Naomi Wallace (1995)

Over a remarkable playwriting career of more than 20 years, Naomi Wallace has demonstrated a sustained and fierce commitment to the examination of identity and power—in terms of race, class, gender, age, nationality, and sexual preference. Nevertheless, her plays are more poetic than rhetorical in structure. They develop searing images and compound metaphors—linguistic, gestural, and theatrical—that avoid didacticism as they focus an audience's attention on the power dynamics at work in social and economic relations. While her sympathies are clear, her plays do not argue for a political orthodoxy so much as they evoke the forces of history that leave a mark on the individual. As the Vietnamese woman Lue Ming says in *In the Heart of America*, "The past is never over" (Wallace 2001, 125). The past penetrates the present again and again in Wallace's plays, in the form of a historically significant setting or event, a mysterious figure who travels magically through time, a theatrical reenactment of an earlier event, a ghost girl who is dead and gone yet walks among the living, or the permanent scars that experience has left on the bodies of her characters.

My focus here is on the last of these historical coefficients: the discourse of the body, especially the wounded body. The poem that serves as an epigraph above is a reminder of Wallace's virtual obsession with the flesh-and-blood physicality of her characters, dead or alive. The woman working in a morgue reanimates the cadavers she attends to: giving them a name, bearing witness to their hardships, touching them with tenderness, and even turning the application of a toe tag into the occasion for a round of the tickling nursery rhyme "This Little Piggy." In Wallace, a character's body is conspicuous as the living record of past experience. The peasant character Hesp Turner in *The Inland Sea* (2002) describes losing her thumb at age 12 while slaughtering pigs with her father, concluding "My mother says our hands, our bodies even, are the history of insults that have been inflicted against them" (Wallace 2002, 45). And in *Things of Dry Hours* (2004), the African-American Cali Hogan holds a dying Corbin Teel in her arms and responds to his appeal to "Let me touch you" by taking his white hand and guiding it to places on her black body: "Here is where I cut myself as a child. Here, where I burned when the fields caught fire. Here is where my mother touched me. I can't remember, but I know it's her" (Wallace 2007a, 90). Wallace's interest in how individuals are marked by social, political, and economic forces leads her to create characters whose bodies are marked by their lived experience. They exist in the present but they carry their pasts with them—etched in the flesh.

Over time, Wallace has developed a variety of techniques, tactics, and tropes that foreground physicality and corporal being. In this essay, I want to examine one particular dimension of the discourse of the body in her works by looking at three early plays that established her as a playwright to be reckoned with: *In the Heart of America* (1994), *One Flea Spare* (1995), and *Slaughter City* (1996). Each is 20–30 scenes long, divided into two acts, with a cast of roughly a half dozen characters. Each is strongly rooted in a tangible, real-world situation conditioned by crisis and danger, a time and a place that by their very nature pose a threat to the human body. *In the Heart of America* takes place during the Gulf War of the early 1990s and includes scenes in the Iraqi desert, on the outskirts of Baghdad, and in a US military camp in Saudi Arabia. *Slaughter City* takes place in a meatpacking plant at a moment when workers have just returned to the shop floor after an unsuccessful strike for better working conditions. *One Flea Spare* takes place in London in 1665, the year of the bubonic plague that ravaged the population and devastated the city.

In typical fashion for Wallace, characters in all three plays are plotted out by their gender, race, ethnicity, nationality, and social class. *In the Heart of America* hinges on questions of national and ethnic identity: it includes a brother and sister who are first-generation Palestinian-Americans and a woman who is Vietnamese; the other two characters are Americans, both soldiers. *Slaughter City* hinges on matters of race and occupational status: two characters are African-Americans, the rest are white; all characters are affiliated either with labor or management. *One Flea Spare* features a similar division into class. There are the 'haves,' William Snelgrave, a wealthy merchant capitalist who imports tea and spices from the East, and his wife, Darcy Snelgrave, and the 'have-nots,' Morse, the daughter of a housemaid and orphaned by the plague, and Bunce, an itinerant seaman eager to avoid conscription into the navy. In all three plays, gender and sexuality are prominent aspects of a character's identity, which is often shown to be radically unstable by the events of the play.

A character defined by social or demographic type is often individuated by a singular history that includes illness, injury, or some form of physical violation that has resulted in permanent scars, a wound that will not heal, or other lasting effects. In *In the Heart of America*, this character is Fairouz, who is trying to find out exactly how her brother, Remzi, came to be killed by so-called "friendly fire" while serving in Iraq. As a child, Fairouz was attacked by bullying schoolchildren trying to confirm rumors that her Muslim identity meant she had hoofed feet; they beat her, crushing her foot so that she ended up walking with a permanent limp. In *One Flea Spare*, there are two characters with lasting wounds. The aristocratic Darcy Snelgrave wears long gloves and high-necked dresses that completely cover her skin, which was burned from head to toe in a stable fire when she was 17, leaving her permanently disfigured and effectively ending conjugal relations with her husband. In the play, the Snelgraves are quarantined in their London home with the tramp sailor Bunce, who wears a bloody bandage wrapped around his midsection to protect a hole in his side that never properly healed after he was stabbed by a guard for protesting his brother's death in a mineshaft collapse.

In *Slaughter City*, the injured party is Brandon, a white slaughterhouse worker who claims to be a virgin at 22 because of "The white marks. Like a halo around my mouth" (Wallace 2001, 223).[1] Even though he is a quick study, dyslexia prompted him to quit high school at age 15 and go to work for a man who owned a chain of jewelry stores. He tells this story to his co-worker Roach, an African-American woman in her mid-30s who is the object of his romantic interests:

> One day I dropped a box with some china in it. He hit me until I passed out. When I came to, he was sitting beside me. He had a lure box with him. He said I'd cursed him. I couldn't remember, up 'til then I'd never said a thing but "Yes, sir." He said he'd make sure I never spoke against him again. He took some fish line and a hook out of his box and he sewed my mouth shut. That's why I never could kiss a girl. Because it's always bleeding where the line went through. How can you kiss a girl when your mouth is always bleeding? (223)

Taken metaphorically, this question sums up the predicament for many of Wallace's desiring characters. They gravitate towards each other with a sexual longing that is conditioned by a history of violence, complicated by social and political divisions, and in some instances gratified in startling and theatrical ways. Their wounds—and there are more of them in these and other plays—are the outward physical signs of a legacy of pain and a life of oppression. In Wallace, the body is the thing that is poked, prodded, pierced, penetrated, and pulverized, revealing a vulnerability that is reinforced by gruesome imagery and a general air of carnage. *Slaughter City* invites the scenic display of huge sides of beef, suspended on hooks and rolling by on a conveyor belt, dripping a trail of blood. In *One Flea Spare*, the watchman on patrol assigned to enforce the London quarantine provides graphic descriptions of bodies ravaged by plague all over the devastated city. *In the Heart of America* includes a scene in which the soldiers Remzi and Craver (his buddy and eventual lover) collect corpses and body parts to bury in the Iraqi desert. In effect, the plays themselves take place in an open wound.

The present-tense action of each of these plays seeks to redress the legacy of corporal pain that defines certain characters and to re-dress the figurative wound that is the play's setting. These danger zones and the character's actual wounds become erogenous zones, sites of eroticized contact that resist the vulnerability of the flesh. In *In the Heart of America*, Fairouz visits Craver in a Kentucky motel room to find out what really happened to her brother, and their encounter leads to him caressing her foot, just as Remzi did when she was young. She recalls how, "Sometimes when we were children he would soak my foot in a bowl of warm water, with lemon and orange rinds. He would blow on my toes to dry them. He thought if he cared for my foot, day by day, and loved it, that somehow it would get better" (112). In *One Flea Spare*, Bunce will not allow Darcy to look at the open wound in his side, but he does allow her to touch it (Figure 2.1). "It's warm," she says, after delicately lifting the bandage and placing her finger in the hole: "It feels like I'm inside you" (53). By the end of this scene, he in turn is touching her scorched skin all over—which seems somehow tender and callous at the same time—on the arms at first, watching her face to see what she can feel, looking for the threshold between pleasure and pain, and eventually reaching up under her long dress between her legs, touching her higher and higher.

There is a delicacy in these sexual encounters that is eerily dispassionate, almost a bit cold. In image and action alike, sexual relations are so grounded in woundedness and so surrounded by the threat of new pain that the contact can register as clinical, an-esthetic in a sense, a feeling without feeling. It is still erotic, but it is not particularly sensual, except perhaps in a vaguely sado-masochistic way that emphasizes the enactment of power in sexual relations. In Wallace, sexual dominance and submission need to be seen here as a correlative for political dominance and oppression. The body politic manifests itself in the politic body, a kind of geo-corporal entity that is subject to invasion, occupation, colonization, and other territorial maneuvers. The skin functions as a kind of 'international' boundary.

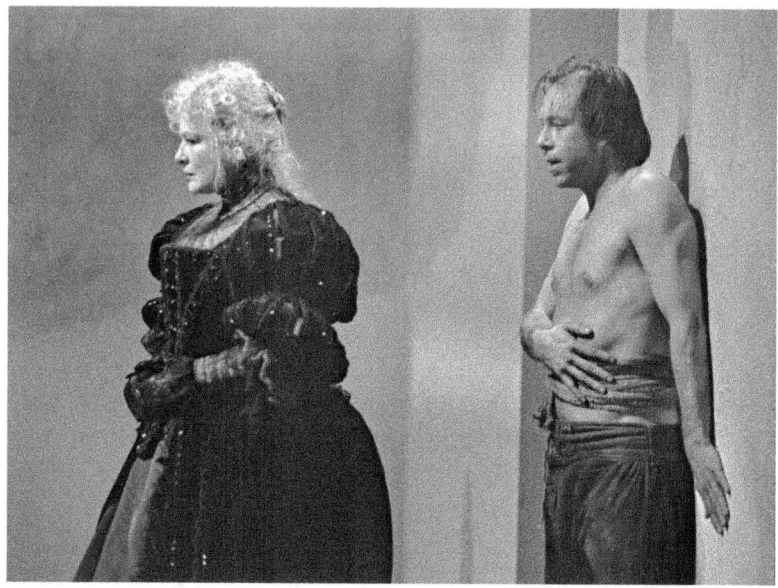

Figure 2.1 Dianne Wiest (Darcy Snelgrave) and Bill Camp (Bunce) in the 1997 Public Theater production of *One Flea Spare*. Director: Ron Daniels. Photo © Michal Daniel, 2007.

Darcy's sexually tinged insertion of her finger into the hole in Bunce's side is just one example of a theatrical crossing of the border of the body. In *One Flea Spare*, William Snelgrave expresses a salacious interest in how Bunce handled his "natural instincts while so long at sea":

> You're halfway to Madras and it's sweltering hot and you wake with the hunger of a shark. But not for food. The Devil is foaming at your lips. What do you do, man? You're frothing with desire. What do you do? (48)

To get an answer from Bunce, as a form of payment in advance, he tosses him an orange, a rare treat in the midst of the plague. But Bunce is coy and demure. "I don't know as I ever frothed with desire, sir," he says. Snelgrave commands him to speak, but Bunce responds with an elaborate, nonverbal gesture. He takes Snelgrave's raised index finger, forces the orange in his hand down upon it, twists it slowly back and forth, lifts it off, holds it over his own head, and squeezes it so that juice falls into his mouth and down his chin. Staring at his wet finger, Snelgrave is so flabbergasted by this homoerotic exchange that all he can say is, "I issue commissions to the Navy Board. I draft resolutions to send to the king" (49).

Erotically charged exchanges such as this occur in the other plays. Early in their relationship, Remzi teaches Craver the proper way to eat a fig. "Eating is like walking," he says, "My sister taught me that. There's a balance involved. You have to eat the fig gently. As though it were made of the finest paper. Look. I'll put the fig in my hand and without touching my hand, you pick it up. Gently." When Craver reaches forward to pick it up with two fingers, Remzi stops him and tells him to use his mouth. So Craver leans over Remzi's open hand, carefully lifts the fig with his teeth, and then allows Remzi to reach forward and push it onto his tongue. "There," Remzi says, "How does it taste now?" (108). In *Slaughter City*, when Brandon does finally get a kiss on his wounded mouth from Roach, it comes with a price. "I'll give you a kiss," she says, "if you can take this knife from me" (257). And she takes one of Brandon's razor-sharp trim knives and puts the thin blade between her teeth, so that their kiss takes the form of the delicate passing of the knife from her mouth to his. "A kiss is a dangerous thing," she says.

And so it is. Nevertheless, the threat of opening up old wounds, literal and figurative alike, elicits a peculiar tenderness from Wallace's characters. Sometimes that tenderness is an expression of genuine love or affection; sometimes it is the cruel mask of oppression or dominance. In either case, the wounded body operates as the physical ground on which power is activated, negotiated, contested, or forfeited. These transactions take on added dimensions when regarded theoretically using the apparatus outlined in Stanton B. Garner, Jr.'s *Bodied Spaces: Phenomenology and Performance in Contemporary Drama*. Garner's book seeks to delineate, "the set of variables and principles fundamental to a phenomenology of the theatrical body." Its secondary objective is to affect a rapprochement between poststructuralism and phenomenology as potentially complementary modes of dramatic criticism and performance analysis. In the process, he looks at twentieth-century plays by Beckett and Pinter, David Mamet and Sam Shepard, and Caryl Churchill and Maria Irene Fornes.

Garner draws primarily on the 'second generation' phenomenology of Maurice Merleau-Ponty, which privileges sentient experience and the perceiving I/eye as subject over the abstract extrapolations of the strictly rational, objective, and conceptual mind. It accentuates the world as lived over the world as idea. As Garner writes, "Merleau-Ponty posited a consciousness caught up in the ambiguity of corporeality, directed toward a world of which it is inextricably and materially a part" (Garner 1994, 27).[2] This ambiguity is represented by two different conceptions of the body: the thing-body (Körper) and the lived-body (Leib). The thing-body is the body as it is given to observation from the outside-in, the body as anatomical object, like the ones ministered to by Wallace's "woman working in a morgue." The lived-body is the body as it is experienced from the inside out, the body as sentient subject, the body you take out for dinner and dancing. The lived-body is the body as self (filled with presence), while the thing body is the body as other (marked by absence, or at least a degree of alienation).

For Merleau-Ponty, the ambiguity of the thing-body and the lived-body is fundamentally irreducible. As Garner writes, "The body is that by which I come to know the world, the perceptual ground against which the world has existence for me; at the same time, it is an object in this world, much (though not all) of which is available to my direct perception...my material body is charged with sentience, while the field of my lived-body is impinged on by a thingness, imperfectly grasped, from which it can never extricate itself" (50).

Garner goes beyond Merleau-Ponty and draws on contemporary phenomenologists Elaine Scarry (*The Body in Pain*) and Drew Leder (*The Absent Body*) to point out that the thingness of the lived-body is heightened and foregrounded when the body is in pain or physical distress. In such situations, the thing-body imposes itself on the experience of the lived-body, occludes, and eclipses it, triggering what Garner describes as "a radical materialization of the body as object" and "an equally radical derealization of the world itself." He continues, "As consciousness contracts in the circle of pain and the bodied subject is displaced by body as object, the subject/body/world continuum is characterized by increasing disengagement: the body toward thingness, and both subject and world toward a condition of disembodiment" (183).

With Garner as model and guide, we can see how Naomi Wallace captures and stages the inextricable phenomenological ambiguity of Körper and Lieb, mainly through her depiction of characters whose bodies are marked by wounds. Consciousness for them has already long since contracted into the circle of pain. When we first meet them, their old wounds have led to a condition of disembodiment.

What happens in the present-tense action of the plays can be seen as a twofold process of re-embodiment. First, through the activation of the wound as the site of sentient experience and a surrogate or symbolic coitus, the thing-body and the lived body are re-engaged. Then, through the renegotiation or realignment of political relationships that this regained sentience signifies, the subject and the world are re-engaged. The characters make love in a wound—Fairouz's crippled foot, Brandon's bleeding mouth, Darcy's leathery skin—and by that action both the subject and the world are reembodied.

As it turns out, this re-embodiment is only temporary. No sooner does a disembodied character finally make contact than he or she sustains a fresh—and fatal—wound. In *In the Heart of America*, when Remzi and Craver are caught making love behind the barracks, racist, homophobic American soldiers attack them and Remzi is killed. In *Slaughter City*, three scenes after Brandon and Roach share their knife-kiss, an industrial accident causes Brandon to inhale vapors from a liquid ammonia spill and his lungs burn until he suffocates. In *One Flea Spare*, not long after Darcy and Bunce fully consummate their attraction, Darcy exhibits the telltale symptoms of the plague. When Bunce cannot bring himself to help her take her own life, she turns to Morse, a street urchin also under quarantine and the ministering angel of the play, who places her hands on the knife Darcy holds to her chest and helps her to drive it into her heart.

There is nothing overtly tragic or heroic about these deaths, just as there is nothing overtly romantic or passionate about the erotic actions that precede them. In sex and death alike, the phenomenological dialectic remains unsynthesized and the existential doubleness of thing-body and lived-body is maintained. Wallace is careful not to offer up some sort of compensatory fantasy of transcendence or redemption: the wounds do not heal; the bodies that come together do not remain together; the forces of oppression—capitalism, patriarchy, racism, homophobia—are not vanquished. Wallace is too realistic for that. But the action of re-embodiment does testify to the will of the oppressed to engage and resist those forces in an attempt to forge an identity of one's own making, to achieve personal liberty or the sovereignty of the individual, and even to claim for themselves a human dignity that is variously identified as "a quiet sense of pride," balance, grace, and even the proper way to eat a fig. In this regard, Wallace attends to her characters in much the same way as the working woman in the opening poem attends to her wards in the morgue, as thing-bodies with lived-bodies buried deep inside them, as delicate cadavers subject to violent rupture and a penetrating care, with unfulfilled dreams lodged like a whisper in the throat.

Notes

1. Naomi Wallace, *Slaughter City*, in *In the Heart of America and Other Plays* (New York: TCG, 2001). All subsequent references to *Slaughter City*, *In the Heart of America*, and *One Flea Spare*, all in the TCG volume, will be made by page number in the body of the text.
2. Stanton B. Garner, Jr., *Bodied Spaces: Phenomenology and Performance in Contemporary Drama* (Ithaca: Cornell University Press, 1994), 27. All subsequent references to Garner will be made by page number in the body of the text.

3

Messianic Marxism in Naomi Wallace's *Slaughter City* and *Things of Dry Hours*

Buell Wisner

Over the past two decades, Naomi Wallace has established herself as one of the most important voices in activist theatre. All of Wallace's best plays address Empire—past and present—from the standpoint of social justice. In works as separated by time as *The War Boys* (1993) and *The Fever Chart* (2008), the playwright has consistently voiced her opposition to global capitalism and the violence that maintains it. Wallace has asserted, "We live in a culture that is hostile to creativity and original thought that does not serve capitalism, empire, and the most virulent by-products of those forces: racism, homophobia, classism, and sexism" (Wallace 2008, 98). Exposing both these "virulent by-products" and their origin has been the dramatist's focus since the early 1990s.[1]

Even more than contemporaries Tony Kushner and Suzan-Lori Parks, Wallace brings an explicitly Marxist political outlook to her drama. She employs the conventional socialist themes of industrial labor, class conflict, proletarian revolution, and Communist Party politics in such plays as *Slaughter City* (1996), *The Trestle at Pope Lick Creek* (1998), *Things of Dry Hours* (2004), and *The Hard Weather Boating Party* (2010). To these themes is added a Marxist faith in history. And Wallace is seemingly obsessed with history: *One Flea Spare* (1995) is set in Pepys's London during the plague of 1660; *The Inland Sea* (2002) dramatizes the transformation of the English countryside and rural economy during the eighteenth century; and both *The Trestle at Pope Lick Creek* and *Things of Dry Hours* are set in Depression-era America. Like Brecht, Wallace's plays use historical settings both as *verfremdungseffekt* and as a means of underscoring the impact of politics on individuals' daily lives. As she tells Vivian Gornick in a *New York Times Magazine* article, "Politics is history...and history is what sparks my imagination. That's where my fire comes from (Gornick 1997, 27).

Furthermore, Wallace continues the tradition of the 'classic' socialist theatre that blossomed in both America and Europe between World Wars I and II. Reviewing *Slaughter City*, for instance, Benedict Nightingale declares, "At root, this is a traditional Marxist protest play...All this could have been written by Odets for New York's Group Theatre in the 1930s" (1996, 1). Meanwhile, Claudia Barnett argues, "Wallace employs Brechtian themes and techniques in her plays to become the consummate Brechtian feminist" (2002, 156). While she is perhaps best known for the lyrical sexuality of her work, Wallace is at heart a historical materialist working in the Marxian tradition. What then, is one to make of her explicit Marxism?

This effort to continue the tradition of Brecht and Odets and her intense focus on the historical permutations of capitalism might be seen as a form of postmodern nostalgia for an earlier epoch when political activism was effective and possible. In the wake of Lyotardian poststructuralism, Marxist dialectic has often been characterized as "contemptible attempt" to construct "grand narratives" and "totalizing (totalitarian?) knowledges" (Ahmad 1992, 69). In a rather different diagnosis, Fredric Jameson has lamented that postmodern writers, thinkers, and artists—unable to see beyond the late capitalist illusion of timelessness and political stasis—have "forgotten how to think historically" and by extension politically (Jameson 1991, 1). From a Jamesonian perspective, Wallace's plays might be seen as nostalgic for a practicable Marxian radicalism, the playwright taking dialectic from its origin in rational inquiry and sensationalizing its key concepts as aesthetic formulations.[2] Yet Wallace's politics cannot be dismissed as just another example of postmodern nostalgia.

Wallace's fascination with Marxism can be understood in relation to a postmodern crisis in historical thought. In *Sublime Desire: History and Post-1960s Fiction*, Amy J. Elias claims that this postmodern "crisis in history" (and, by extension, macropolitics) can be characterized as an impasse between the desire for a meaningful history and the conviction that such meaning is impossible; she writes that, as a result, postmodernists tend to envision history as a kind of "secular-sacred" knowledge, one rooted in the chaos and ultimate inscrutability of what she—borrowing from Hayden White—calls the "historical sublime" rather than in a rational, scientific history (Elias 2001, 187). According to Elias, this postmodernist secular-sacred history is expressed in the fabulist counter-realism of what she calls the metahistorical romance. Along similar lines, Marxist dialectic provides just such a secular-sacred foundation in Wallace's plays. Faced with the impossibility of claiming—as Brecht did—a scientific basis for her plays, Wallace hopes instead to recuperate dialectical materialism in quasi-theological terms.[3] The Marxism of her plays reflects an effort to think dialectically in an age where history and grand political narratives can be seen only in terms of the sublime, the transcendent. For Wallace, this generally theological and specifically messianic Marxism offers the foundation for a utopian politics. Comparing *Slaughter City* and *Things of Dry Hours*, two plays that appeared more than a decade apart, reveals not only the consistency of this faith in Marxism, but also the playwright's evolving strategies for staging it.

While Wallace's plays are closely linked to other postmodern literature (such as the metahistorical romances described by Elias), her theological Marxism can be traced to a specific source: Walter Benjamin's "Theses on the Philosophy of History," which offers a thorough revision of Marx's philosophy of history. Having seen in the rise of Nazism the horror that history brings, Benjamin rejected the vulgar Marxist concept of Europe progressing steadily towards utopian socialism and proposed instead that historical materialism—which he considers an objective, rational, scientific radicalism—enlist the services of theology (1969, 253). Borrowing from Jewish ideas of messianic time, he conceived history not as a chain of events culminating in a perfected state, but as a continuum of catastrophe, a piling of "wreckage upon wreckage" (257). Any given catastrophe, however, might usher in messianic revolution and a millennial utopia of social justice and equality; for Benjamin, as for the Jewish theologians, "every second of time was the strait gate through which the Messiah might enter" (264). Thus the practice of history becomes a search through the rubble, an effort to find traces of revolutionary immanence (and imminence) in historical crises. Instead of a positivistic, linear history, Benjamin saw one perpetually occurring catastrophe interpenetrated by messianic time, what he called *"Jetztzeit,"* or, as Hannah Arendt translated it, the "presence of the now."[4] Wallace's own understanding of Marxism and of history derives largely from this theological revision. Most of her plays dramatize historical crises (ranging from the plague of 1665 to the Iraq War) while reflecting Benjamin's notion of historical time; in them the catastrophic violence of social conflict is shot through with utopian potential, what Benjamin calls "chips of Messianic time." Wallace's plays are notable for their adherence to a messianic concept of historical materialism, one, which underlies both the aesthetics and political sentiments of the playwright's oeuvre.[5]

Wallace's 1996 fantastical factory drama *Slaughter City* is, of all her plays, the one most central to her art and ideas. Reworking the territory of such precursors as Sinclair's *The Jungle* and Brecht's *Saint Joan of the Stockyards*, the play's action occurs in a factory that exists "now and then" in "Slaughter City, U.S.A." Prefaced by Wallace's account of her interviews with meat-industry workers in the 1990s and arriving on the stage weighted with the association of labor themes with social realism, *Slaughter City* nevertheless aims for something very different from realism. Instead, the play remakes factory drama as an elaborate fantasia of spectral visitation, symbolic action, and the sensationalism of bleeding flesh—human and otherwise.[6]

The play's central characters work on the floor of a meatpacking plant that is haunted by the Sausage Man, seemingly the ghost of a turn-of-the-century meatpacking tycoon. The play's narrative is driven by the arrival of the worker Cod, later revealed to be both a woman in disguise and the Sausage Man's metaphysical adversary.[7] Over the course of the play, Cod organizes the workers and leads them into an apocalyptic strike. Central to the play is the classical Marxist paradigm of dialectical materialism, which Wallace presents by using the strategies of spectacle and fantasia. Using these strategies, Wallace updates the rationalist dialectic of 'classic' socialist drama to include a postmodernist, revisionary utopianism that is rooted in the historical-political sublime.

Slaughter City's spectacular fantasia is erected explicitly on the foundation of Marx and Engels's *Manifesto of the Communist Party*, establishing the play as an allegory about class conflict and the imminence of radical social change. This can be seen as an effort to reimagine socialist theatre for postindustrial capitalism. Writing about contemporary visual art, Craig Owens identifies the increasing presence of allegory as one of the characteristics of postmodern aesthetics. For Owens, allegory occurs in contemporary art, "whenever one text is doubled by another... Allegorical imagery is appropriated imagery; the allegorist does not invent images but confiscates them. He lays claim to the culturally significant, poses as its interpreter" (1992, 53–4). *Slaughter City* must be read in light of this; the setting, characters, and events of Wallace's play reflect her interpretation of the *Manifesto* as a work prophetic—in virtually a theological sense—of sudden and radical social change.

The characters fall generally into two categories that embody the *Manifesto*'s "two, great contending classes." Representing the bourgeoisie are the factory's manager Baquin and his foreman Tuck, who—despite his misgivings—is generally complicit in Baquin's schemes to increase worker productivity. On the other side are the union workers: Roach, Maggot, and Brandon. The chief allegorical characters of the play, however, are the two ghostly figures that haunt the packinghouse, representing the adversarial classes described in the *Manifesto*. The Sausage Man, aligned with Baquin and Tuck, wields a hand-held sausage grinder and waxes nostalgic about the "old days" when visionary capitalists refused to let unions stand in the way of production. Constantly brandishing his symbolic grinder, the Sausage Man recognizes that his power—and that of his industry—derives from exploiting the "refuse" of progress: the proletariat itself. The Sausage Man recalls, "I made sausages. All the little bits of bone and gut and cartilage that the rest of the world threw away, I made into something useful. Something edible... With my two hands I created an empire out of a single sausage" (Wallace 1996c, 19).[8] Meanwhile, his adversary Cod straddles the two temporal dimensions of the play, interacting with both the Sausage Man and the play's flesh-and-blood characters. Victory for her means awakening to her role as Slaughter City's revolutionary leader.

Wallace uses these two characters to produce not only an allegory of the *Manifesto*'s contending classes, but also to articulate a vision—derived from Benjamin—of the historical sublime. Using metaphors from the meatpacking industry, the Sausage Man conceives progress as a great animal: "Can there be history without the poor? Small people die small deaths and their place in history is the flick of a pig's tale, part of the machinery of the living beast, but the tail end all the same... There will always be refuse in this world, so there will always be a place for me" (44). Described by The Sausage Man as the mechanical production of refuse—the process described by Benjamin as the piling of "wreckage upon wreckage"—historical time is, from the first scene, destabilized. Cod, the eternal animating spirit of labor activism, may lead the fight in Slaughter City, USA, but she has led it elsewhere and 'elsewhen' as well. Appearing throughout the history of labor conflict, Cod nearly personifies Benjamin's concept

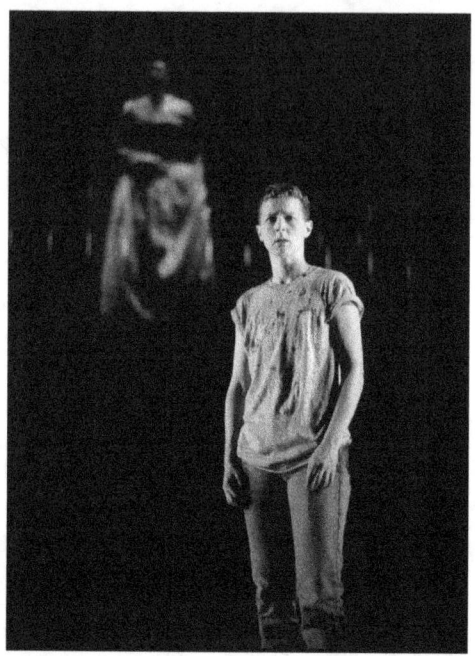

Figure 3.1 Phoebe Jonas (The Textile Worker) and Sharon Scruggs (Cod) in the 1996 American Repertory Theatre production of *Slaughter City*. Director: Ron Daniels. Photo: Richard Feldman. Courtesy of American Repertory Theatre.

of an interpenetrating *Jetztzeit*. Delivering a trance-like litany of her personal history, she recalls:

> I used to be union. A miner. Long time ago…Harlen [*sic*.] County …Kentucky…No…It was the Colorado coal strike. Dug our own graves underground. Ate coal, pissed coal, shat coal. After years of it, we went on strike…Rockefeller called out the National Guard. They came down on the Ludlow colony, burned our tents and opened fire. Sixty-six of us dead (16).

Cod remembers more labor tragedies in this same dream-like manner during the play; like Tom Joad, she has been there, fought oppression in a thousand guises, observed countless catastrophes, and witnessed, in Benjamin's terms, the wreckage piled at the feet of history. Cod embodies also the spiritual gifts of the revolutionary, bringing to the workers at Slaughter City those things that according to Benjamin, "manifest themselves in this struggle as courage, humor, cunning, and fortitude" (1969, 255). Thus Cod, who represents Labor's indomitable spirit of resistance, is furthermore a messianic figure.

For Benjamin, the ultimate goal of such revolutionaries is the disruption of history. *Slaughter City* ends with a revolution brought about by catastrophe. As Brandon dies from an ammonia-line rupture, Cod removes her shirt to use it for first aid. Because she has been disguised for the duration of the play as a man, this act is dually catastrophic, sparking both a worker revolt and a gender cataclysm. As Roach prepares the chains that the workers will use to seize the factory, Maggot unwinds the bandage that restrains Cod's breasts. When the bandage drops to the floor, two revolutions occur at once: "Maggot and Cod kiss. At the moment of the kiss we hear the very loud sound of heavy doors being pulled shut and locking, echoes of many doors locking and locking. Then silence" (83). Roach proclaims the new order of affairs in Slaughter City: "My friends. Welcome to Slaughter City. This is a place where things go and go and go. Now this is a place where things stop. Machinery stops. Cows stop. Pigs stop. We stop. And most importantly, profits stop. And whenever profit stops, things heat up fast. From now on, anything can happen" (86).

As the workers' takeover of the plant commences, the Sausage Man faces his old adversary Cod in a final showdown: "The two of us here, together. At last. But will both of us be here to mop up the mess?" (86). The scene is permeated by the failures of the past and the potentialities of the future, illustrating what Benjamin terms, "a history which does not occur in homogeneous, empty time, but time filled by the presence of the Now" (1969, 261). For Cod, this threatens to be overwhelming. She scarcely remembers the place or hour, stuttering, "I'm with the Knights of Labour...No...With the United Mine" before she can locate herself (86). At last, however, she is able to do just that, throwing off the Sausage Man's yoke by remembering, just in time, to call out "fire" and ostensibly prevent another defeat. As Benjamin describes it—ironic here considering Cod's transvestitism—the revolutionary, "remains in control of his powers, man enough to blast open the continuum of history" (1969, 261).

Both the utopian politics and fantastical aesthetics of Wallace's play derive from her adoption of Benjamin's theological Marxism. Where the rationalist dialectic of classical Marxism led to a realist discourse of industrial labor, Benjamin's theological revision engenders in *Slaughter City* a fantasia of immanence in which the workaday world of a meatpacking plant is interpenetrated by a ghostly conflict between capital and labor. Furthermore, each crisis brought about by this conflict, each new catastrophe, offers the possibility of a revolution that will redeem history by establishing social justice. Thus, *Slaughter City* creates the paradigm by which Wallace's other historical and political plays can be understood.

Wallace's *Things of Dry Hours*, first produced in 2004, likewise features factory workers' resistance to the ideological pressures and political oppression propagated by the bourgeois establishment. Additionally, the play reflects the development of Wallace's dramaturgy away from the fantasia of *Slaughter City* and towards a minimalism that suits the play's overt didacticism. In accordance with *Things*' somewhat closer observance of 'realism' (although an element of 'magic' remains), there is little of the *gestic* spectacle that characterizes Wallace's earlier plays. The scale of the play's setting is much reduced, as is the number of characters, who generally 'talk more' (while 'acting less'). Nevertheless, *Things of Dry Hours* is of a piece with the earlier play in its focus on messianic time. Drawing from Robin D. G. Kelley's *Hammer and Hoe* (1990), a history of Communist activism in Alabama during the 1930s, *Things of Dry Hours* takes for its subject the Depression-era struggle between Tennessee Coal and Iron (TCI) and the radicalized workers—many of them African-American—in Birmingham's steel industry. The play is tightly focused on just three characters. Tice Hogan, an out-of-work, aging African-American Sunday School teacher and Communist Party member, is forced to open the home he shares with his daughter Cali to Corbin Teel, an illiterate, itinerate, white worker who asks for refuge after fatally striking his foreman and who is probably a company stool pigeon. With the exception of Tice's framing chorus, the play occurs entirely within the Hogan's home and between these three characters. Reviewers of the play were nearly united in finding the eponymous 'dry' an apt description, though Sam Marlowe, even while terming the production "relentlessly stark" and "arid," praised its "cool, reflective intellectual rigour" (2007, 18). This 'dryness' is recognizable as a shift in Wallace's dramaturgy, yet *Things of Dry Hours* maintains the sense of messianic Marxism that drives *Slaughter City*.

Even more explicitly than in Wallace's earlier plays, *Things of Dry Hours* conflates the spiritual and the political. This combination stems from the historical fact that homegrown communism among African-American laborers in Alabama often borrowed from the New

Testament rhetoric of religious utopianism (Next Stage, 6). Thus Tice is at once a devout Christian and a disciple of Marx, teaching from the Bible every Sunday while piously noting, "I pay my two cents a month dues as a member and unit leader of the Communist Party of Alabama. Hallelujah" (Wallace 2007, 5).[9] Throughout the play, Tice claims to follow two books. The first is a very large Bible, while the second is "the little book," one of the three secret copies of the *Manifesto* in Birmingham (31). As he is fond of observing, "these two books agree on a lot of points" (11). For Tice, the books provide complementary radical utopian visions. He explains the relation between his theology and his political activism to Corbin: "Jesus Christ says the poor, that's us, are all brothers. And his right-hand man, a quick little fellow, boils on his ass, goes by the name of Karl, says those who labor, that's us again, even if we are out of work, to make the wealth are one" (39). This underscores Tice's—and the playwright's—belief that the gospels of Christ and of Marx both offered a powerful utopian alternative to the realities of economic and racial oppression in the 1930s. As Wallace tells Kwame Kwei-Armah, "they are interconnected—the spiritual with the political—in the end, all change comes from dreaming...And dreams are magical. I wanted to show the magic of that world. To show that these things were inseparable—dreaming of a different kind of America" (Wallace and Kwei-Armah 2007, 7). Throughout the play, historical materialism is reimagined as a kind of gospel for evangelical radicalism.

Of central importance are Tice's efforts to proselytize the nihilistic Corbin Teel. Corbin has heard the rhetoric of communism before, but he mocks it with the same condescension that he feels toward religion. Tice suspects the fugitive to be a company stooge from the beginning, but he nevertheless undertakes to educate him in the Marxist dialectic that he understands as both a "hard truth" and a "calling." From the play's beginning, Tice provides a dialectical appraisal of class and race in both the present and the historical past, following the dialectician's creed: "How would Marx consider the situation?" (6). Though Cali worries that her father is "dryin' up into a set of words," Tice eventually convinces her that educating others is the most important aspect of his activism, noting that to Marx's words he adds, "Du Bois, the Bible. Lots of things. All good words of justice they come from. Some kind of Heaven" (59). Tice is able to analyze, for his daughter and their 'guest,' not only the current conflict between Birmingham's proletariat and Tennessee Coal and Iron, but also the peculiarities of race in America (62–5). This is the education that he extends to the illiterate Corbin by teaching him to read from the *Manifesto*:

"we'll start with the reading and we'll keep with reading until you love it. Until your face looks like a page" (31). Although he doubts that Corbin will ever be useful to the Party, Tice instructs him with a missionary's zeal, explaining to Cali that only by planting such seeds will activism flower in Alabama: "No, he may never get to a meeting, but I tell you he's going out of this house a changed man. He had no eagerness when he came in. Spirit all flickering dull in the back of his skull, 'bout to go out. And a meanness in his eyes, like small change. All these days, I've been stoking that little flame... bringing it back to life" (69). *Things of Dry Hours* re-invents classical Marxism as a sacred scripture that requires careful study and application.

This draws upon Benjamin's belief that historical materialists—as revolutionaries—work to "blast upon the continuum of history" by introducing messianic time into the piled wreckage of historical catastrophe. This catastrophe is represented in the play by what Tice refers to as, "that deeply underrated and American phenomenon: the persistent murdering of resistance" (91). Thus Wallace focuses on the violence that destroys both the bodies and the wills of those who labor for others. For instance, Tice recounts the story of fellow foundry-worker Joe Holton, dwarfed and bent by his job of ladling 60 pounds of molten iron a hundred times a day before finally dying

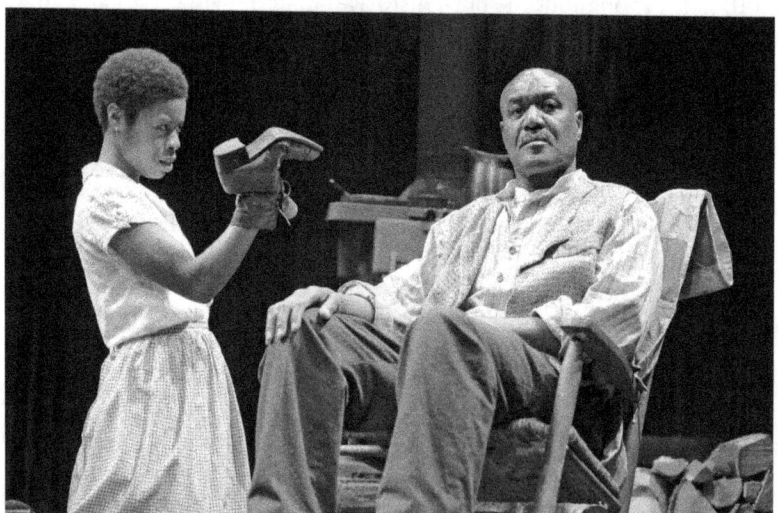

Figure 3.2 Roslyn Ruff (Cali Hogan) and Delroy Lindo (Tice Hogan) in the 2009 New York Theater Workshop production of *Things of Dry Hours*. Director: Ruben Santiago-Hudson. Photo: Joan Marcus.

in a horrific accident in which both of his feet are burnt to nothingness by the liquid metal (23). Cali, meanwhile, suggests that she has been the victim of sexual domination by white, privileged employers in her job of laundering the sheets and towels of Birmingham's affluent families (54–7). To this is added the counter-revolutionary violence of Tennessee Coal and Iron, which maintains a private police form that is, as Corbin says, "more law than law" (20). It is the company that has sent Corbin to the Hogans in order to find names of Party members, and it is the company that eventually murders both Corbin and Tice.

This oppressive power is opposed in both a Benjaminian and a gospel sense by the evangelism of the party. As in *Slaughter City*, 'soapboxing' for the Party is translated into preaching the good news of social justice. Meanwhile, Tice's description of his conversion to Marxism at a protest led by historical agitator Hosea Hudson evokes the crowds of the gospels: "We were shouting for work relief. Shouting 'gainst segregation. But it wasn't just the words that took me up. It was a kind of. Humming... it was the first time I didn't feel. Alone" (79). This is revolution as revelation, and—like the Christian scriptures—the movement is abounding in martyrs, including Tice, who reveals in the epilogue that his framing narration has been a spectral visitation. Like the executed Wobbly in the folksong "I Dreamed I Saw Joe Hill Last Night" (and like other characters in Wallace's plays, most notably Morse in *One Flea Spare*), the murdered Tice is now outside of history, speaking from beyond the grave and directly to the play's audience out of Benjamin's *Jetztzeit*. While the company has murdered Tice, they have also martyred him. Even in what seems like defeat, his story continues to inspire faith in a redemptive political activism. Like martyrs in the Christian tradition, Wallace's historical martyrs serve to glorify the utopian imagination and to anticipate the arrival of the just, equitable society: one that results not necessarily from the proletarian revolution advocated in the *Manifesto*, but from the sudden, unexpected occurrence of what Benjamin calls the messianic redemption of history.

The thematic consistency of *Slaughter City* and *Things of Dry Hours* underscores what may be the central political idea in Wallace's drama: her conviction that Marxian dialectic possesses a redemptive power conceivable in theological terms. Inspired by her mentor Tony Kushner's use of Benjamin's "Theses" in *Angels in America*, she has made messianic Marxism the bedrock of her political and historical drama since her earliest major productions. While her politics have been consistent, the considerable formal differences between

Slaughter City and *Things of Dry Hours* show Wallace working away from an avowedly postmodernist, fantastical appropriation of the factory drama toward a didactic minimalism. Ultimately, these two plays contextualize the obsession with history in Wallace's other plays and showcase her efforts to work out a new Marxist drama in an era that has been mostly hostile to utopian socialism.

Notes

1. This essay represents an extension of my earlier piece Wisner "'Waiting in the Angel's Wings': Marxist Fantasia in Naomi Wallace's *Slaughter City*," which appeared in *The Journal of American Drama and Theatre* 18 no. 1 (2006): 54–70. Some of the ideas here, as well as several passages analyzing *Slaughter City*, first appeared in this earlier essay.
2. A possible analogy is E. L. Doctorow's historical novel *Ragtime*. See Jameson (1991, 21–25).
3. See, for instance, Bertolt Brecht, "The Epic Theatre and Its Difficulties," in *Brecht on Theatre: The Development of an Aesthetic*, ed. and trans. John Willett (New York: Hill and Wang, 1964), 22–24.
4. "*Jetztzeit*" might be translated as, "now time," but Arendt notes that the term should not be confused with "the present," but refers instead to "the mystical *nunc stans*," when "normal" time stands still. See Benjamin (1969, 261).
5. Wallace shares this debt to Benjamin's "Theses" with Tony Kushner, whose two-part *Angels in America* brought a camp version of Benjamin's ideas first to Broadway and later to a widely-acclaimed HBO production. See Roger Bechtel, "'A Kind of Painful Progress': The Benjaminian Dialectics of *Angels in America*," *Journal of Dramatic Theory and Criticism* 16 (2001): 99–121.
6. Both the word 'fantasia' and my concept of the aesthetic are taken from Kushner's *Angels in America*.
7. For more on the many ghosts in Wallace's plays, see Beth Cleary, "Haunting the Social Unconscious: Naomi Wallace's *In the Heart of America*," *Journal of American Drama and Theatre* 14 no. 2 (2002): 1–11 and Erica Stevens Abbitt, "Getting Out, Flying and Returning from the Dead: Girl Ghosts in Live Performance," *Journal of Dramatic Theory and Criticism* 21 no. 2 (2007): 143.
8. This and all subsequent quotations from *Slaughter City* come from the 1996 Faber and Faber edition of the play.
9. This and all subsequent quotations from *Things of Dry Hours* come from the 2007 Faber and Faber edition of the play.

4

An American Exile in America

Vivian Gornick

This profile appeared in the New York Times Magazine *on Sunday, March 2, 1997 on the occasion of Wallace's New York debut downtown at the Public Theater. At that moment, Wallace was a virtual unknown on the American theatre scene.*

* * *

Naomi Wallace is an American playwright whose work has gone largely unproduced in America, her plays routinely described as 'strong but political,' whereas in England she has had four major productions in as many years, with a striking amount of critical attention awarded each of them. Last year, however, her newest play, *One Flea Spare*, was the consensus hit at the Humana Festival of New American Plays in Louisville, Kentucky. Now, having won a raft of awards, it is set to open next Sunday at the Joseph Papp Public Theater in New York, with Dianne Wiest in the lead role. Wallace is finally about to be discovered by her compatriots—although some of them have known for years that recognition at home was foregone conclusion.

In England, Wallace has been widely responded to. Her adaptation of William Wharton's *Birdy* is opening this week in the West End, and a film script she wrote, *Lawn Dogs*, has been produced in Britain and will be released this year. Wallace has also had a book of her poetry published in, yes, Britain and not yet in the United States. But her four plays—not only political but often imbued with an almost otherworldly sexuality—are what have made her reputation abroad. It is precisely that blend of politics and sexuality, laced with relentlessly lyrical writing that seems to have made her welcome in Britain and a stranger in her homeland.

In *The War Boys*, Wallace's first play, three young men are hunting illegal immigrants on the Texas-Mexico border for bounty. The second, *In the Heart of America*, concerns a pair of gay marines who get caught in the internal viciousness of the Gulf War. In the third, *Slaughter City*, a strike is taking place in a meatpacking plant. In *One Flea Spare* (the title comes from a John Donne poem), a group of Londoners, low and high, are quarantined together during the 1665 Plague. Each of the plays is set against a piece of social realism, but none of the plays are presented realistically. All are made to serve a language, rich and poetic, that is associative and dreamlike, often surreal and in every case haunted by history.

History is what excites her, history and politics. "Politics is history," Wallace says, "and history is what sparks my imagination. That's where my fire comes from. For me, politics and art can never be divided. Once you see that politics affects our daily lives—our loves, our desires, our needs—that's terribly exciting." She knows that this is not a fashionable way to approach the making of art. "But it's my way," she says, and her intelligent, serious face breaks up unexpectedly. "Hey, listen," she grins, "whatever stirs your soup."

Tony Kushner, whose *Angels in America* seems to have led the way to a resurgence of serious, often political playwriting, has been a champion of Wallace's since 1990. "I was doing a one-week stint at the playwriting program at the Iowa Playwrights' Workshop," he says, "The students were all okay, smart, talented, some of them better than okay. And then there was Naomi. I'd given them all this theory, Marx and modern drama—you know, that stuff doesn't go over well in playwriting courses. She not only loved it, went right for it, she already knew a lot of it. I remember thinking, 'Who is this?'"

"She gave me *War Boys* to read, and I was blown away. The power of language in it! And the way she thought, the things she was thinking about," Kushner laughs at the recollection. "I said to myself: 'Now, take it slow. Don't overwhelm her.' Then she walked into class the next day and I gushed: 'This is one of the most astonishing plays by a student I've ever read.' I came back to New York and took her play to my agent. I said to her: 'This woman is going to be big someday. Please read her play and take her on.' And she did. Naomi's language bowled her over, too."

Naomi Wallace was born 36 years ago on a farm in Kentucky to a son of the gentleman-farmer class who had once been a *Time-Life* reporter and a vigorous Dutch mother who had once been a member of the Netherlands' Communist Party. Wallace has been marching in protest parades since age eight, which made it exciting to go to Washington but not so easy to stay home.

The Wallace farm was set in a conservative area outside Louisville where independent-minded politics was not welcome. Naomi's grandfather, Tom Wallace, had been the editor in chief of *The Louisville Courier-Journal*, and when Naomi was growing up, her parents were considered radicals. Inevitably, the Wallace children became social oddities in the neighborhood.

Life inside the family was complicated as well. Naomi's mother, an artist, was a city girl from a working-class family who was alarmed to find herself rearing five children on a farm in Kentucky. She made so many trips back to Amsterdam that the marriage ended in divorce and with her return to the Netherlands.

Ill at ease almost everywhere, Naomi hung around the only people she felt at home with—her neighbors, the children of the rural poor. She spent all her time after school inside the houses of kids whose parents were sometimes farmhands, sometimes mechanics, sometimes unemployed. She ate what they ate and drank what they drank. She shopped with them and she danced with them. She listened to the rhythms of their speech, heard their secret thoughts and marveled at how both got put into stories. They had a habit of turning every small event into a story so wonderfully told that it was like listening to poetry.

What she saw and felt and heard among the rural poor in Kentucky 25 years ago entered into her: the poverty, the richness of language, the peculiar grace of hard-worked lives. Hard-worked and going nowhere. She knew even then that she would get out, and that most of them would not. When she looked in the mirror, she saw a face that looked just like the faces all around her. What made the difference?

"Class," she says quietly, matter-of-factly, over a plate of Indian food in Iowa City, where she lives with her husband, who teaches literature at the University of Iowa, and their three daughters. "It's all a matter of class." The class she came from, she explains, invited her into her own mind; the class her friends came from not only didn't invite them into theirs, but did everything it could to keep them out and break them down. Her expression is intent as she speaks, the forkful of food in her hand forgotten midway to her mouth.

Wallace is thin and angular, somewhat raw-boned, with a thatch of cropped black hair that frames a long, narrow face and a manner strongly marked by a kind of reserve common to country people. The reserve makes her face in repose very nearly inexpressive—the eyes opaque, the features immobile. But ask a question, elicit an opinion, and the impassivity instantly collapses into an unbroken flow of speech. During the two days I visited Wallace in Iowa the conversation was constant and without closure. It consisted entirely of a discussion—focused and urgent—not of how her plays get put together, but of the ideas and experiences out of which they grow. It's not so much that Wallace thinks about politics all the times as that she is continually registering its consequences on the lives of all the people she knows.

"I don't know why everyone doesn't see this," she says. "We live in a culture where social forces are so present. They make us what we are. As an artist, how can I ignore what has created us?"

'The system' is a reality for her, and inevitably, perhaps even reluctantly, she rates the people she knows according to how responsive they are to the meaning of politics in ordinary life. At one point I idly asked her is she like her father. She turned the question over in her mind (as with every question I asked) and then, with her usual quiet reserve, said: "I think he must be a good man. Two of his daughters are gay. That can't be easy for him." Her face lighted up. "But he marches in the parades." She likes him because he's a good man. He's a good man because he resonates to social injustice.

This is homegrown American radicalism, the kind that has been coming out of the heartland for one hundred years and more. It is a radicalism rooted not in theory but in a vivid, emotional flash on the way social inequity pushes lives out of shape. "I am moved," Wallace says, "by the way the system breaks people in half, and still they rise up to tell their story again, with grace and eloquence. People I went to school with have become farmers and factory workers and electricians. They pump gas and drive trucks and dig wells, and they are old in their mid-30s. One of my schoolmates, a man of 35, has been laying carpet for twenty years. The last time I was home he told me that his back and his knee hurt so much now that he can't get on top of his wife when they're making love. But he told me in a kind of wild, funny, self-mocking tale full of Kentucky humor and smarts, and I could see, not in what he said but in how he said it, that he was trying to make sense of things. Just behind his words, he was saying: 'What did I do wrong? How did I end up like this?'"

Wallace left Louisville for Hampshire College in Amherst, Massachusetts, then the writing program at the University of Iowa. But the voices in her head, the ones that pull language from her, are back there in Kentucky. It's the carpet layer whose life seems metaphoric to her. "He's a man whose body has been used up by the system and then thrown away," she says. "In our society, the body is a thing made instrumental use of, and then asked to be—meant to be, unable to be—a thing of love." This, above all else, is the contradiction that excites her. "Capitalism," she says, quoting Terry Eagleton, "plunders the sensuality of the body," and her eyes shine as she repeats the British Marxist's poetic indictment.

The most striking element in Wallace's work is the use she makes of the erotic. Invariably, at the unexpected moment, between an unlikely pair of characters—an old woman and a young man, two boys, two women—a sexual flare will occur that is mysterious and disturbing. "In Naomi's work something is always being done to the body," says Ron Daniels, who is directing *One Flea Spare* at the Public and who also directed *Slaughter City* at the Royal Shakespeare Company. "It is always being touched, caressed, burned, perforated, poured on, and spat on. It's standing in a river of life-and-death fluids: alive to blood, sweat, snot, running sores, and oozing wounds. For Naomi, it has to do with making the body—for which read 'class'—burst its bounds. Now here's the catch: it's all in the name of change, hope, possibility."

This intimate relation among sensuality, the cruelty of politics and the hope of redemption is crucial in Wallace's plays. Sensuality has not much to do with romantic love and everything to do with the primitive longing to connect. "Desire—that's really what I'm talking about," she says. "I don't mean love. I'm not sure I know what that means. Desire serves the need to end one's singular state. It creates the space in which to reimagine oneself. That alone ends loneliness."

One Flea Spare is, at this moment, a culminating work. The play is set in London during the great plague of 1665 in the stripped and boarded-up house of William and Darcy Snelgrave, a wealthy, elderly couple quarantined because their servants died of the plague. Their confinement period is about to expire when Bunce, a seaman fleeing impressment, and Morse, a 12-year-old girl also seeking refuge, steal into the house. This condemns the Snelgraves and the intruders to 28 days of shared quarantine.

Angry, frightened, confused, and unable to escape, these people will engage with one another—and therefore with themselves. It

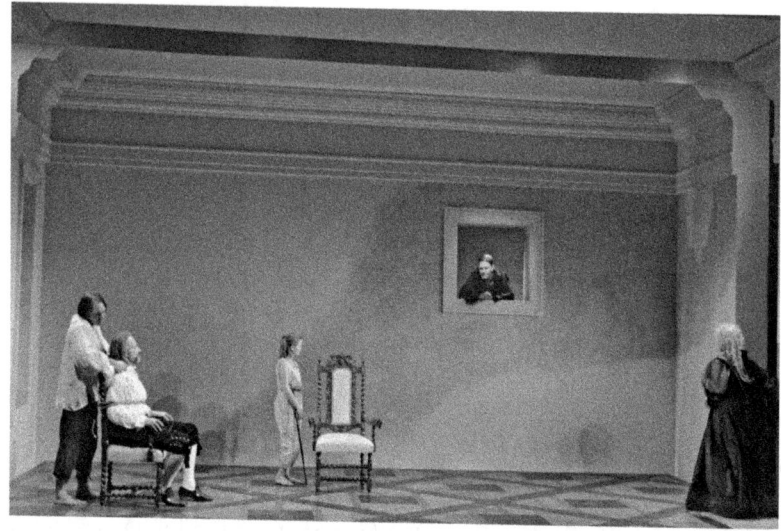

Figure 4.1 (From left to right) Bill Camp (Bunce), Jon De Vries (William Snelgrave), Mischa Barton (Morse), Paul Kandel (Kabe), and Dianne Wiest (Darcy Snelgrave) in the 1997 Public Theater production of *One Flea Spare*. Director: Ron Daniels. Scenic design: Riccardo Hernandez. Costume design: Paul Tazewell. Lighting Design: Scott Zielinski. Photo © Michal Daniel, 2007.

will soon transpire that Darcy Snelgrave, married at 15 to William Snelgrave, was hideously burned in a stable fire at 17 and has not been touched in 30 years by her husband or any other human creature, and that Bunce has a wound in his side that refuses to heal, and that Morse is a mysteriously wise child who will become the catalytic force that brings the play a dramatic power. At last, in a memorable and remarkably erotic scene, Bunce will 'touch' Darcy, and she will 'penetrate' his wound.

The situation may be contrived, but the language is stirring and the play brilliantly constructed. "There are at least two moments in it," Kushner says, "when everything comes together—emotionally, symbolically, intellectually—and you hear the voice of the play. Not of the playwright, but of the play. Those are thrilling moments, and they don't always occur."

The London reviews for *One Flea Spare* were spectacular, praising not only the richness of the language, but also the way the language serves the subtext. "What the plague throws into relief about class division and the nature of human intimacy comes under a scrutiny both poetically sensitive and beadily comic," wrote a critic in *The Independent*, echoing many others in England. And indeed, this was the play that would bring Wallace home. "I did find it ironic," she says, "that the play I wrote about a young gay man from Kentucky who goes to the gulf war—that Louisville passed on that play. And they passed on *Slaughter City*, about a meatpacking plant twenty minutes away from the theater. Then my British play, about the plague, that's the one they took."

It was actually the Los Angeles riots in 1992 that started Wallace on *One Flea Spare*. "I'd been reading Daniel Defoe's *Journal of the Plague Year* when the riots broke out," she recalls, "and I began to see them both—L.A. and the London plague—as the same event. A time of crisis. A time when rich and poor get thrown together—and, suddenly, one sees alternatives. I began to think about what happens when the containment of a presumed danger through the regimentation of space breaks down, such as when South-Central L.A. began to 'invade' Beverly Hills. I wanted foreground a society in crisis. By writing about a time other than our own, it's possible for issues that have become locked in rhetoric, or dismissed as too over determined for the stage, to become visible anew."

Naomi Wallace is a playwright who thinks of herself as a public intellectual with a responsibility to make theatre audiences feel and understand the urgencies of their time. Deeply influenced by modernist theatre, she is nevertheless, in spirit, a descendant of 1930s and 1940s social realism. This apparent anomaly has created major problems for her poetic plays, at least in this country. "There's a more open tradition for political theatre in Britain," she says. "Somehow, the British are able to say, 'Yes, there's a class culture and it's still worthy writing about.'"

But 30 years of liberation politics and a culture steeped in therapy have made most Americans feel the reality of their lives in a language strongly at odds with the one that focuses on class struggle. To American ears, Wallace's work can sound like Beckett rewriting Clifford Odets. Yet her talent is large, her intelligence strong; the work reminds us of how often writers like Brecht, Yeats, and Gordimer have felt compelled to celebrate life and still bear open, undisguised witness.

When asked if she is bitter about having been so long ignored in her own country, Wallace says: "Hey, I'm happy to have my plays done anywhere. If I wanted to be romantic, I'd think of myself as a writer in exile. But I have never thought of myself that way. Oh, sure, I've been frustrated. I'd think: 'Why the hell is Louisville taking so long to recognize me? I'm from here!' But there's always been a small core of good people who've supported me." The country reserve gives way to that irresistible grin. "I always knew that sooner or later it would get itself organized."

5

The City that Embraced Naomi Wallace

Walter Bilderback

In the fall of 2001, theatres in Atlanta, Georgia collaborated on a citywide festival of Naomi Wallace plays, one that took on an added resonance in the wake of current events. This account, reprinted by permission, first appeared in the February 2002 edition of American Theatre *magazine.*

* * *

To call Vincent Murphy, artistic producing director of Atlanta's Theater Emory, a fan of the work of Naomi Wallace is an understatement. Her writing, he says, is, "Brecht seen through the lens of Faulkner and Caryl Churchill."

Murphy illustrates his admiration by describing a scene from Wallace's 1998 drama *The Trestle at Pope Lick Creek*. The couple Gin and Dray, rural factory workers in Depression-era Kentucky, are discussing their situation: Dray has been laid off from his job, and Gin works in a glass factory where a new process has turned the hands of the women workers glow-in-the-dark blue. Their teenage son is in jail on suspicion of murder, and they're having difficulty remembering why, years ago, they fell in love with each other (a love that, as in all of Wallace's plays, is frankly sexual). As they talk, Wallace's text requires that they throw a plate back and forth and that it shatter at the end of the scene.

"Who does this? Who thinks this way?" Murphy marvels, as he remembers being, "blown away," by the scene when the play debuted at the Actors Theatre of Louisville Humana Festival. "This is a voice we don't understand"—which for him is the mark of a potentially great writer. Never one to let his enthusiasms lie untested, Murphy asked himself and the entire Atlanta theatre community a question: "What if a dozen theatres across Atlanta got together to present the works of this not-so-well-known American playwright, Naomi Wallace?" His colleagues were mostly unfamiliar with Wallace's work (none of her plays had ever been produced in Atlanta), but Murphy's case for her literary importance was as convincing as his ardor was contagious. In short order, the theatres of Atlanta had signed on to Murphy's mammoth challenge.

As plans for the autumn-long festival developed, Wallace's stock grew, especially when the Kentucky-born writer was named a MacArthur 'Genius Grant' winner in 1999. Murphy served as yenta for the project, attempting to match Wallace's plays with the strengths and styles of the theatres taking part. In most cases, his suggestions worked out. "I didn't think *One Flea Spare* was the right play for us," commented Hope Mirlis of the four-year-old Synchronicity Performance Group, "Then I read the play." Synchronicity's Michele Pearce credits Murphy with, "a knack for matching companies with plays," which comes from a deep understanding of, "who these Atlanta companies are."

The final pieces fell into place when Wallace agreed to allow Theater Emory to workshop *The Inland Sea* (formerly titled *Fugitive Cant*), a new play commissioned by the Royal Shakespeare Company, this past April as part of its Brave New Works series, and to participate in the festival herself over the course of a week in November, when she would see the various productions and answer questions for the public. The prospect of having personal access to Wallace electrified the theatres involved and brought the Georgia Shakespeare Festival into the mix. Artistic director Richard Garner asked to direct a further developmental reading of *The Inland Sea* for the festival, saying he was, "smitten with the imagery, the poetry, the mystery, the lustiness, the gutsiness—all the good Naomi stuff."

In the end, three theatres agreed to mount full productions. In addition to *One Flea Spare* at Synchronicity, Murphy would direct *Trestle* at Theatre Emory, and (most ambitiously) PushPush Theatre would take on three plays in rotating rep—*In the Heart of America*, *The Girl Who Fell Through a Hole in Her Jumper* (a children's piece co-written with Wallace's partner Bruce McLeod) and *The Bone*

Gardens, an early work that had never received a professional production—all under the direction of PushPush founder Tim Haberger. Other theatres staged readings or site-specific performances of Wallace plays, monologues, and poetry.

As preparations continued over the summer, there was a growing sense of excitement at being involved in a common endeavor. Then came September 11.

The day before the terrorist attacks, the Naomi Wallace Festival was an interesting experiment in theatrical community-building for the participants. By the next day, like so much else in the world, it had become something else: a laboratory of questions about what theatre can and should provide in a time of crisis, an examination of the role of art in the wake of tragedy.

Rehearsals for *One Flea Spare*, set to begin on September 11, were delayed for five days when director Rachel May was unable to fly out of Boston's Logan International Airport. Was this kind of theatrical enterprise even 'necessary' (some of the artists involved asked themselves) given the situation? What would the reaction be to a festival of works so charged with a left-wing critique of society? Two of the plays, *In the Heart of America* and *The Retreating World*, dealt with the aftermath of the Gulf War. The former tied American military involvements over the past half-century to male fear of otherness; the latter, a monologue scheduled at Actor's Express, was told from the standpoint of an Iraqi solder reeling from Desert Storm. Would these pieces be seen as unpatriotic? Was it appropriate to present notions critical of the American government's past Mideast policies during the new 'War on Terrorism'?

At Actor's Express, director Wier Harman and actor Brad Davidorff discussed dropping the production. Davidorff worried that the piece might be "anachronistic" in the changed climate. But watching the television coverage of the World Trade Center and the Pentagon, the actor found himself thinking that Americans had a "new vulnerability" that would help them understand the horrors inflicted on the retreating Iraqi army described in *The Retreating World*. Harman began to see the show's carefully delineated character, a man opposed to Saddam Hussein yet conscripted into his army, as an antidote to stereotypes of Arabs and Muslims.

"It would have been inappropriate to do it at this time if it had just been agitprop," Harman told interviewer Jennifer Deer in a half-hour special on Atlanta public radio. Instead, he found his "emotional investment" in the project soaring. "At a time when a lot of artists are questioning the value of art, I'm reminded of its clarifying value in a moment like this, when I am lucky enough to be working on a piece that is so meaningful," the director declared.

Other artists shared Harman's response. Events in the plays gained deeper meaning as connections to the larger world presented themselves. Pearce, listening to the first run-though of *One Flea Spare*, a tale of the London plague of 1665, found, "the fear of dying striking me in a way it never had before." Stranded in Boston, May found new relevance in a play, "about an invisible enemy, and people isolating themselves to keep from getting hurt." Flea actress Kathleen Wattis was struck by other parallels: "We're all suspicious of each other and the air we breathe and the water we drink. Are we in danger?"

Wallace herself was strongly affected by the convergence of the festival and the tragedy. "I was feeling like less than nothing, as many are, in the face of all this," she wrote in response to an email confirming the Atlanta theatres' dedication to the festival. "That you and others are doing my work gives my spirit a purpose and a lift."

From the festival's first performance—a testosterone-infused staged reading of Wallace's *War Boys* (like *Bone Gardens*, never professionally produced in the United States) at Dad's Garage Theatre Company—it was obvious that something special was happening, and that Murphy's brainstorm had been visionary. The sense of purpose the artists found radiated off the festival's stages and individual performances. *Flea* and *Trestle*, both excellently directed, featured superb ensembles, made more remarkable because their central characters were played by adolescents (most notably, 15-year-old Rachel Durston in Flea) whose work melded seamlessly with that of their experienced cast mates.

The opportunity to take in so much of Wallace's work in a short time seemed to justify Murphy's belief in her importance as an American writer. Taken as a whole, her body of work is far less didactic than it may appear on the page or in individual productions. She doesn't shy away from genuine complexities, and the plays raise questions that urge us to find connections everywhere—among such phenomena as homophobia, racism, militarism, gender attitudes, sex, the body, and poetry. The plays (with the exception of *Trestle*) exhibit a surprising amount of humor and an unexpected sense of the craving for forgiveness, or rather the craving to forgive.

Finally, there is the eroticism of Wallace's writing: In the worlds of her plays, breath or the imagination can be as potent as an embrace. (Indeed, directors and actors would do well to examine skeptically any urge for physical contact not specified in Wallace's stage directions.) She speaks to, and for, the body as eloquently as any American writer since Walt Whitman. And, as director Gayle Austin points out, Wallace's imagination and generosity of spirit allow her to speak for both women and men. Murphy admires the playwright's, "recognition that we're all halves of something, that we're all much more erotic and tender and forgiving than we can allow ourselves to be," due to the impact of society.

At the end of the month of readings and productions, this observer felt an almost crazy sense of optimism, of hope for the future. Murphy praises Wallace for, "actually believing things can be different," and I found myself sharing some of that conviction in Atlanta theatres. This was not a bad goal before September 11; it feels all the more important now.

Wallace herself felt similar emotions. In an open e-mail to festival participants, she wrote: "Attending the festival of my plays in Atlanta was the most moving experience I have ever had in theatre, and perhaps may ever have. It wasn't only the sheer volume of work that was done, nor the consistently high quality, but a feeling of my work having a dynamic home in Atlanta that is not just for today, but for tomorrow as well. The festival gave my work a wide-open space in which to be considered and challenged and debated. That is what my work longs for."

* * *

Author's Afterword

Rereading this article more than a decade after the fact brings back a ton of memories and raises questions about impact. It certainly felt as if working on the Festival led to a relative sanity on the part of the participants that often felt sorely lacking in September and October of 2001. I moved away from the Atlanta area in 2004, so it's difficult to gauge a lasting impact on the Atlanta theatre community. I wrote my old friend Vinnie Murphy, who organized the Naomi Wallace Festival, and received this response, via Facebook (September 18, 2012):

> The Naomi Wallace Festival opened four days after 9/11 with work that viewed the world through Arab eyes *(The Retreating World).* It scared many here and made many of us learn how to listen to a voice—Muslim, Arab, other—in a new and empathetic way. I

think theaters should use this model and band together to present a single artist, theme, or period. It elevates the dialogue, publicity, and audience interrelationship... Although I'm no longer an Artistic Producing Director I believe the Atlanta community would step up if a project with vision and need was offered.

"Vision and need" are important terms to consider here. In Philadelphia, where I moved from Atlanta, I have been involved in two multitheatre projects in recent years—the Philadelphia New Play Project (2007), which led to a month of new plays presented by a consortium of theatres, and the Philadelphia International Festival of Arts (2012), which resulted in dozens of productions inspired by Paris before World War I. Neither had the same feeling of community among the theatre artists involved. In fact, it was common for artists involved in the projects to admit they hadn't been able to see most of their peers' work. Both projects seemed full of vision at the outset: it's unclear in retrospect whether there was a strong 'need' for them. The Naomi Wallace Festival in 2001 began with the vision of Vinnie Murphy; its synchronicity with 9/11 generated an unexpected and tremendous need.

6

Naomi Wallace and the Dramaturgy of Rehearsal

Lindsay B. Cummings

In Naomi Wallace's play *In the Heart of America*, set during the first Gulf War, the character Remzi poses the following questions to Craver, his fellow soldier and soon-to-be lover: "Let's say I'm lying over there, dead as can be, and then you see it's me, from a distance. But you still have to walk over to my body to check it out. So, how would you walk?" (Wallace 2001, 88).[1] In this scene, the first in the play between the two men, Remzi is asking Craver to define their relationship. He is also asking Craver to travel the distance between them, a distance delineated by race and class—Remzi is Palestinian-American and Craver is self-described "White Trash" from Kentucky. It is a distance, furthermore, created by the military ban on same-sex relationships then in effect. In what follows, the two men improvise, revise, and negotiate the most appropriate physical representation of their relationship.

If you were in this situation, how would you feel? How would you act? These are questions that every actor who has studied Konstantin Stanislavski's system of acting has asked, and this includes nearly every actor in the United States. Many students and teachers of Stanislavski understand this system of actor training as one that requires the actor to imagine herself into a situation and respond emotionally. But Remzi's question also calls for a critical response: in this case, for the production of Brechtian *gestus*. Here, as throughout her plays, Wallace draws on the techniques of both theorist/practitioners, calling our attention to the affective and critical demands of *acting* in each of these systems. She does this by depicting characters engaged in rehearsals for social change—rehearsals that employ a range of acting techniques, from affective to cognitive to physical. In rehearsal, we practice feeling and responding differently, letting our responses derive from unfamiliar circumstances and exploring the perspective of a character who might be quite different from ourselves. In this essay, I argue that rehearsing, as it is presented in the context of Wallace's plays, requires estranging *and* empathizing. The empathy achieved under these circumstances will be changeable, subject to constant negotiation—empathy, in other words, that consists not in 'arriving' at understanding, but in an ongoing labor that requires continual engagement with the other.

By inserting play-acting, games, and rehearsals into the narrative of her plays, Wallace explores how the improvisational and collaborative techniques of theatrical rehearsals might offer us tools for pursuing social change. On one level, these scenes resemble a child's game of 'let's pretend'; on another level, they are attempts to revise the past and to create an as-yet undetermined future. Rehearsals, Richard Schechner has argued, are subjunctive ("as if"), while performance is indicative ("is") (1985, 104). Performance *does* while rehearsal *proposes, explores, pretends, simulates,* and *hypothesizes.* As such, rehearsals are liminal processes, often requiring us to question that which seems "normal" or "natural" in life. In rehearsal, "strips of behavior" are broken down and reassembled in new ways, a process that Schechner refers to as "re/membering" the past—disassembling it and putting it back together in a way that may never have existed before (48). Through these processes, rehearsals may help us work out what it means to live in the world and what it would take to change that world. As Amy Steiger writes, "Wallace's plays are full of moments of embodied teaching and learning, in which characters remember and repeat the movements of others to transform their bodies to fit particular social roles." She continues: "teachers and pupils in these plays are also *actors* who manage to change their worlds through performances that combine real bodies and history with courageous acts of imagination" (2011, 21). They do this, I argue, through a complex blend of affective and cognitive acting methodologies. Her characters do not engage in uncritical and all-encompassing empathic attachments or identifications; they enter tentatively into affective relationships, sensing boundaries, exploring limits, and deliberating over the results of their endeavors. If we are to use theatre as means of creating social change, Wallace's work suggests, then we must understand theatre as labor, as process, as *rehearsal.*

Brecht, Stanislavski, and the Actor's Labor

In spite of a wave of recent scholarships devoted to rethinking the relationship between Stanislavski and Brecht, the two theorists have retained their reputation as being largely oppositional, an opposition often characterized as one between affect and cognition, or between empathy and estrangement.[2] In Stanislavski's system, the actor uses her imagination to place herself within the "given circumstances" of the play so as to achieve "truth of the passions" (a phrase Stanislavski borrows from Pushkin).[3] He writes, "You must sincerely believe that such a life is possible in the real world. You must become so used to it that it becomes an intimate part of you. If you can do that, then the truth of the passions or feelings that seem true will arise of their own accord" (Stanislavski 2008, 53). Brecht, of course, was not interested in making what happened on stage seem "true," but rather constructed and thus changeable, and frequently cited "empathy" (*Einfühlung* in the German) as an enemy of this goal. While Stanislavski did not use the term "empathy" to describe an actor's process, what Brecht meant by it is, admittedly, quite, similar to what Stanislavski describes as "truth of the passions": for Brecht, empathy entailed the complete acceptance of the characters' thoughts and feelings as natural and inevitable, an acceptance that was in turn passed on to the audience. "Our dramatic form," he wrote, "is based on the spectator's ability to be carried along, identify himself, feel empathy and understand" (Brecht 1992, 25).

It was precisely the notion of a "truth" of feeling that caused feminist theorists and performers to turn away from Stanislavski in the early 1980s. Sue-Ellen Case famously argued that a female actor utilizing Stanislavski's system is forced to both represent and internalize misogyny: "In building such characters as Amanda in Tennessee Williams's *The Glass Menagerie*, the female actor learns to be passive, weak and dependent on her sexual role, with a fragile inner life that reveals no sexual desire" (1988, 122). By demanding that women adopt their characters' emotions as their own in order to produce "believable" performances, feminist critics argued, Stanislavski's system reinscribes patriarchal values.[4] This problem was not limited to gender politics: feminist critiques of the Stanislavski system, Rhonda Blair explains, targeted its tendency to naturalize ideas like the "self," identity, social relations, and other constructions, aligning it with, "the humanist project of reductively universalizing about experience in order to erase difference" (2002, 179).

Turning to Brecht, feminist theorists and practitioners simultaneously tended to turn *away* from emotion, focusing instead on the Brechtian notion of complex seeing: viewing the world historically and dialectically (Brecht 1992, 44). This notion has been central to the work of scholars like Case, Janelle Reinelt, Alisa Solomon, and Elin Diamond. Brecht's theatre, Solomon argues, "demands that we perceive things as they are and, at the same time, as other than they are" (1997, 74). In her seminal book *Unmaking Mimesis*, Diamond explores how critical seeing impacts the representation of gender, writing that the Brechtian feminist performer, "connotes not 'to-be-looked-at-ness'—the perfect fetish—but rather 'looking-at-being-looked-at-ness' or even just 'looking-ness'" (1997, 52). These arguments privilege the act of viewing and the negotiation of representation that occurs between a performer and a spectator.

Without negating any of these lessons, I argue that there is much more that we can learn from a Brechtian feminist theatre—particularly from the practice of *doing* such theatre—especially when it is practiced in conjunctions with empathetic methods of acting. What does it *feel* like to estrange our world? How might critical seeing be aided by imagining the other's point of view or embodying new behaviors? I am proposing a Brechtian feminist theatre that acknowledges the imbricated labor of mind and body, affect, and intellect. As I rethink the ways in which feminist theory might draw from Brecht, I am also rethinking what we might draw from Stanislavski. We can productively put these two theorists together, in part, by reevaluating the role of empathy in Brechtian theory, understanding it not as an all-consuming identification, but rather as a dynamic and dialogic process. To explain this shift, I need to first contextualize Brecht's use of the term "empathy."

One Word, Many Meanings

Einfühlung is a term with a short but complicated history. Attributed to the German aesthetic theorist Robert Vischer, who first used it in his 1873 essay "On the Optical Sense of Form: A Contribution to Aesthetics," *Einfühlung* was quickly adopted by the fields of philosophy and psychology (Vischer 1994). When Brecht adopted it in his own work, it was already a term with many different meanings—describing anything from how we perceive feeling in a painting to how we understand another person's experience of the world. There was also much disagreement over how empathy worked. Vischer had described it as the process by which we imagine ourselves and our feelings *into* an aesthetic object, coming to feel at one with it. As Vernon Lee explains it, when we sense that a mountain in a picture 'rises': "The rising of which we are aware is going on in us" (1913, 62). In psychology, Theodor Lipps used the term to describe an automatic and involuntary "inner imitation" of another person's feeling.[5] Edmund Husserl, meanwhile, described it as a process akin to analogy by which we understand others as other Ego-subjects with their own, independent phenomenological experience of the world.[6] In the early twentieth century, then, empathy could mean anything from a process of reasoning by analogy to an involuntary emotional response. Brecht's use of the term hews most closely to its usage in aesthetic theory, but with some key differences. He describes the *Verfremdungseffekt* as distinct from styles of acting in which the audience is "worked up" or "swept away" (i.e., empathetic acting), suggesting that for him it is the aesthetic object that takes over the spectator, rather than the other way around (Brecht 1992, 136). In either case, empathy is imagined as a unidirectional flow from one body to another, which in turn produces our response to that object.

I find these aesthetic definitions of empathy problematic in regard to the theatre because they do not take into account the dynamic exchange of a live encounter. To consider how the live encounter impacts empathy, I turn to more recent developments in the fields of psychology and philosophy, where empathy has generally come to be understood as both a cognitive and affective process between two or more people, rather than between a person and an object. This process may or *may not* lead to a shared affective experience. Martha C. Nussbaum, for example, defines empathy as the, "imaginative reconstruction of another person's experience, without any particular evaluation of that experience" (2001, 302). Empathy need not consist, as some have described it, of putting yourself in someone else's shoes (thereby assuming a correspondence between your reactions and theirs), but might instead involve using all that you understand about the other to imagine *her* feelings and reactions in that particular situation. In *On the Problem of Empathy*, Edith Stein, a student of Husserl's, takes great care to distinguish empathy from identification and emotional contagion. Stein is adamant that empathy maintained a self/other distinction and argues, furthermore, that empathy is *not* a form of emotional projection. As soon as you *feel* the feelings that you sense through the imaginative act of empathy *as your own*, Stein asserts, what you are feeling is no longer empathy, but rather your own affective experience (1989, 13). As Stein's description makes clear, empathy is a process—one which might fail, and which should be undertaken with care. American psychologist Carl Rogers, who championed the importance of empathy in his client-centered therapy, described empathy as, "temporarily living in [another's] life, moving about in it delicately," and noted that the empathizer must not assume too much or try to uncover things for the other (1975, 4). This is not to say that empathy never slips into identification, that it always involves caring, or that it is a foolproof means of understanding others. This *is* to say that empathy requires work, and when that work is undertaken in a particular way, it can encourage a more dynamic, dialogic exchange.

Empathy, as an imaginative act that may help us understand how another feels, might provide a crucial dimension to our critical understanding. What I am proposing is not only a revised consideration of the role of empathy in Brechtian dramaturgy, but also of the role of emotion in Stanislavski's system. Stanislavski's techniques have been mischaracterized as relying exclusively on emotions, a problem that Blair attributes in part to "a mistrustful attitude toward feeling and the biological body in general" in feminist theory (2002, 177). Many feminist scholars, Blair argues, find that feeling is too easily essentialized and naturalized. Blair refutes this argument, asserting that this particular critique of Stanislavski overlooks the importance of action and embodiment in his work: "Stanislavsky's thought reached its culmination with the method of active analysis—not, I note 'emotional' or 'psychological' analysis (180).[7] Emotional memory was only one of several ways of generating emotion, and a less favored way at that. Emotions also emerge from physically acting the role; as Blair puts it, "the actor puts her body where her mind needs to go" (181). This leads to Blair's second point, which is that mind, body, emotion, and consciousness are not separate in Stanislavski's system. Our emotional responses are part of how we understand our physical circumstances. Knowing and feeling cannot be separated. Suggesting a link between Stanislavski's system and recent work in the field of cognitive neuroscience, Blair writes, "[B]eing aware of feelings allows us to be innovative and creative—conscious, not just automatic—in our responses to the thing causing our emotion" (187). Acting, as a kind of embodied empathy, lets our bodies take us where our minds and imaginations need to go. Merging Brechtian and Stanislavskian methods creates for a performance practice in which the character's point of view is affectively and critically engaged, but not necessarily adopted. In the remainder of the essay, I analyze the labor of this embodied, critical empathy. In this sense, I am taking up Brecht's own argument that empathy is a useful tool for rehearsal and expanding that idea to argue that rehearsals are useful tools for empathy (Brecht 1992, 137).

In the Heart of America: Rehearsing the Future

In the Heart of America shifts temporally between the 'present,' which takes place in Craver's hotel room in Kentucky, and the past, in Iraq. In the present, Remzi's sister Fairouz has tracked Craver down in order to find out what happened to her brother, who never returned from the war and who the army has classified as "missing" (111). Remzi and Craver's relationship unfolds through flashbacks, until we learn that his fellow soldiers beat Remzi to death after they discovered him with Craver. The question Remzi poses to Craver early in the play, the question quoted at the outset of this essay, thus foreshadows the future. But in as much as it is a call to friendship in addition to a prefiguring of death, Remzi's question also engages Craver in a hypothetical future in which they are "pretty good friends" (90).[8] The scenario Remzi proposes is at once highly critical and highly affective. He asks Craver, literally and metaphorically, to travel the distance between them. In this sense, the walk can be viewed as a metaphor for empathy, since empathy is often characterized as the "bridging of difference between self and other" (Gardiner 1989, 1). But as noted earlier, because the moment also requires both men to enact a physical representation of the social distance between them, the walk can be understood as a *gestus*—one built, crucially, through a complex melding of Brechtian and Stanislavskian techniques.

Brecht defined *gestus* as an expression of the characters' relationships to each other and to their social environment, a representation of who they are historically and culturally. Walking is arguably the central gestic action of *In the Heart of America*. Fairouz walks with a limp, the result of a childhood injury caused when schoolchildren took a hammer to her foot to prove that the "Dirty Arab devil" had cloven hooves (128). The Vietnamese ghost named Lue Ming walks hunched over, like all the women in her country, she explains, so as to be "less of a target" (91). Fairouz and Remzi's mother limps from an injury probably sustained at the hands of Israeli soldiers (93). Each step these women take is encoded with a history of ethnically motivated hate, religious conflict, war, and violence.

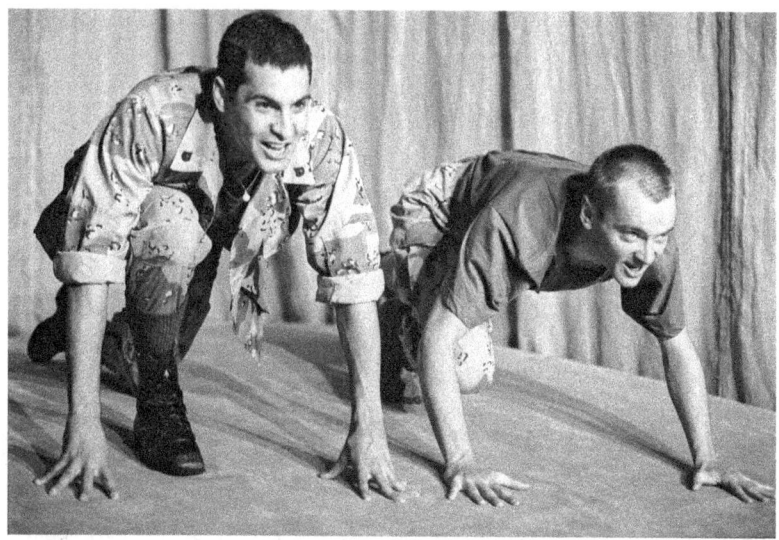

Figure 6.1 Zubin Varla (Remzi) and Richard Dormer (Craver) in the 1994 Bush Theatre production of *In the Heart of America*. Director: Dominic Dromgoole. Photo © Mark Douet/ArenaPal.com.

Craver and Remzi, on the other hand, create the opportunity for a different kind of *gestus*—one that expresses, to be sure, the trauma inflicted by Remzi's hypothetical death, but also one that engages both men in imaginative acts of empathy as they "cross" perspective from self to other.[9] They approach the situation much as actors might. "This is something important I'm talking about," Remzi says, first establishing the 'stakes' of the situation: "Let's say I'm you and I see me lying up ahead, dead. I stop in my tracks. I'm upset. We were friends, and I've got to cross the thirty or so feet between us" (88). The crossings described in this passage are more than just physical. Remzi "crosses" to Craver's point of view, seeing his own dead body as he imagines Craver might see it. Craver, meanwhile, studies 'his' actions by watching Remzi perform them, a technique that Brecht recommended for the rehearsal process. The men then consider the 'given circumstances' of Remzi's scenario: the heat of the desert bearing down, Craver's understanding that he could easily have been the one killed (in the scenario, Remzi has been shot by an Iraqi), Craver's happiness at still being alive, and their status (in the context of the scenario) as "pretty good friends" (90). Remzi's first walk, the men determine, is "too confident," while Craver's attempt is "too careful" (88). Remzi then devises a combination of the two walks, which both men find appropriate. Craver attempts to reproduce it, pausing first to pose a question evocative of Stanislavski's system—one having to do with the actor's motivation: "Why do I want to get closer if you're dead and I know it's you? I mean, there's nothing else to figure out, is there?" To this, Remzi replies, "Because...I'm your friend, and you'd rather be the one to report my death than some jerk who doesn't know I exist" (89). Finally, the two men *"link arms and walk in unison"* (90).

By inviting Craver to perform in an imaginative scenario in which they are "pretty good friends," Remzi asks that Craver experience, physically and emotionally, the possibility of this kind of relationship. Earlier in the scene, Remzi had responded to what he perceived as an anti-Arab sentiment from Craver by attempting to highlight their mutually minoritized status, stating, "You're broke and I'm Arab. That about evens it out, doesn't it?"—a question Craver ignores (87). At this early point in the play, they seem unsure of the nature of their friendship, as well as how to address their racial and class differences. To realize the possibility of friendship, the men must establish what this distance between them means. Are they 'about even,' or are they not? By accepting Remzi's invitation and engaging in the imaginative scenario, Craver accepts the challenge that he has previously ignored. He responds to Remzi's call to friendship.

As they exchange roles, traveling the space between them, Remzi and Craver attempt to see the situation from the other's perspective, but never by simply presuming knowledge of that perspective. Instead, they ask questions and respond to the other's comments. Their fluid trading of perspectives evokes Anna Deavere Smith's notion of acting as a continual travel: "To me, the search for character is constantly in motion. It is a quest that moves back and forth between the self and the other" (1993, xvii). Their respect for one another is revealed in the dialogic nature of their empathy and the extent to which each man regards the other as having his own, distinct understanding and experience of the situation. Both men are, furthermore, working in the subjunctive mode: while they agree to *assume* the relationship of "pretty good friends," this is, at this point in the play, merely an imagined condition. Neither man is sure what this condition looks or feels like, and consequently neither is imposing a particular emotional state or critical response on the other. They are, rather, *trying it out*. Their empathy is contingent, able to move in new directions as new ideas and emotions surface. Emotion, after all, comes from the Latin *emovere*, meaning 'to move' (Oxford English Dictionary). As they experience emotions, they are moved to new places, inspiring new ideas, questions, and responses in the process. When Remzi suggests that Craver would not be feeling very confident because he would be thinking, "that could just as easily be me lying there as him," Craver agrees (88). But when Craver turns this idea around, proposing that, "I might be feeling in a pretty nice way, thinking about being alive and not quite as dead as you," Remzi concedes, "You've got a point there" (89). First one possibility is imagined, felt, and enacted, and then another, until both feel that they have explored all the possibilities, and that they both understand where they finally end up.

The empathy practiced here contrasts markedly to the monologic and unidirectional forms described by theorists like Vischer and Brecht, for whom empathy consists of an engagement with a relatively passive body. These bodies either become a canvass onto which the empathizer projects his or her emotions or an involuntary receptacle for emotion and ideology. Augusto Boal reiterates the latter understanding of empathy in *The Rainbow of Desire*: "The emotion of the characters penetrates us, the moral world of the show invades us, osmotically; we are led by characters and actions not under our control; we experience a *vicarious* emotion" (1995, 42). Under these circumstances, the spectator feels that she must "surrender empathetically" (27). Empathy is seen as an emotional invasion, more of a one-way street than a bridge, and the feelings and thoughts that travel it remain un-affected by the act of transmission. These models of empathy, furthermore, imagine a clear exchange between a stable, coherent 'I' and an 'other'—and, while empathy may threaten to disrupt that coherence, it does so in a way that is always invasive, with the power located only on one side of the exchange.

Remzi and Craver, however, open themselves willingly to one another, inviting respectful exchange that is not only multi-directional, but is also constantly shifting as the two subjects engaged in the project grow, change, and respond to one another. In this respect, their exchange is more characteristic of clinical empathy than aesthetic empathy. As Warren S. Poland argues, "Emotional traffic goes two ways" (2007, 90).[10] Craver and Remzi reflect this as they carefully, slowly establish trust and understanding. But even this model of exchange suggests stable subjects transferring emotion back and forth from stable origin to stable destination. We must keep in mind that this exchange is complicated by the ways in which Craver and

Remzi each change through their encounter. As Robert L. Katz writes of clinical empathy, "the client with whom we empathize is far from static" (1963, 25). This is presumably true of the clinician as well, and it is certainly true of Remzi and Craver, who are in the process of reimagining their relationship, and thus themselves, as they undertake this empathetic exchange. By engaging in this dialogic, contingent empathy in their rehearsals for an imagined future, Remzi and Craver render themselves vulnerable to change not because they risk being invaded by the other's emotion, but because they are willing to *respond* to the other and possibly change in the process.

As they enact different possibilities, the two men rely on affective and embodied knowledge to measure the "rightness" of each possible walk. When Craver tries to copy Remzi's walk, he concludes, "That didn't feel right" (89). Whether this is because the solution was too much Remzi's and not enough Craver's, or whether it is simply not the right solution, is unclear. What is clear is that we are unlikely to adopt solutions that we cannot comfortably embody, a lesson reminiscent of Boal's work, and one that highlights the importance of embodiment to social change. Wallace's characters learn and change by *doing*, and embodying new ways of being takes practice. Most new things are uncomfortable the first time we try them. Sara Ahmed has suggested that discomfort can be generative; it tells us something about our relationship to our environment. She aligns this with her notion of "queer feelings," which, "may embrace a sense of discomfort, a lack of ease with the available scripts for living and loving, along with an excitement in the face of the uncertainty of where the discomfort may take us" (2004, 155). As spaces where we might explore our discomfort, rehearsals not only offer us the chance to acclimate to new ways of being, but also to understand why and how particular ways of being are more 'comfortable' than others.

Rehearsals offer an important corrective to existing notions of how theatre might inspire social change—notions that are often based on instantaneous emotional or cognitive conversions. Brecht often described the *Verfremdungseffekt* as breaking a spell or shocking the audience out of trance—a realization that comes like a splash of cold water to the face (1992, 26). In "Theatre for Pleasure or Theatre for Instruction" he writes, "What is 'natural' must have the force of what is 'startling'" (71). Gradual changes, he believed, are not effective because we do not consciously notice them (1965, 32). Jill Dolan's notion of the utopian performative also relies on a *momentary* experience: utopian performatives are the, "small but profound moments in which performance calls the attention of the audience in a way that lifts everyone slightly above the present, into a hopeful feeling of what the world might be like if every moment of our lives were as emotionally voluminous, generous, aesthetically striking, and intersubjectively intense" (2005, 5). Building on Dolan's work, Shannon Baley has suggested that Wallace's plays offer multiple examples of utopian performatives originating in *gestus* (2004). Remzi and Craver's democratically attained union certainly seems to evoke a possible, utopian future. Both Baley and Dolan focus on the moment of the performative itself—the achievement of the utopian goal, in this case, the walk in unison. But Craver and Remzi do not simply *perform* a utopian moment; they *build* one through rehearsal. They do not express a *gestus*; they devise one through careful improvisation and negotiation. Unlike the moment when an actor sums up a character's social situation, like Helene Weigel snapping her purse closed as Mother Courage, Remzi and Craver use the methods of rehearsal to explore what their relationship *might be*, to make discoveries, to create *gestus*, and to rehearse their own possible future. In the process of building a 'reading' of their relationship, Remzi and Craver perform that relationship into being; they rehearse their way into friendship.

What did it take to get there? What other possibilities were tried along the way? What mistakes and missteps? What needs to happen *before* we can experience Brecht's "shock" of recognition or the elevation of a utopian possibility? Wallace calls our attention to a key difference between *performing* and *rehearsing*, suggesting that we must engage not just the affective moment of the utopian performative or the critical realization evoked by the *Verfremdungeffekt*, but also the creative labor that produces these moments: labor that requires trust, listening, attending to your own thoughts and feelings as well to those of others. It is labor that requires empathy (and an empathy, more specifically, that requires labor). This listening, collaborating, risk-taking, and empathizing is physical, emotional, and intellectual work. It is the work of rehearsal.

Lest we get too carried away by the radical potential of rehearsals, however, Wallace contrasts her characters' attempts to build new ways of being in the world with the rehearsals and repetitions that structure the social world—the ones that resist change. As identities and social structures are made and remade through the re-inscription of social norms, Wallace's characters are faced, to paraphrase Judith Butler, with the problem of when and how to repeat. Remzi and Craver are taught how to interrogate Iraqis by acting out the interrogation with their lieutenant, Boxler, who shouts insults at the pair until they hit and kick him, insisting that they "Hold on to that anger," so they can use it later (99). Successful learning requires not only enacting the correct behavior, but also strategically deploying emotion, turning their own frustrated sense of minoritization against the designated, appropriate 'others.' Through rehearsals like these, Remzi, in particular, tries to remake himself to fit neatly into the United States military's one-size-fits-all scenario for interpreting the world—a scenario in which 'America' is constantly threatened by an 'Other' who goes by the various names "gook," "Indian," and "sandnigger" (135). As the ghost Lue Ming comments, "what's done is often done again and done again" (118). Just as Peggy Phelan argues about performance, we encounter in these rehearsals "the impossibility of maintaining the distinction between temporal tenses, between an absolute singular beginning and ending, between living and dying" (1998, 8). The past is remade in the present. The genocide of Native Americans, the wars in Vietnam, Panama, Iraq—all are depicted in the play as repetitions of a perpetually re-activated scenario of invasion and destruction.

Remzi and Craver's embodied scenario differs from that orchestrated by the lieutenant, though, in that theirs is other-focused. Whereas Boxler wants them focus on their own hurt and anger, Remzi

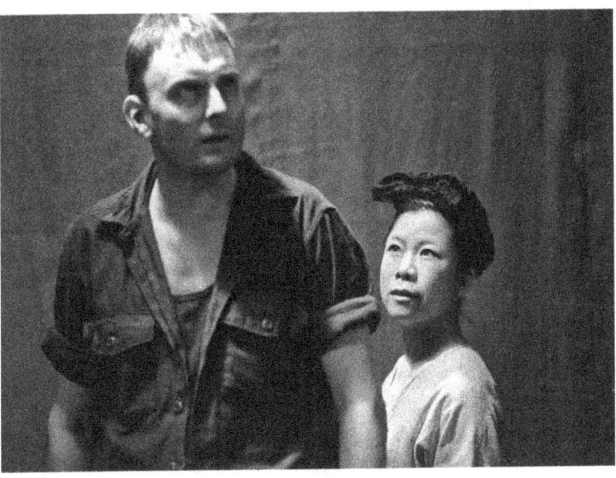

Figure 6.2 Robert Glenister (Boxler) and Toshie Ogura (Lue Ming) in the 1994 Bush Theatre production of *In the Heart of America*. Director: Dominic Dromgoole. Photo © Mark Douet/ArenaPal.com.

and Craver attempt to step away from themselves, allowing them to imagine their relationship from other perspectives. This willingness to be other than they are opens the way to friendship, and eventually to a love that prompts them to approach their environment differently. The more violence Remzi sees around him and the more love he feels for Craver, the more Remzi begins to rethink both his role in the invasion and his desire to overcome his hyphenated identity. As he watches the bombs fall on Baghdad, he recites the Humpty Dumpty nursery rhyme and asks Craver, "Do you think he really wanted to be whole again?...I think he was tired of being a good egg" (119). (You can hear the echo of "good subjects"/"bad subjects" here.) The more Remzi sees Iraq shattered—"like a body with every bone inside it broken"—the less he wants to feel whole (130). Wholeness, or self-sameness, after all, is itself a kind of violence, the negation of disparate selves, which, in Remzi's case, comes at the price of remaking himself according to the racist, sexist, and homophobic norms of the US military (Diamond 1997, 97).

Remzi's ultimate refusal to be the person the military wants him to be is made clear in the moment of his death. He and Craver are caught together, beaten, and then brought before a group of officers, where they find an Iraqi man being beaten to death. Remzi—who, as a child, stood by and watched when his sister was attacked—cannot stand by this time. Recounting the event to Remzi's ghost, Craver describes how Remzi fought the other soldiers: "I shouted for you to stay down but you wouldn't stay down" (135). Fairouz once told Remzi, "There are three kinds of people. Those who kill. Those who die. And those who watch" (96). When Fairouz was attacked, Remzi watched. The military made him a killer. If these are the choices available to him, Remzi chooses, ultimately, to die.

Wallace refuses utopian endings. "I'm not utopian," she says, "I know we're never going to live in a society where there's no injustice (Greene 2001, 471). But we can and must work to create better opportunities, better choices for people like Remzi. Hope resides in the message that is passed on: when we let others in we are unmade in terrifying and wonderful ways. At the end of the play, Fairouz and Craver discuss the need to tell Remzi's story, acting as witnesses to his life and his loss. Fairouz comes to understand that watching is not *necessarily* a passive act. Witnessing is a form of activism for Wallace, a means of attesting to the parts of each other that, "were clipped or squashed or strangled because they didn't fit in with the norm" (Greene 2001, 463). Fairouz muses about something Remzi once said to her: "balance could be a bad thing, a trick to keep you in the middle, where things add up, where you can do no harm." She then admits that Remzi did not actually say this, "But he might have" (138). In this example of a Brechtian "not...but," the thing *not* said is as vital as that which has actually occurred. And Fairouz is right, in a way. While Remzi went to Iraq looking for stability, balance, he failed to find it. His 'failure' reflects a growing willingness to challenge the identities available to him through mainstream sources, a willingness manifested in his final act of defiance. It is in the unsettled, unbalanced space where we may fall in unanticipated directions at any moment that we encounter the possibility for change: for unexpected love, for an end to war. As Fairouz and Craver cope with their loss, they, too, are unbalanced, carrying change into the future. Remzi and Craver's rehearsals initiated this change, creating new possibilities for the future.

Conclusion

In *The Messingkauf Dialogues*, Brecht writes, "The audience shouldn't see characters that are simply people who do their own particular deed[,]...but *human beings: shifting raw material, unformed and undefined, that can surprise them*" (1965, 54 emphasis added). What better way to show human beings *in process* than through rehearsals? It is only through these types of characters, Brecht claims, that the audience can experience "true thinking": "that is to say thinking that is conditioned by self-interest, and *introduced and accompanied by feelings*, a kind of thinking that displays every state of awareness, clarity, and effectiveness" (54 emphasis added). As we watch Wallace's characters embody new ways of being, testing new thoughts and experiencing new feelings, we see not only the choices available to them, but also the ways in which new behaviors create new choices and new versions of ourselves.

In Wallace's play, the quintessentially Brechtian goal of understanding the self in process is *aided*, not hindered, by empathy. When we empathize—at least, when we empathize in a way that maintains the alterity of the other and which respects the other's responses as potentially quite different to those that are 'natural' or 'familiar' to us—we imagine ways of feeling other than our own. And this may change us. Crucially, empathic acting need not *force* other ways of being on the actor or spectator. It may, instead, create a space for *exploring* alternative ways of being in the world, helping us understand, to paraphrase Schechner, that to be "not me" is also to be "not not me"—that there are other ways of being ourselves. Rehearsals provide an environment in which contingency, experimentation, and uncertainty are not only permitted, but also encouraged and supported (Schechner 1985, 6). Wallace's pedagogy involves teaching not just the tools for changing our world, but preparing us for the moment of being "not me," for the fear of self-displacement that comes with change. This unsettled, unbalanced feeling is not a utopian one, but it is nevertheless vitally necessary to the work of social change.

Notes

1. All subsequent quotations from the play, cited by page number only, are from this same edition: Naomi Wallace, *In the Heart of America and Other Plays* (New York: Theatre Communications Group, 2001).
2. Reevaluations of the two artists' relationship have been offered by Jean Benedetti, Michael Morley, Duane Krause, and others, and are part of a scholarly trend of reexamining Stanislavski's theories. Benedetti has argued that Brecht's initial rejection of Stanislavski's "system" was based on limited, second-hand exposure via interpretations of Americans like Lee Strasberg, and that Brecht eventually became interested in Stanislavski's writings, particularly the idea that it was the actor's job to serve the "supertask," or the main goal of the play (1995, 107). Morley has similarly cited numerous likenesses between the two men, noting that in both of their work we find, "the same rejection of the classical psychology of fixed character-types, of the 'in general'; the same breaking down of the text into concrete series of action; the same careful analysis of the characters' social and historical backgrounds" (1997, 197). See Jean Benedetti, "Brecht, Stanislavski, and the Art of Acting," in *Brecht Then and Now/Damals und Heute, Brecht Yearbook* 20, ed. John Willet. The International Brecht Society, 1995. Also see Michael Morley, "Brecht and Stanislavski: Polarities or Proximities?" in *I'm Still Here/Ich bin noch da, The Brecht Yearbook* 22 (Ontario, Canada: The International Brecht Society, 1997).
3. Elizabeth Hapgood omits the Pushkin reference in her translation of Stanislavski.
4. This critique also extended to Stanislavski's concept of the "supertask." Some feminist performers felt that the linear nature of this notion was inherently masculine, and thus not representative of how women experience the world (Case 1988, 123).
5. See Gustav Jahoda, "Theodor Lipps and the Shift from 'Sympathy' to 'Empathy,'" in *Journal of the History of the Behavioral Sciences* 41 no. 2 (Spring 2005): 151–63. *ArticleFirst* (accessed June 21, 2010).
6. Edmund Husserl first uses "empathy" or "*Einfühlung*" in *Ideas: General Introduction to Pure Phenomenology*, trans. W. R. Boyle (London: Allen

and Unwin, 1969). He expands his discussion of the term in the fifth meditation of *Cartesian Meditations: An Introduction to Phenomenology*, trans. Dorian Cairns (The Hague: Martinus Nijhoff, 1977).
7. Blair here repeats the widely held belief that Stanislavski's system was developed in "stages," and that America versions of his system have overemphasized the first "stage" at the expense of the second. Recently, Benedetti has argued that this conception of Stanislavski is an accident of history resulting from the separation of his text into two separate books. Benedetti writes, "Stanislavski had serious misgivings about dividing the book. He feared that the first volume, dealing with the psychological aspects of acting would be identified as the total 'system' itself, which would be identified as a form of 'ultranaturalism.' His fears were justified." Blair's point about the importance of embodiment in Stanislavski's work stands, if her sense of its teleological status does not. See "Translator's Forward," in Konstantin Stanislavski, *An Actor's Work*, trans. and ed. Jean Benedetti (London and New York: Routledge, 2008): xvi.
8. While Remzi's scenario begs the question of whether or not Craver is only able to entertain the possibility of their friendship under the condition of Remzi's death, I believe Remzi's choice of scenario is motivated, above all, by the fact that he has trouble imagining himself as a whole person. Remzi feels fragmented by his hyphenated identity. At the point in the play when he proposes this scenario to Craver, I suggest that the only way he can see himself as whole is in his own death.
9. In her reading of this essay, Sara Warner has questioned why it is the two men who get to devise this potentially liberatory *gestus*. While I do not have space to address all characters here, I want to note that the women in the play are not simply reduced to victimhood. Both Lue-Ming and Fairouz undertake their own quests for retribution and justice, a fact that Emily Rollie explores in her astute analysis of this play. I focus on Craver and Remzi because their imaginative play most closely resembles the work of the actor in rehearsal.
10. Of course, emotional traffic may go more than two ways. In the case explored here, the audience to the play creates a third node of exchange.

7

Naomi Wallace and the Politics of Desire

Josephine Machon

Some years ago, a colleague handed me a copy of Naomi Wallace's *Slaughter City*, suggesting I might want to explore it on an undergraduate project as part of my research/teaching exchange. I read it and responded in an overtly embodied fashion. I felt touched (both physically and emotionally) by the ideas and narratives in the text. I felt excited and somewhat scared to meet the challenge of making them manifest in performance. I also felt inspired by the style of writing itself: dense in its philosophical and historical knowledge and deftly textured in its lyrical grasp of relationships, individual empowerment through friendship, and the reclamation of the body. Here was a play whose form and substance seemed to provide a blueprint for exploring and exposing critical theories of 'writing the body.'[1] This initial visceral response and my subsequent practical exploration of *Slaughter City* proved to be a crucial formative experience underpinning my own theory of '(syn)aesthetics' (Machon 2011).[2]

"(Syn)aesthetics" derives from 'synaesthesia' (the Greek *syn* meaning 'together' and *aisthesis*, meaning 'sensation' or 'perception'). 'Synaesthesia,' in scientific discourse, defines a neurological condition where the stimulation of one sense automatically and simultaneously causes a stimulation in another of the senses, resulting in an acutely felt fusing of sensations; an individual may perceive scents as certain colors, or a word as a particular smell, or experience tastes as tangible shapes. Synaesthetes often have unusual, sometimes extraordinary, powers of cognition and memory. My appropriation of certain features of scientific analysis of synaesthesia to define the parameters of (syn)aesthetics is intended to emphasize the human capacity for perception, which shifts between realms; between the sensual and intellectual; between the literal and lateral. Further to this, (syn)aesthetics emphasizes 'aesthetics,' as the subjective creation, experience, and criticism that constitutes artistic practice. My merging of these terms and concepts as '(syn)aesthetics,' with a playful use of parenthesis, encompasses *both* a fused sensory perceptual experience *and* a fused and sensate approach to artistic practice and analysis. The parenthesis is also intended to distinguish this performance theory from the neurological condition from which it adopts certain features and to foreground various notions of slippage and fusing together in arts practice and analysis.

(Syn)aesthetic analysis is useful when the form and content of the artistic work is executed and received in a way that fuses the somatic ('affecting the body' or 'absorbed through the body') and the semantic (the 'mental reading' of signs). (Syn)aesthetics thus emphasizes the shift between the sensual and intellectual, the literal and lateral in both the work and the process of comprehending that work. The appreciation process is distinguished by a *felt* appreciation of 'making sense' in a cerebral fashion and '*sense* making,' embodied perception via *feeling* (both sensory and emotional). In (syn)aesthetic practice the process is often fused as a making-sense/*sense*-making experience.[3]

(Syn)aesthetic performance practice is always imaginative and embodied, in form and execution (Machon, 2011, 54–81). Wallace's work perfectly illustrates the notion of the (syn)aesthetic *play*text, which reclaims performance writing as a sensate and multilayered form, a visceral act that has the ability both to stir innermost, inexpressible human emotion and to disturb those viscera that cause aural, visual, olfactory, and haptic perception. (Syn)aesthetic *play*texts connect social, historical, and cultural issues with the individual and the personal in a noetic manner. Here, 'noetic' (from the Greek derived, *noēsis, noētikos, nous*, meaning inner wisdom, subjective intellect or understanding) further embellishes aspects of the visceral in that it denotes knowledge that is experienced directly and can incorporate sensations of transcendence. Noetic understanding makes physically manifest complex emotional or social experiences that defy explanation yet are *felt* and consequently the thing shown *feels understood*. Wallace's plays represent a unique model for this sort of embodied practice. Her writing challenges social and theatrical conventions through a radical poetic-politics executed through metatheatrical techniques; playing with transgression *in both form and in concept*.[4]

The emphasis of 'play' in a (syn)aesthetic *play*text draws attention to work that is inherently ludic (a playfulness that is subversive, curious, imaginative, and pleasurable) in form. Wallace's *play*writing plays with the possibilities of live performance, in part through her experimentation with visceral and poetic stage imagery. Light, sound, costume, spatial design, and choreographic movement are woven into the fabric of the *play*text itself in a manner that fuses and extends the theatrical ideals of Antonin Artaud and Bertolt Brecht. Consequently, embodied rehearsal techniques are crucial to the practical interrogation of Wallace's writing. In her work, the body is the key signifier; it speaks for itself. It is the site, sight and cite of performance in a manner more commonly associated with the multilayered signifiers of Dance Theatre. The body of the performer, as sensual, working material, becomes the vehicle through which the full force of the play's transgressive transformations are seen and experienced. I became acutely aware of this when directing *Slaughter City* with an ensemble of young, beautiful, undergraduate Drama students, with physical forms so different to the character descriptions in the text. Compelling performances aside, this experience proved to me the importance of casting appropriate bodies for her plays because these *bodies*—by virtue of their gender, their color, their age—have stories to tell before they utter a word.

Wallace's writing demands that an ensemble is made up of bodies with human histories that match their spoken narratives, bodies from head to toe that look like the lives they have lived. Wallace's body of work demonstrates an ongoing exploration of a 'politics of desire' that is played out on and through the human body and that valorizes its unique capacity for nonverbal communication (Machon, 2011, 132–43). Emphasis is placed on a very real, live(d) body conveying its own history through a corporeal politics that reveals the individual transgression and transformation at the heart of personal, social and historical experience.[5] To illustrate the (syn)aesthetics of Wallace's work, this essay examines the politics of desire in *Things of Dry Hours* and *And I and Silence*.

Set in Alabama in the early 1930s (although an ambiguous time-play is also written into the text from the first stage direction onwards), *Things Of Dry Hours* explores the points at which poetry, philosophy, and live(d) history converge in an imaginative and provocative manner. This is embodied in Tice, a committed Christian, an African-American, and a member of the Communist Party (at a time when Communist Party membership in the United States was a very dangerous choice for any human being). He and his young, widowed daughter Cali, give shelter to Corbin Teel, a white man, seemingly on the run for a murder, who turns out to have more sinister reasons for entering their lives. This play serves as a celebration of the black Communist agitators of the Depression-era and opens out to speak against injustice and the infringement of democratic rights in general. The play received its British premiere at The Royal Exchange Theatre, Manchester and the Gate Theatre, London in 2007, directed by Raz Shaw. It received glowing accolades for its 2007 Center Stage production in Baltimore, directed by the British playwright and director Kwame Kwei-Armah, now the company's Artistic Director.

And I and Silence is set at the beginning and end of the 1950s, "somewhere in the U.S.A." in a prison and a sparse, single room. It is the story of two incarcerated young women, Jamie, an African-American, and Dee, white and working class, played by two sets of performers to denote their younger and older (by nine years) selves. Young Dee and Young Jamie forge an immediate and powerful bond, strengthened by shared dreams of freedom through hard work once on the outside. Yet these dreams to rise above poverty and racial inequality are violently dashed when life outside of prison proves to be harsher, more confining, and ultimately more destructive than their earlier incarceration. The structure offers a dreamlike time-plane where the future is seen in the present through the lens of the past. *And I and Silence* premiered at The Finborough Theatre, London in 2011, directed by Caitlin McLeod.

Embodied Histories

The idea of the body as a complex history, a vessel of mixed emotional, political, and social narratives, is paramount in Wallace's work. The body acts as a force of resistance, often at the point that it is most oppressed. In *Things of Dry Hours*, Cali provides an illustration of a body that is resistant to class and gender inequalities yet also capable of consenting to tenderness. This is emphasized at the point she controls/reveals the narrative of her body, according to her own rules and desires, finally allowing Corbin to touch her by placing his hand on each anatomical point in her history:

> Cali moves his hand to different places on her body as she speaks—not necessarily sexual places, but also on her ribs, her breastbone, her arm, elbow.

CALI: Here is where I cut myself as a child. Here, where I burned when the fields caught fire. Here is where my mother touched me. I can't remember, but I know it's her. This is where I stripped the corn. This is where I slept too long. And this place, here, you can never know.
CORBIN: Cali.
Corbin is still. He is dead.
CALI: And here is where you knocked on the door.
Cali takes his hand from her body and puts it gently on the table (Wallace 2007, 90–1).

In the Center Stage production this sequence was acted out earlier, before Corbin dies, the latter occurring off-stage. Shifting the action in this way, demonstrated an intuitive and embodied understanding of the ideas, beyond the romantic narrative, at the heart of this power play. By giving both Cali and Corbin "agency" through showing a tactile "negotiation" of their relationship, this interpretation allowed the play to become "much sexier" and "to be more dangerous in its desire, in its moments of power" between them (Wallace in Machon 2011, 136–9). This sequence demonstrates how "the body is not static in any way, it's in continual movement, continual transformation, the body itself and the signs it takes on" (135). It shows Wallace's *play* with a politics of desire via a corporeality that reveals personal, societal, and historical experience all in the same moment. Transgression exists in the act of touch itself, touch that has been previously denied, accentuated by the fact that the touch crosses barriers of race. Transformation occurs in the interplay of philosophical and emotional ideals, all played out on and through a live(d) body.

Wallace's style also encourages a verbal delivery where the experiential potential of words is carried by the quality of the voice, the physical and emotional shaping of the ideas, and the choreography of the words in the space. The visceral-verbal here incorporates the sensual sounds of the words *and* the noetic expression of ideas so that the language is apprehended as both an earthly physicality and an imaginative dream. This was demonstrated in the intense performances in McLeod's production of *And I and Silence*, where both emotions and ideas resonated in the intimate space. Kwei-Armah's production of *Things of Dry Hours* exposed how wrestling with the verbal delivery stimulated a visceral interpretation of the work, which led to a poetic and profound realization of the ideas: "the language, the stories, everything became embodied in the actual bodies of those characters on stage" (Wallace in Machon 2011, 138). This corporeal exchange of live(d) experience from playwright through performer to audience member encourages a fusion of body and mind in comprehension of these ideas and narratives. In this way Wallace's writing establishes a paradigm shift in production and appreciation by requiring that a making-sense/*sense*-making process is deployed at every stage; in subject and form it invites a (syn)aesthetic embodiment by directors, performers and spectators alike. This prevailing corporeality, in rehearsal, production, and interpretation, ensures that it is a very real *writing* of the body in concept and form.

Things of Dry Hours and *And I and Silence* also allow spaces for silence—and for the narratives that bodies tell in that silence—to be felt. These distilled moments of silence cut to the core of the particular circumstances to communicate something essential about/within the prevailing social and personal relationship and to express the *feeling* of the experience as it is undergone. This is illustrated in the repeated and reflected moments of waiting in *And I and Silence*:

> [Scene 2] *Young Jamie is standing alone in her cell, looking out at something we can't see. After some moments, Young Dee enters… They say nothing for a long moment, just looking at one another…* [Scene 4] *Young Jamie in the cell. Alone. Waiting. Waiting. Young Dee finally comes, breathless…* [Scene 5] *Dee in their small room. Standing still, waiting. Jamie enters, tired* (Wallace 2011, 12–30).

This repetition of the silent, still, looking, and waiting conveys *in one and the same moment* a waiting for freedom, an acceptance of the here and now, expectancy, postponement, time passing, time held, and—most potently—a longing for the other to arrive and complete the picture, the partnership. This minimalist action communicated in a cerebral/corporeal manner in the McLeod production where the pregnancy of the moment held the weight of the history of Dee and Jamie's relationship *and* the charge of hope, expectation, for the future. The loaded nature of this waiting was consequently felt in the body as much as understood in the mind.

The *Play* of the *Play*text: Shifting Performance Paradigms

From *The War Boys* (1993) onwards, Wallace has demonstrated a sensitivity to theatre as a multidimensional medium that has the power to communicate experiences in a political and vital way. She has played her own part in reclaiming the *play*text, the task of writing for performance, as a sensate and multilayered practice that can reignite a visceral quality in communication. In this regard, Wallace's practice squares with other playwrights, such as Samuel Beckett or Caryl Churchill, who have been responsible for redefining contemporary theatre. The experience of Wallace's writing, at every stage of the production process (from reading to interpreting through performance to appreciating in performance as an audience member), engenders a double-edged quality of making-sense/*sense*-making where ideas as much as narratives are *felt* and thus deeply understood. This is illustrated by the final sequence of *And I and Silence*:

> *Young Jamie and Young Dee are suddenly with them now. The two realities happen simultaneously...Jamie abruptly stabs Dee in the stomach. At the same time Young Dee lets out a wild, loud celebratory call...Jamie, with Dee helping, pushes the knife into her own stomach...Jamie comes to kneel beside Dee. The women are both calm, as though at the centre of a storm* (Wallace 2011, 63–8).

Past and future are fused in a visceral present where time coils, helix-like, to communicate the power of hope amidst the destruction of dreams. The mutual stabbing of the older protagonists resonates alongside the simultaneously played out dreams for and belief in freedom evoked by the chillingly apposite parting dialogue between their younger selves as Young Dee embarks on her/their future journey beyond the prison walls. In this instance, the imaginative leap that the audience is obliged to take is fundamental to the immediate experience of the work and any subsequent processes of individual interpretation. This live(d) moment of *And I and Silence* communicates the brutal harshness of the impossibility of freedom in a society yoked by economic and ideological inequality alongside the reminder that aspirations for personal freedom and social change remain presently possible if the dream is *enabled* to be achieved.

Dreams and Desires—Rupturing History, Metaphor, Ideology

As this illustration demonstrates, Wallace manipulates montage as a theatrical convention to make sense/*sense* of contemporary social, cultural, and political experiences by mirroring these with previous moments in history. These concurrently played moments take on the visceral quality of a glitch in time, like the skipped heartbeat caused by sexual, emotional, aspirational desire:[6]

> I've always felt that not only is the past not over, but that the present is also history. History is always rupturing the present. It's just a matter of recognising that and realising that in order to change our future we have to deal with our past (Wallace in Stephenson and Langridge 1997, 170).

The time-play in Wallace's work, the fusion of past, present, and a potential future, work as a distancing device to become a poetic representation of the dialectical form; thesis and antithesis are *shown* in the same moment to infer all possible courses of action and to accentuate past/present moments of decision that dictate the future trajectory of a character's personal life as much as social (and socio-economic) consequences. Wallace's nonlinear form weaves together narratives across different times and places to confront issues surrounding inequalities of race, gender, sexuality, class, and age.

This historical jarring in the time/space continuum of the world of each of these plays is central to an interrogation, through metaphor, of the ideas at its core. The dialectic of each situation is played out through the characters' relationships, situations that feel very real (in a representational sense) yet are filtered through an otherworldliness evoked by the metaphorical/historical jarring. Furthermore, the time-play occurs in spaces that are confined, that feel both of and adjacent to the outside world. These settings have their own hierarchies and histories and are inhabited by characters that have narratives that exist within and beyond these spaces and times. These intimate spaces heighten the experiences presented and expose each detail of the stories shared, which generates a sense of bearing witness both to the immediate moment and to the past that marks each character's present. For example, in *And I and Silence*, Jamie and Dee's recounted maternal narratives that lead to their respective state incarceration; the stories of cleaning clients (Jamie's mother's and their own), which contrast enduring aspiration with ongoing inequality. These live(d) histories exist outside of past and present confinement and are finally underscored by Dee's revelation of the truth about her client and the actual services rendered, a story that 'could be seen coming' in the construction of her future/present history.

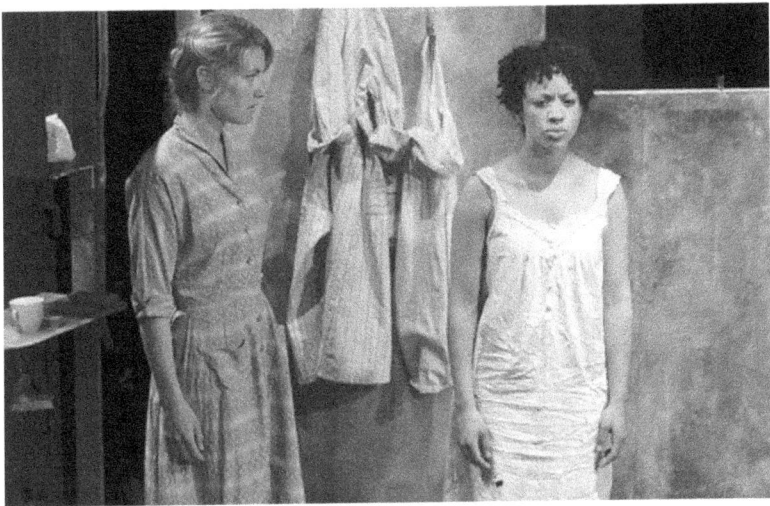

Figure 7.1 Sally Oliver (Dee) and Cat Simmons (Jaime) in the 2011 Finborough Theatre production of *And I And Silence*. Director: Caitlin McLeod. Photo: Andrew Reed. Courtesy: Caitlin McLeod.

As this suggests, Wallace stages the experiences in her plays through poetic encounters that involve the sharing of embodied history and lead to compelling moments of revelation. This serves to emphasize the witnessing of these histories between all parties present (including the audience), both within the time-space of the play and within the time-space of the performance. The repetition of verbal motifs adds to the sense of past/future and freedom/constraint intertwined in the present. In *And I and Silence*, this is made spine tinglingly tangible in the double reference to Korea and the linguistic echoes of hope and aspiration, such as the chilling reiteration in the past and present of "spiffy" and 'flittering'; the repetition of these linguistic tics in the past serves as an indicator of the power of imagination and dreams in the struggle for social change; in the present, it underscores the destruction of those dreams.

Wallace uses metaphor to distil speech and physical imagery to convey ideas in an essential, resonant way and to point up the complexities *within* the ideas and experiences shown. She focuses on the meaning that words and bodies together can generate: words become experiential and tactile; bodies become textual. Prelinguistic processes of human communication are activated when transgressive poetic and embodied signifiers come into play, becoming at once material and metaphysical, tangible and intangible.

In *Things of Dry Hours*, shoes become a metaphorical motif that conveys layers of meaning. Initially, they represent the economic poverty of Cali and Tice alongside Cali's resistance to that poverty by keeping shoes that wealthy clients carelessly discard amongst the laundry. They are the puppets through which Cali plays out the inequalities and abuses of her daily grind; they demonstrate her bold subversion of the situation in role-play, resisting/exposing the unsolicited sexual desires of a predatory male. Finally, the polishing of shoes becomes the object/action through which Corbin displays his newfound education and self-respect, gained through his relationship with Tice (Wallace, 2007: 5, 15–8; 55–6, 73). In both The Gate and Center Stage productions, the inherent physicality of the shoes made their metaphoric potency manifest; as objects, each suggested its own perceptible history and retained an eerie human presence in its unique worn-ness.

In *And I and Silence*, the metaphors resonate with a mythic quality, invoking Beckett's use of the same imagery. Alongside the loaded 'waiting' there is also the window looking out (to another world? to freedom? a view denied to the audience) and the tree denoting time passing, natural cycles, hope. The predominant metaphor, however, is spatial: the setting denoting past and present confinement. In the Finborough premiere, the shift from past to present captivity was realized via a simple removal of the table. Furthermore, the enclosed space of the venue (a small, fringe theatre above a pub), enhanced by the minimalist and confined design of the setting, ensured each moment was intensely perceived. The sparse, gray frame accentuated the minute detail of the pared down action played out between the Jamies and Dees.

Wallace's evocative metaphors—verbal, physical, and spatial—ignite the imagination of practitioner (performer, director, designer) and audience alike. Her layered worlds are at once familiar and 'understood' yet also disquietingly unfamiliar and conspicuous. In this way, they correspond both to the Artaudian idea of dream worlds that expose our unconscious human drives and desires and the Brechtian idea of defamiliarization via the gestic play that demonstrates social experience, economic status, and the power struggle between (personal) freedoms and (state) control.[7] The poetic fusion in Wallace's metaphors takes on a magical quality in the way that it makes tangible the dreams, aspirations, and desires—personal and political—of the characters.[8] Her plays incorporate concentrated symbolic moments that exploit a visceral fusion of space, object, bodies, sound, and speech. Crafted on the page and choreographed in the space, these moments communicate somatic experience and intellectual attitudes, which the audience can appreciate (syn)aesthetically through the form itself. This is demonstrated by the sheet sequence from *Things of Dry Hours*.

> *In the dark, Cali is asleep on the floor among the largest pile of sheets we have yet seen. These sheets seem to glow in the darkness with a strange, ethereal light. Magically, a sheet rises from its pile and floats in the air above Cali. If possible, more than one sheet rises up, perhaps many. The sheets float around the stage like ghosts. Cali sits up in her "dream," and marvels at the floating sheets. She reaches to grab one, but it evades her. She tries again.*
> CALI: Come back here, you.
> *Cali follows the sheet/s around the room, mesmerised by it, jumping for it, laughing as it evades her, enjoying the strange game* (Wallace, 2007, 51).[9]

Such beautifully constructed transcendental imagery, in the simplicity of the action, transmits sensual experience without falling into a trap of esoteric fancy; instead it pulls the audience towards the live(d) history (the sheets are both Cali's emancipatory flight and her economic oppression). Such a provocative play with form engages the noetic within interpretation, demanding that an individual's imagination is engaged within the active appreciation of the work. The sensual interplay of verbal, architectural, and physical imagery taps into human consciousness on a prelinguistic level. These (syn)aesthetics appeal to the imagination in an acknowledgement that the sentient body is able to understand sensual, image-based expression at a deeply somatic level.

Conclusion: The Politics of Desire

A politics of resistance, demonstrated through the ownership of the body and the taking back of control played out in expressions of desire, is central to Wallace's work. *Things of Dry Hours* and *And I and Silence* exemplify this quality. Both are marked by the presence of provocation, invention, imagination, transgression, and transformation in form and content. Hers is a fundamentally (syn)aesthetic theatre that requires innovative interpretation from directors, designers, and performers. When realized imaginatively and effectively, her plays engender a visceral response to their political and emotional narratives and themes. In this way, Wallace reclaims the craft of playwriting as an intensely sensual act.

Wallace's characters are a source of sociopolitical criticism. They become revolutionary in that they *demonstrate*, in metatheatrical moments and in pared down expressions of tenderness, how the body is a site of struggle and change. Wallace's visceral poetics allow intimate personal stories to meet epic socioeconomic and historical narratives, both played out on and through the body. Her work allows for an experiential interrogation of deep-rooted philosophical concerns and suggests that history *can* rewrite itself from a starting point of shared humanity and collective ideals. Cali's embracing of Corbin before he dies (literally and on a deeply emotional level) or the glitch in time that allows the *belief* in freedom for Dee and Jamie to remain *physically* present, despite circumstances proving otherwise, serve to remind the audience that even in despair there remains that potential for society. Both demonstrate the persistence of the possibility of change, which remains the hope for humanity.

In reflecting on my own performance explorations with Wallace's work and the way in which it proved inspirational to me and empowering to the ensemble with which I collaborated, I am mindful of how her unique writing style has given authority and pleasure to my students in other ways. Whilst discussing the formalistic and thematic features of her plays, I have heard shared embodied histories, from women students in particular, who have profoundly connected with the narratives of the strong, female roles. I recall a student who, inspired by discussing the magic of the feather sequence in *The Trestle at Pope Lick Creek*, went on to direct this scene for a final performance project, intuitively uncovering the delight in life that existed in this image by simply *playing* out the directed action. I am reminded of another's unbridled ability to own and articulate challenging theoretical concepts in and through *The Things of Dry Hours*, passionately expressing advanced ideas on paper in a way that she had never done before. Wallace's plays allowed these individuals to consider their own philosophical, ideological, educational, and emotional desires, to connect with different experiences and alternative histories, and, in so doing, embrace some kind of liberation in their own lives.

Notes

1. "Writing the body" is a theoretical concept that crosses many disciplines. Initially associated with *écriture féminine* (literally feminized writing) and the French critical theorists, Hélène Cixous and Luce Irigaray, the concept now covers a broad range of critical and artistic thought around the body, language, and how meaning is made and contested. The notion is also related to Antonin Artaud's practice. Many performance practitioners have interrogated ideas around the body as the site/sight upon which representations of difference and identity are inscribed.
2. I use "visceral" in this essay in its fullest sense: to define those perceptual experiences that affect the innermost, often inexpressible, emotionally sentient feelings a human is capable of as much as to describe the strong emotional and physiological effect of the upheaval of our viscera. The term "experiential" describes performance events that directly activate this combined quality of the visceral to affect us in a manner that draws attention to the fusion of the cerebral and corporeal, the fleshly and the arcane.
3. The duality of 'sense' is fundamental to (syn)aesthetics. The term 'making-sense/*sense*-making' plays on the fact that human perception translates received information through the sense organs and simultaneously combines this with perception as cerebral insight, involving memory, cognition, and expectation. Thus, perception as sensation, that is, corporeally mediated, and perception as cognition, intellectually mediated (accepting that the latter also involves cultural and social mediation).
4. "Metatheatrical," defined by Lionel Abel, is a dramatic device where characters subvert roles enforced by society through role-play. In so doing, "metatheatre" provides an imaginative evocation of how situations might be changed (Abel, 2003). The role-play is seen as a transgressive act that can be dark and reflective of social control (as in the plays of Jean Genet) or can celebrate the human capacity for imaginative thinking, providing alternative ways of being that indicate the potential ease of desired social change. Wallace exploits this form in poetically unsettling ways.
5. By employing parenthesis with live(d) I draw attention to the way in which, in experiential performance practice, the performing bodies and perceiving bodies that undergo the experience within the duration of that event are charged by the sensual aesthetic and the specific energies of the piece in a live and on-going present. This underpins comprehension of lived histories in the subject matter of the performance.
6. "[T]here is something that is inarticulate about desire. It's that skipped beat. There's a space there and we're talking in metaphor to a degree, but if you skipped it there is a new space there and that is where possibility is. In that moment when someone literally takes your breath away...everything about them stirs you up, puts you upside down, that's when I say even desire in itself can become a form of resistance...What dynamics are set up in that moment for that skip to be able to happen?" (Wallace in Machon, 2011, 141).

7. "Defamiliarization" is associated with the Russian Formalists in relation to a subversive play with poetic language and, in an interdisciplinary form with Brecht's Epic Theatre and his *Verfremdungseffekt*. With Brecht's techniques, the intention is that performance processes are made clear, designed to awaken an audience to an active and political way of receiving theatre. With the Russian Formalists' approach, language is made unusual in the fabric of the text and thus in an individual's perception and appreciation of that writing. This accords with an Artaudian desire to manipulate speech so that it resonates with that which we experience in dreamworlds (see Artaud, 1993; Mikhail Bakhtin et al, 1965; Willett, 2001).
8. [I]n the end, all change comes from dreaming…folks sitting down and dreaming what they want to be different. And dreams are magical. I wanted to show the magic of that world…dreaming of a different kind of America. It's not magical thinking, but the power of the imagination to create a different world in a community's mind. And it is magical, to be able to sustain that dream (Wallace and Kwei-Armah, 2007, 7).
9. "In the material…what we are taught that we can do with our bodies or with an object can be pushed to a different space so that it's re-envisioned." These metaphors retain an ineffable quality for Wallace, "you can feel them work but why they work is the question" (Wallace in Machon 2011, 142).

8

Crucial Unspeakables, or Pedagogies of the Repressed: Directing Sex in the Plays of Naomi Wallace

Beth Cleary

There is no faculty handbook for staging sex with college actors. Those of us who do theatre with students know the importance of scheduling special, separate rehearsals for any intimate physical interaction—violent or sexual—that a play requires, building trust before working on 'those scenes' and talking through the power dynamics to make sure emotional safety is acknowledged and ensured. Everyone—the student actors, the faculty director, others in the rehearsal room, and even ultimately the audience—needs to feel prepared before tackling the parts of the play where somebody can get hurt. If this is true of staging, say, *Romeo and Juliet*, it is profoundly and problematically true of staging the plays of Naomi Wallace, where feeling unsafe is part of the process. Sex is never innocent or easy in Wallace's theatrical world, and it is *always* political. Two characters may come together in private, erotic exchanges, but they are always also indices of history, of family and work, of race, class, and gender.

Wallace stages the politics of sex. She does this in part by writing sexual acts that are strange—strange in the Brechtian sense of the familiar-made-strange so as to be seen anew, and strange in the more pedestrian sense of being unusual, even abnormal, in the sexual values of the dominant culture. She wants us to *see* why the tomboy Pace Creagan cannot gratify young Dalton Chance with a normal kiss or a normal blow job, to *see* why Bunce, the sailor, makes Snelgrave, the trade merchant, "fuck" an orange so that Bunce can drink the juice of New World fruit. But it is one thing to write a scene with stage directions to this effect and it is another thing altogether to come into a cold rehearsal room on a Tuesday night in February and have two student actors put down their book bags and cell phones and do it.

For the past 15 years, my teaching at Macalester College has been engaged with the plays of Naomi Wallace. I have taught all of them in a variety of courses and used many scenes for performance training in laboratory classes. I have directed two of her short monodramas, *Standard Time* and *The Retreating World*, with Macalester students, and I have directed three of her full-length plays: *Slaughter City* in 1998, *In the Heart of America* in 2005, and *The Inland Sea* in 2011. This work has relied on conventional directing strategies, but it has also led me to rehearsal problem-solving with my students that none of us foresaw during auditions, callbacks, or even early read-throughs, when bodies sit safely at tables, scripts open conventionally, studiously. It has called on me to transgress the mythical faculty handbook on directing in order to prepare them to talk about, rehearse, and then perform the body politics of Wallace's plays, with their myriad motivations, complicated stakes, and micromoments of flirtation, foreplay, and intercourse. Awkward? Sometimes. Worth the effort? Empathically, yes. In this essay, I offer encouragement and practical advice to directors who wonder how to approach this mature material with college students.

However cool, sex-positive, dis-identified, and inter-sexed they may be, college students are still 20-ish and exactly the demographic that stands to benefit most from linking their tribal-personal ethos with the contemporary political. In play after play, Wallace writes *youth*: how the young fight to become agents of their own destiny within terms already set by the apparatuses of capitalism, nationalism, patriarchy. Students respect Wallace's playwriting, her fierce imagination, her confusing but compelling sexual politics, and they want to understand or at least to explore their reactions to her characters and the rebellions they attempt against forces as totalizing as empire, militarism, even genocide. They get—and some even get off, intellectually—on how Wallace uses sexual encounters as rehearsals for revolution. Her ambivalent endings speak directly to students at a small liberal arts college like Macalester whose education in critical theories makes them skeptical of plot structures that wrap up with happy endings that betray the complex anguish they felt in earlier scenes. Wallace's plays *describe their fury* at the ways they have learned that they are always already interpellated as subjects. The rehearsal-and-performance process, as well as the panel discussions and informal conversations that follow, allow students to speak *from* those troubled sites of interpellation. They know those sites are their own personal starting points as they move into adulthood, and they know the compasses that might orient them have been smashed. They feel it with every notice from the student loan office, every rejection or non-answer for a summer job, and each time they attend a Hollywood film or log-on to websites clogged with ads and product placements. In the tradition of Brecht, but with an utterly contemporary sensibility, a Wallace play gives them a chance to embody the problems of history, to examine agency and the fatality of tragedy, and to question and support each other in the meaning-making process that is part of rehearsal. The potential for the growth of the students and even the chance of a transformative experience are worth the risks and the challenges that come with entering Wallace's theatrical territory.

Directing sex is one of the challenges, and there are risks involved. The richness, contradictions, and surges of human desire and rebellion in a Wallace play demand a process as variegated as the forces she summons. What follows are reconstructions of my approach to staging three Wallace plays and specifically to rehearsing sexual and violent content, which are often intertwined.

Slaughter City: Anger and Desire as Meat

When I undertook *Slaughter City* more than 15 years ago, I did so from a place of *not knowing how* to direct it. Upon first reading, I was bewildered by the play's historical ghosts and by its intertextual mingling of labor history, Karl Marx, the fierce poetries of Thomas McGrath, and, coyly, Raymond Williams's *Modern Tragedy* and his take on Brecht and the recovery of history as the subject of tragedy. I had just staged *Waiting for Lefty* with several other short labor plays from the 1930s, and I felt that my knowledge of labor theatre (and that of my students) would be deepened by this troubling contemporary play that significantly sexed-up "the conditions" referred to by Odets' characters. In effect, I wanted to know the difference between Agate yelling "Strike! Strike!" at the end of *Waiting for Lefty* in 1935 and Cod yelling "Fire!" at the end of *Slaughter City* in 1998 (when we did the play at Macalester). I knew I had to stage the play to find out, but I was not sure where to begin. The bibliography facing the final page of the script offered a map toward understanding.

Wallace often provides bibliographies in the published versions of her plays. Each bibliography—listing texts by historians, poets, biographers, and cultural critics—is a map of the reading material she drew on in constructing her play, and as such, it offers initial coordinates for research projects among director, designers, cast, and crew. Wallace's bibliographies always draw me to the pedagogical possibilities of her plays, and so, in my practice, I have come to assign research to students in a production, getting them started well before rehearsals begin and scheduling whole evenings of presentations early in the process. The quality of these presentations varies, but the evenings generate information, images, stories, and questions that come up again and again as rehearsals continue. This research is the ground on which the production stands.

Set inside a meatpacking plant at a time of labor unrest, *Slaughter City* includes a hierarchy of characters: a captain of industry, the plant manager and his middle-management underling, a union rep, and the lowly workers on the kill floor. The work of killing is the explicit labor in "Slaughter City, USA," and it structures and threatens to destroy the relationships among the workers. It tends them toward violence and hurt, injures them, implants chronic pain, and lowers their horizons of possibility. Their brave and creative resistance to the external and internalized violence of the workplace is the drama of the play.

To galvanize the rehearsal process and to make the-kill-and-the-cut of the play's gory setting palpable for the student cast, I sought to arrange a tour of a real-life slaughterhouse. As it turned out, the Hormel plant in Austin, Minnesota, was off-limits, and though the outdoor pens are in plain sight in South St. Paul—where Union, Swift, Armor, and Cudahy all operated until 1984—there was no tour available. Through family connections, our scenic designer, Tom Barrett, managed to arrange a solo visit to the partially defunct Cudahy plant in Milwaukee; he visited archives at the Milwaukee Historical Society as well, and his report and the photos and tools he brought back proved crucial to the play's design and to our understanding of the vastness and ubiquity of the meatpacking industry in the upper Midwest: the transport from farm to city, the labyrinthine outdoor pens, and the gigantic indoor processing facilities. As a cast we did manage to tour the Ford Truck Assembly Plant in St. Paul, where we witnessed middle-aged union workers with a high level of job seniority doing hard work continuously and repetitively. The massive scale was instructive: the relentlessness of the automation, the chemical odor, the din of the machinery, and the way the whole apparatus seemed to render the individual worker small and mechanical.

Wallace's research for *Slaughter City* led her to consult the work of labor historians James R. Barrett, Peter Rachleff, David Roediger, and Sheldon Stromquist. From these sources and from talking with a former packinghouse worker, we learned about the workers' obsession with knives. Knife pride is an occupational necessity on the kill floor because the care and expertise used in sharpening one's knives can make a difference in job performance and in safety. Knife sharpening time is a matter of collective bargaining, and sick jokes involving knives, carcasses, and animal guts are commonplace among slaughterhouse workers. We began to understand the literal and metaphorical significance of the knives, and particularly the knives' edges, and the preciousness of leisure time: a beloved hobby like fishing is savored not only for its intrinsic pleasures, but also for the challenge it poses to the segmented time of the conveyor belt, the time clock, and the workday.

Processing this research served and supported our work in rehearsing the transgressive sex encounters called for in the play. Our work on Act 1 Scene 9 offers a good example. The scene centers on the young, white worker Brandon, who after another long day on the kill floor is discovered at the top of this scene with his portable music player, "alone after everybody has gone home" (Wallace 2001, 221). In private, he cuts down a large, wrapped side of meat hanging from the ceiling, lays it on the ground, and speaks directly to it, quoting Albany from *King Lear* (Act 5, Scene 3): "Let sorrow split my heart if ever I did hate thee." He slices open the outer wrapping of the meat, essentially ripping its bodice, and coos to the carcass as he kisses it again and again, "See the light comin' off my feathers, Love? See it? I'm an angel, and I'm gonna reach my wing so far inside you, I'm going to disappear." Then, he plunges his hand and forearm deep into the meat, enacting a desire for Roach, an African-American coworker in her 30s. He does not know that Roach is watching his bizarre antics until she comes up behind him and puts a knife to his throat. Wallace indicates that all this should be "both sensual and frightening."

In approaching this scene, "J", the actor playing Brandon, and I recognized that the key was to show how a knife that is used all day to kill and to carve can be turned into an instrument of tenderness, transformed from the industrial weapon of Brandon's "formal combat with the meat" (210) into a seductive tool for undressing and making love to it. At the time of the production, J was a 19-year-old college student whose work experience included a summer in a locally infamous ice cream joint in a riverside town. The repetitive action of digging and twisting his forearms into deep buckets of cold hard dairy products was a useful point of reference for him, as was the more general feeling of being a dispensable seasonal employee. We rehearsed this scene at first using a cardboard box as a surrogate for the carcass of meat, which led us to consider different staging possibilities. Did Brandon perform this 'show' often or was it a new 'breach' for him, the eruption of a repressed or thwarted desire for Roach that suggests that love is possible amidst the death of the slaughterhouse? The scene seemed to suggest that flesh is both object and subject, both commodity for consumption and membrane to be caressed and penetrated. When the sound designer, Michael Croswell, picked INXS's *Fuck You Like an Animal* as the music Brandon plays for his seduction, the song's frank, even shocking lyrics amplified J's sense of transgression, of 'crossing over' into some new kind of self. When the scenic designer, Tom Barrett, carved the foam that would be the prop slab of meat, he checked several times with J to get the correct length of his forearm.

In short, the materialist research inspired by Wallace's bibliography helped to deliver J into the fullness of an action that at first seemed merely titillating or gratuitous. This collectively held knowledge served the rest of the cast as the frame for the play's many other erotically charged confrontations. In Act 1 Scene 5, Maggot berates Cod for being a scab and then kisses him hard on the mouth until he pushes her away. In Act 1 Scene 12, Baquin, the plant manager, orders Maggot and Roach to strip out of their work uniforms in front of him and then to wash themselves clean with a wet sponge; he stops Maggot in the process so that Roach, object of his possessive gaze, stands nearly naked on a chair in a manner that echoes a slave auction block. In Act 2 Scene 6, Cod talks about pickup trucks with Maggot and spears a screwdriver between Maggot's thighs into a workbench (or toolbox) and then uses it to demonstrate his gear-shifting abilities. In the next scene, Brandon and Roach finally consummate their desire and share a first kiss by passing a razor-sharp knife from her mouth to his.

These and similar encounters need to be seen and shaped as gestic. They may puzzle or confound audiences with their dialectics of delicate language and physical force, but the questions and provisional understanding developed in preliminary research and tablework discussions help young actors to achieve the capacity to embody these moments not as weird or kinky one-offs but as manifestations of desire struggling to undo and redetermine workers' history.

In the Heart of America: A Quiet Sense of Pride

Wallace's 1994 play asserts that all 'new' US military conflicts proceed from previous ones. History is never over: the dead haunt the living and the living seek to learn how the dead died. Love and familial loyalty develop despite the entrenched militarism of US society, but they are compromised by the ineradicable jingoism of empire. The heart of America, the play suggests, is making war: it perpetuates itself, sustains its administrations and pleasures, gives pet names to its weaponry, and even writes its own porn. As in *Slaughter City*, killing and practicing to kill are strange aphrodisiacs.

In 2005, when I directed *In the Heart of America* at Macalester, Operation Iraqi Freedom was well into its third year. The Desert Shield/Desert Storm conflict of the early 1990s to which the play refers had technically ended 13 years earlier, but US-Iraq tensions had simmered until the outbreak of the new war in 2003. The students in the cast were in high school during 9/11. None were from military families, though some had relatives who had served at the time of the Gulf War or in Vietnam. The play's linking of these two conflicts brought the issue of conscription versus an all-volunteer army home to them. Had the draft been in effect in 2005 they would have had to respond: either by signing up or by protesting, claiming an educational or other exemption, leaving the country, or otherwise 'dodging' the draft. The personal immediacy for them of such questions as what 'service to one's country' really means paved the way to other poignant and unsettling reckonings with issues of class and privilege, and certainly race, gender, and sexuality.

Here again, dramaturgical research, including assignments and presentations for each actor, provided a rich and evocative context for their work. Two significant activities involved combat veterans of Desert Storm/Desert Shield and the Vietnam War. We met for two afternoons with members of the local chapter of Veterans for Peace. Their stories were searing. A woman Air Force veteran of Desert Shield, stationed in Kuwait as part of air traffic control, described the traumas that all the soldiers, and particularly female soldiers, faced:

sexual harassment and rape, drug use, alcoholism, military-issued porn to ramp up for missions, and then, back home, the nightmares, lack of health services, employment issues, and suicides and near-suicides. This same trauma defines the characters in *In the Heart of America*, and after our meetings with these vets, we felt all the more motivated to convey the severity of their wounded psyches.

The other activity was more physical in nature and played a role in how we handled the sexual encounters in the play. Three of the play's five characters are soldiers who are involved in fight sequences in the play. Our combat choreographer was a former marine whose restitution for having committed acts of violence, he explained, was to become certified in fight work and to teach people how to use stage combat for artistic purposes. He asked me in the first rehearsal how graphic I wanted to get, and I said, "go for it." Stage combat is a matter of learning precise, second-by-second sequences of physical actions and reactions and then speeding them up to quarter time, half time, three-quarters time, and eventually full speed. The actors must calibrate these differences in tempo to ensure safety and to build the 'drama' of the fight scenes. Our ex-Marine choreographed the scenes in question—where Boxler trains and/or humiliates Craver and Remzi, as well as other partial fights and military crawls—graphically, almost sadistically, knowing that the action would be close to the audience.

The first time I saw the actors execute the fights in rehearsal, I felt physically ill. But the mechanics of the fight sequences taught me about the politics of the sex scenes in the play. If we were going to commit to the violent impulses in the play, then we surely had to make an equal commitment to the expressions of desire and sexuality. The sheer intimacy of the fights—the physical contact, the precise timing and coordination, the connection to the partner—helped me to recognize that the erotic bits not only had to be just as intimate and just as precise but also informed by a tenderness that is the opposite of aggression and that attests to the human capacity for love, even in the midst of war, even in the heart of America. The sex scenes in Wallace's plays need to be approached like combat sequences, all the more because the nature of the contact is less familiar and more 'dangerous' than a conventional stage kiss.

Take Act 1 Scene 9 for example. Craver and Remzi, two soldiers in Kuwait, one from Kentucky and the other a Palestinian-American from Atlanta, are talking in the barracks after Remzi returns from a leave in the Occupied Territories. There is a wariness between these two friends, stemming in part from a violent confrontation in the previous scene, but Remzi is eager to practice his new Arabic, to tell stories about his trip to the West Bank, and to share with Craver the varieties of figs he has brought back for him to try. Remzi chastises Craver for "not eating them right," for plugging a fig in his mouth "like a wad of chewing tobacco," for not eating them with grace, purpose, and "a quiet sense of pride," a phrase they used earlier in the play about how to be a soldier (Wallace 2001, 107). Remzi proceeds to teach Craver how, "to eat the fig gently. As though it were made of the finest paper." Remzi places a fig in the palm of his own hand and challenges Craver to pick it up—with his mouth. He bends, takes the fig, and holds it between his lips.

> REMZI: Now take it into your mouth. Slowly.
> *(Remzi helps the fig inside Craver's mouth.)*
> REMZI: Slowly. There...Well. How does it taste now?
> CRAVER *(After some moments of silence)*: Did you take a lot of pictures? (108)

The scene is self-evidently homoerotic, but that did not tell us exactly how to play it. Or how to talk about playing it. Figs, hanging from trees, look like testicles. I knew this and I thought the actors should, too, but as a white woman directing sex between two young men, one white, a senior, and personally-politically queer (playing Craver) and the other of color and as-of-yet sexually undisclosing (playing Remzi), I balked at saying the word *testicle* for fear of making one of them tense or embarrassed. I remember saying that I had seen figs growing on trees and that the sight was suggestive of male genitalia; I left it to them to do the research.

We approached the scene as an extension of earlier moments in the play when the two guys horse around in flirtatious ways that either one can call off at any moment. Remzi's visit to the territories confused his Palestinian identity and seemed to activate a desire for connection. We discussed Craver's willingness to play along with Remzi's fig lesson and when this little pick-up game, a simple, silly way to pass the time, became something more than that. Seeing Craver *mouth* the fig out of his hand, his lips on his palm—this would be exciting, curious. We imagined Remzi would see, from this improvisational moment, an opportunity: the mouth of his soldier 'buddy' with something delicious, desired, in it. As I recall, it was the actor playing Craver who remarked that what was sexy about the exchange was the finger pushing the fruit into the mouth and that that is where we would find the crux of this seductive faux-blowjob.

When it came to rehearsing with the actual fruit, we were very technical at first. Extend the hand out here, place the fig just so, Craver's decision to play along, lean down, sit back up, hold fig between lips, eye contact, Remzi's impulse to go further, reach forward, finger pushing the fig slowly into the mouth, lingering there where the fig was, turning the finger. Guided by our work on the combat sequences, we put these motions—action and reaction—together with the same clinical, mechanical precision, and this helped us to discuss and to discover where the impulse to 'keep going' at each step would come from (sensually, imaginatively). How close should their bodies be? What should their eyes communicate? Why not go further? They are alone, after all. Which one of them ends the moment, pulls back, pulls out? Or do they stop at a moment of mutual consent united around the fruit that comes from Remzi's ancestral homeland? How does it taste now?

Despite being men at different stages of their psychosexual development, the two actors playing Craver and Remzi developed a bond and a trust through the fight training that facilitated the choreographed tenderness required of them in the sexually charged moments. Days before the show opened, as a publicity move, the two of them, each with buzz cuts, donned their full combat gear and stood in front of the Student Center handing out fliers for the show. Fellow students, even their friends, did not recognize them, seeing only their uniforms and assuming they were recruiters. They came to rehearsal that night describing how they were told by the 'progressive' students of their own school to get off campus, to take their war and go home. They were shaken and furious and all the more determined to tell the stories of these two young men who they all might have been.

The Inland Sea: Anatomy Lessons

A landscape remade for the pleasures of the aristocracy—this is the terrain of *The Inland Sea*, Wallace's little-known play about the transformation of the English countryside in the eighteenth century by wealthy estate holders and the havoc it wreaked on the tenants who lived on and farmed that land. The play brings a group of townspeople in contact with the gentry who are threatening to evict them and with the diggers, unemployed shipbuilders, and soldiers who are hired to do the labor of that eviction. Central to this disruption is the major historical figure of landscape architect Capability Brown, who plays a minor role in the play, and the fictional character of his brother Asquith, who functions as Capability's surrogate in the action. By virtue of his gender, class privilege, and attendant sense of entitlement, Asquith assumes that the local women are easy, available, and perhaps even sexually primitive in some exciting, transgressive way. He takes a liking to a widow named Hesp, who proves to have an independence of body, mind, speech, and action that is much more than Asquith bargains for. The course of their ambivalent and awkwardly mutual attraction shapes a major portion of the play's action and leads to perhaps the most graphic sexual confrontation in Naomi Wallace's body of work.

The closer the estate comes to complete renovation, the more emboldened Asquith becomes with the place and the people he commands and the nearer Hesp, her mother, and their neighbors come to removal. The tension between his mounting ambition and the tenants' growing fury fuels their desperation for and against each other. As often as he compliments and delights Hesp, he humiliates and patronizes her. She knows that the only power she has over him stems from his interest in her body, and she is not fully certain of that. By the middle of the second act, their sexual compulsions have become both powerful and confusing. In Act 2 Scene 10, Hesp takes offense when Asquith mocks the "wheezing and grunting" of their lovemaking. He reaches for her, she pulls away, he accuses her of being a tease, and she declares she wants to be more than a quick toss in the hay for him. Her swagger aside, she confesses she wants to win his heart, but he complains that he is no longer "surprised" by her, sexually, and that her willingness to transgress class boundaries and give herself to him also, "was no real surprise, however delightful" (Wallace 2002, 93) Insult is added to injury.

Hesp is caught in the class-driven script of the poor country lass, comely one moment, saucy the next, just bold enough, and then demure, playing hard to get for the gentleman suitor until the moment prescribed for her to succumb to his mannerly charms and acquiesce to his superior will. Challenged to surprise Asquith, she takes the script into her own hands and improvises. She commands him to take down his trousers and drop to his knees. She tells him to turn around and then pushes him forward onto all fours. She reaches up under her skirt—for lubrication, we soon realize—and then, "her hand disappears under his shirt and after a moment Asquith gasps" (94). She is entering him, challenging his penchant for sexual escapade, and satisfying her instinct to take him 'down' and to make him her partner, to feel what she feels, to know her position as a 'bottom.' She perseveres in the fisting, with an odd mixture of cruelty and sensitivity, encouraging him to "keep breathing," saying she's "almost in." Finally, defiant and yet also somehow eager to please, she moves her hand—which is missing a thumb!—back and forth and asks, "Do I surprise you now, Mr. Brown? Are you awake?" Utterly hers, in exquisite pain and pleasure, he can only mutter, "Oh. My. God." as she curls forward over him and the scene ends (95).

With college students. In a 50-seat theatre with spectators—roommates, classmates, professors, parents—less than ten feet away. Early on in the rehearsal process, the preliminary research and analysis of the cast reflected their collective fascination with and terror of this scene and with being affiliated with a play that has this scene in it. The gesture is shocking, to be sure, but they could see how it compressed in explicit terms the complex histories of gender and class that were the subject of many of their courses. This particular penetration, we all came to understand, was a *gestic* cry of rage and pain by the perpetrator, an attempt to level the historical playing field. And it was a rape, too. Was it justified? Was it justice? We could not decide. Unable—and ultimately unwilling—to judge the act, we understood the various logics that led to it and went about building the scene.

"Z," the actor playing Hesp, took the position that Hesp was not sure what she wanted from Asquith but that in this moment she wanted to hurt him by taking him to his most vulnerable place using the only language she knew he would listen to. "B," the actor playing Asquith, understood his character's self-entitled masculinity as the counter-mask of an insecure younger brother who cannot possibly measure up to the standards and ideals of the older Great Man. When we started work on this scene, we had several rehearsals where we did everything but the penetration itself, trying first to understand Asquith's careless and hurtful speech, Hesp's vulnerability, when Asquith becomes aroused, and when Hesp's impulse ignites and she moves with uncharacteristic speed and focus to make him submit. When it came to the fisting sequence, we concentrated on the spatial logistics of the encounter, marking off distances and breaking down movements into step-by-step sequences. Here again, we approached it like a combat scene (which, in effect, it is), repeating again and again the way Hesp spins Asquith around and forces him to his knees, the way Asquith falls forward on all fours, the way Z lifts his shirt and places her hand on the inside of B's right leg so that the actors have some form of communication, the thrust, the gasp, the breathing, and so on. We used an experiential anatomy approach, discussing how the sphincter muscle reacts involuntarily here, and then how Asquith and Hesp each react moment by moment. The sex choreography provided stability for the actors as they rode the emotional currents of the scene. B understood—cognitively, emotionally, and through his preparation—that Asquith is a rebel of sorts, a thrill-seeker, and to the extent that he can think in this moment, he knows only to surrender—and in that surrender perhaps find a release the likes of which he's never known. At the end of the play, the landscape nearly finished, Asquith looks back on this moment in his final reckoning with Hesp and laments:

> In those moments, staring at my own hands in the grass. *(Speaks in a continuous stream.)* Terror and pleasure the land around me going out like a light I could have torn the field beneath us wide open such was the power I thought I'd split in two. *(Beat.)* No. I yearned for it. That I would never be again who I was. But I couldn't. I was. Afraid (111).

With purpose, Wallace ties the moment of anal penetration not only to the possibility of personal transformation (that Asquith might "never be again who I was"), but also to the transformation (if you will, the penetration) of the English countryside over which he has presided.

The action may be shocking, but it is not gratuitous. Neither is Brandon thrusting his forearm into a carcass of meat in *Slaughter City* or Remzi pushing a fig into Craver's mouth and letting his finger linger there in *In the Heart of America*. Or when, in *One Flea Spare*, Lady Darcy Snelgrave unwraps the bandage around the sailor Bunce and places her finger in the wound in his side. Wallace's body of work is marked by these wounds, these points of entry. The scenes of their discovery are highly charged dramas where the powerful and the powerless, the captor and the caught, reverse roles and know as they are doing so that the terms of their usual estrangement could change forever *starting right then*.

Student actors need to feel and understand these stakes. They need the dramaturgical research and text analysis to anchor their approach to the dizzying dialectical turns of Wallace's plays. They need trust in each other and in their director in order to enter into the complex dynamics of the play, including the erotically charged bits that hinge on vulnerability and submission. The emphasis in the plays on laboring bodies confers on the actors the understanding that they, too, are working, that the presentations, discussions, choreographed movement, and moment-to-moment discoveries in rehearsal are all the labor of embodied research. A full and genuine engagement in the production process offers to bring difficult, often dirty, conscripted work—butchering, soldiering, digging—*through* the bodies of middle-class college students such as mine at Macalester, young people who have not yet earned much in daily wages, who rarely come from families who belong to unions and do manual labor. What they learn about the *work* depicted in Wallace's plays takes them beyond the kinesphere of their limited life experience. It nurtures a respect for the living realities of wage-earning life under capitalism. And for the life of the artist under capitalism. If Wallace's plays offer an understanding of the operation of class (*and* gender *and* race), historically and in our own time, the work of rehearsing and performing them reinforces and deepens that understanding, for college students and for all who are willing to engage the work.

9

Mapping *The Inland Sea*: Naomi Wallace's British Epic Drama

Art Borreca

In the theatre of Naomi Wallace, separating the question "Who am I?" from the questions "What is the nature of the society I live in? And can it be changed?" is impossible. While these are hardly new questions in contemporary drama, Wallace has probed them with a remarkable combination of social commitment, theatricality, lyricism, gravity and humor, brutality and tenderness. Her plays dramatize how social forces and constraints—especially those having to do with race, gender, class, nationality, and sexuality—affect the life of the individual at every level of experience, from the personal to the social to the metaphysical. Her characters strive to stem or to transcend those constraints, and their efforts often reach a point at which sexual longing, one of the most inexplicable aspects of human experience, converges with the equally confounding realities of social power, its attainment, maintenance, and display. That collision of person and politics takes elaborate form in Wallace's *The Inland Sea*, a sprawling historical drama that premiered in London in 2002 and has been seldom produced since.[1]

When Wallace set out to write *The Inland Sea* in the late-1990s, it was to be, as she herself acknowledged soon before its opening, her "biggest" play so far (Kushner and Wallace 2001, 37). The work revisits Wallace's fascination with the inseparability of the individual and society, but it does so through a previously untried (for her) historical setting, a strikingly diverse set of characters and stories, and a vision perhaps riskier and more ambitious than in her previous work.

The ambition rests partly in the play's imaginative, empathic presentation of characters from the whole spectrum of eighteenth-century English society, as well as in how they are counterposed to capture a moment of historical transformation, a time when the socioeconomic structure, the network of human-social relations, and the very landscape of England were being reimagined and remade.

The Inland Sea takes place in Yorkshire in the 1760s. It dramatizes the impact on the inhabitants of a local village of an English Lord's transformation of his estate into a landscaped park, a phenomenon linked partly to the accelerating practice of land enclosures at that time. This project, designed by the historical figure of Lancelot "Capability" Brown (1715–1783), necessitates the removal of the villagers to another location. As the most important landscape architect of the era, Brown was involved in many such projects. In the play, he charges the fictional character of his brother, Asquith Brown, with completing the project. While sharing in his brother's grandiosity, Asquith has had greater difficulty transcending their family's working-class origins, and he soon finds himself the object of rage (at the removal), the subject of yearning (for a village woman named Hesp), and the unwitting agent in revealing a buried secret on the estate. While the play centers on Asquith's project and his affair with Hesp, it moves among a diverse range of characters, exploring the ways in which their lives and stories intertwine. These include the villagers, the soldiers, and shipbuilders who have been enlisted or hired to dig up the grounds of the estate, and an aristocratic female cousin of the Lord's who aims to capture the estate in a landscape painting, even as it is transformed into something else before her eyes.

The result is the most epic of Wallace's plays, not only in its historical scope and dramatic sweep but also in its debt to, and extension of, the epic theatre of Bertolt Brecht and a more recent generation of British dramatists from John Arden to Caryl Churchill and beyond, writers who have used the stage to depict the forces of history so that the present society might in some way be changed. *The Inland Sea* stands on its own as a work of theatrical imagination: one need not have knowledge of Capability Brown, eighteenth-century landscape architecture, or the societal conditions of the time to experience the play. And yet, as with any historically based drama, some knowledge of its period and figures can enhance or deepen one's understanding. This essay lays out the historical context of *The Inland Sea* in order to illuminate the action of the play and to demonstrate Wallace's commitment to rooting each of her plays in a specific historical moment.

The Eighteenth Century: A Widening Class Divide

The 1760s stood roughly at the center of major socioeconomic transformations that were taking place over the course of the eighteenth century, transformations which historians, conservative and radical alike, point to as marking the beginning of modern capitalist society—with both its attendant associations with positive socioeconomic "progress" and its noxious impact on individual and collective life. The middle of the century, from approximately the 1740s to the 1770s, saw an explosion in population growth, the extraordinary expansion of capitalism, and a shift from a predominantly agrarian to a rising industrial economy. The shift became visible in a transforming class-structure. Before 1700, that structure had been largely (if not simply) divided between a small aristocratic class and a massive underclass of subsistence farmers, laborers, and working poor. After 1700, there was an expansion of what would come to be called the "middle classes": tenant farmers and yeomen, merchants, and trades people, professionals (including clergymen, lawyers, and surgeons), and manufacturing and industrial workers. Whatever social and economic opportunities this expansion reflected, the structure of society as a whole still hinged—paradoxically—on the retrenchment of the landed aristocracy, its alliance with the landed gentry (persons without titles who had risen from the middle classes to become landowners), and the consolidation of wealth into the hands of this newly developing class-alliance. This shared economic self-interest cut across party lines: the aristocracy were largely Whigs who aimed to check the power of the monarchy over the peerage; the gentry were predominantly Tories who sought to emulate the nobility of old (Briggs 1999, 190–91).

Statistical figures for the period are unreliable, but there appears to be rough historical consensus on the widening disparity between rich and poor, no matter how precisely graded had become the social steps from the top to the bottom through the new middle classes. Oft-quoted figures include: whereas in 1700, the peerage of England owned 15–20 percent of the land, by 1800 they owned 20–25 percent. All landowners taken together, gentry as well as aristocracy, came to own as much as 75 percent of all cultivated land, most of it being cultivated by tenant farmers (Briggs 1999, 175–90; Sutherland 1988, 14–16). While landowners typically had incomes ranging from 20 thousand to 30 thousand pounds a year, laborers and others of comparable social status struggled to survive on an average of five to seven shillings per week (Mingay 1994, 6).

In this emergent capitalist economy, the landed classes led an "agricultural revolution," which entailed new and more productive crops, methods of crop rotation, and agricultural technology (including the mechanical drill and hoe introduced by Jethro Tull (1674–1741), developments that facilitated the production of root-crops such as potatoes. However, alongside the rise in productivity, there was a steep rise in food prices and farm profits as food became more scarce relative to the population as a whole. The new economy created opportunities to farm a portion of a landed estate within a competitive agricultural market; and yet, as Eric Hobsbawm observed, England at this time was losing a peasantry in the continental sense of the term: a class of owner-occupying small cultivators who subsisted on what they grew (Hobsbawm 1999, 16). In its place came an explosion of poverty, both agricultural and urban, a new, modern kind of poverty that resulted not from "the unholy trinity of famine, plague and war" but rather from "undernourishment of a significant portion of the rural and urban population" (to use the words of Christof Dipper (2000, 52). In short, individual suffering, especially of small landholders and squatters lacking in capital and legal rights, became widespread.

Integral to these changes in the social and economic structure was the phenomenon at the heart of *The Inland Sea*: the radical transformation of the English landscape. Around 1700, about one-half of all arable land in England was cultivated on the "open field" system of farming, with common fields broken into strips held by various families. The system worked, in part, because of low population. As the population rose and the agricultural economy changed, the movement to enclose lands quickened. The process began before 1750 with piecemeal enclosures initiated by landowners who sought to consolidate adjoining fields and then accelerated in the 1760s with the spread of agreements to enclose among neighboring landowners. Parliament fully legitimized the practice in the second part of the century through a long series of Bills of Enclosure that favored the owners and inevitably displaced squatters and copyhold tenants from their lands. The stone walls and hedges of East Anglia and the midlands had been an exception at the start of the century; by the end of the century, patterns of walls, fences, hedges, roads, and enclosed fields across England wrote new concepts of absolute "ownership" and "private property" into the land itself. (Hill 1985, 12–20; Mingay 1994, 42). "Not until the late 20th century was there to be such a drastic transformation in the appearance of the countryside," writes Asa Briggs (1999, 194).

Ultimately, the Bills of Enclosure were merely an extension of newly established laws regulating the use of the land over the course of the century. Such laws were established and enforced in direct proportion to the enclosures, and moreover were enforced by local magistrates and Justices of the Peace drawn predominantly from the landed gentry. Such 'gatekeepers' of enclosure and the consolidation of landed wealth required assistants who would carry out unpleasant aspects of their work. And so yet another middle-class occupation was born, or at least proliferated: that of estate managers, wardens, and gamekeepers. The last of these—particularly relevant to *The Inland Sea*—were responsible for enforcing game laws established as a counterpart to the laws of land regulation. With the enclosure of estates, game preservation and game shooting developed into popular sports of the aristocracy and gentry. The gamekeeper's job was to watch over the wild game on the lands of an estate, ironically preserving it to be hunted by the owner of the estate and his peers. The laws against poaching were severe, and the gamekeepers did not always allow their transgressors to make it to a judicial process; if they did, such a process would be unlikely to provide a fair hearing of the accused.

The wealthiest and most powerful landowners went beyond enclosing to "imparking" their estates: transforming the ground into landscaped parks and often tearing down buildings, leveling forests or preexisting gardens, and even relocating, razing, or drowning villages that obstructed the desired view. Viscount Cobham razed the village of Stowe and removed its inhabitants to Dadford. Thomas Coke moved the village of Holkham but later expressed some remorse when he wrote: "It is a melancholy thing to stand alone in one's own country. I look around, not a house to be seen but for my own. I am Giant, of Giant's Castle, and have ate up all my neighbors" (Porter 1982, 75).

Lancelot Brown, the most famous English landscape designer, was nicknamed "Capability" because of his fondness for saying that a country estate had great "capability" for improvement. Eventually given the position of Master Gardener to King George III, Brown's landscapes eradicated architectural gardens of French and Italian classical design, replacing them with sweeping expanses of lawn, undulating hills, and picturesque groupings of trees, some of which, such as North American conifers, were new species to the English countryside. Brown's designs represented a new philosophy of artfully cultivated 'nature,' a practice that went hand in hand with other displays of taste and sensibility, such as the collections of artwork, antiques, and books to which they dedicated entire rooms of their mansions.[2]

These developments—the consolidation of landed wealth, the changing class structure, the enclosure movement, the regulation of land use, and the landscape movement—suggest the complexity and ramifications of country life in eighteenth-century England. A brutal political will lay beneath the aesthetically designed surface of a landscape created by Capability Brown. The aristocracy, often with the assistance of the gentry and the gatekeepers of the estates, sought to secure grants of royal forest as well as common lands and to displace the working poor from those lands, mainly in the interest of lending artistic purpose to the act of enclosure. This is not to deny the aesthetic pleasure of contemplating the late-eighteenth century landscapes created by Brown and others or what remains of them today. The question is: can this pleasure only be gained by suppressing the social and economic realities in which the landscape was created? That question lies at the heart of *The Inland Sea*.

The Inland Sea: An Expanding Epic Vision

If Wallace's *One Flea Spare*, set in a quarantined London household during the plague of 1665, compresses the force of history into a closed, intimate, domestic interior, *The Inland Sea* explores how the same force reverberates a century later across a spectrum of spaces, realities, and classes—without losing the crucial sense of the intimate and personal. The play provokes both empathy with the past and a sharply implied critique of the present through an intricate series of displacements of the purpose or power of one character or group onto or by another character or group. Capability Brown sets the drama in motion by entrusting his brother as his surrogate to oversee the reconfiguration of Lord Heywood's estate. The actual labor of the project is displaced onto the diggers and soldiers who carry it out; they come to this labor having been displaced (or having escaped) from their previous occupations. By virtue of their labor, these workers are in turn displacing the villagers from the land that they have tilled for generations. The question that grounds the play's social narrative and dramaturgical structure is whether the villagers will yield to or resist the force of change embodied in the project designed by Capability, supervised by Asquith, and executed by the diggers and soldiers. They are, in effect, the agents of a present that seeks to forget or erase the past.

Two major strands of action—the Asquith-Hesp story and the Leafeater-Bliss story—are tied dynamically to the tensions and confrontations surrounding the work on the land and the threatened removal of the villagers. Early in the play, when Capability puts his brother in charge of the project, he advises him to stay away from whores and to get a wife. Soon after, Asquith meets a villager in her 30s named Hesp Turner, whose husband died from black fever seven years earlier. She dreams of getting away from the village—"Just step on a boat, my back to the land, and sail" (Wallace 2002, 20)—just as her father and young sister did when they left for the colonies of the New World 15 years before. Asquith and Hesp share an attraction that is mutual, ambivalent, and animated by both libido and class difference. Though the son of farmer, Asquith is a well-mannered gentleman now, self-made by dint of his education and social climbing; though she taught herself to read, Hesp is a potato picker who lost a thumb as a child when she and her father were slaughtering pigs. On a basic level, Asquith wants to play out their seduction by the usual terms of Gentleman and Maid, but as their relationship develops, she takes the lead in a series of surprising and unconventional sexual encounters that are disarming in their intimacy and that bring each of them to the brink of personal transformation.

Leafeater and Bliss are characters who shadow and haunt each other over the course of the play. Bliss is an 11-year-old girl who emerges from a hole in the ground—a shallow grave—and spends much of the play wandering the stage as a restless ghost calling and searching for someone or something. That turns out to be Leafeater, an odd, demented man who was once a "gentle youth" known as Ash Pidduck, the younger brother of Lord Heywood and eventually the gamekeeper on his estate, responsible for catching and punishing poachers. Fifteen years ago, he caught a starving man stealing deer on the property and had him hanged, and when the man's young daughter came out of the woods and attacked him, he beat her to death with a shovel. This girl is Bliss, who is Hesp's sister, and the poacher is Hesp's father as it turns out, the two of them did not flee to the colonies after all. Bliss will not leave Leafeater in peace until he reminds her of exactly how she died and returns her tiny skull to her, which has been disinterred by the work on the land along with her bones, her father's skeleton, and the noose used to hang him.

There are other characters who play secondary roles in the action but whose profiles are crucial to the demographic and ideographic spectrum of figures in the play. Jayfort is a black sailor turned boxer born in London of Jamaican parents who sailed the world on merchant ships but confronted the concept of empire in learning to read John Milton. He is someone who has gained a special knowledge of the world and how it works and has a vision of possible transcendence beyond this world. Simone Faulks is a landscape painter in her 30s and a distant cousin of Lord Heywood who has come to his estate to render on canvas a landscape that is already in the process of being destroyed. She, too, is a visionary of sorts who sees the evanescence of all life, human and natural, as "an impermanence that *is* infinite" (75) The stories of these and other characters make clear that in the world of Naomi Wallace the past is not so easily displaced by the present. In the final scene, as Jayfort shadow boxes and Bliss chants a parting refrain, Asquith takes up a handful of mud from the ruined landscape, his project sabotaged by flood. He tastes the mud and speaks of "a world leaning into the future, a world that did not look back. That could have been our paradise" (115). But for Wallace, history is too strong to be ignored. A moment later, Asquith calls for silence: "Listen. Shhh. The years are coming up from behind us, fast, fast, hear how they choke on their own thick breath?"

The Inland Sea combines elements of a costume pageant, a people's history, a ghost story, a Brechtian epic, a sexually charged romance, and a concrete social drama to represent a particular moment in English history—socially, politically, and economically—and to suggest how that history affects the lives of individuals who live and work and struggle within it. The play is bold in its ambitions, and on a formal level, a certain untidy amplitude is intrinsic to the work. While the play benefitted from a sustained developmental process, Wallace never succumbed to dramaturgical neatness or the temptation to put all of its stories 'in their place' in a manner inimical to the strange, off-center, and exciting ways in which they coexist in her dramatic vision. Rich and deep in content and form, rigorous in its attention to historical scholarship, the play remains true to its original intent to represent a significant moment in the history of England. In this regard, it offers a paean of sorts, albeit a critical one without jingoism or naïveté or imperial zeal, to Wallace's adopted home since the mid-1990s. In the play's penultimate scene, when the two gentlemen brothers assess the failure of their landscape project on the Heywood estate, it is Lancelot "Capability" Brown, the only character in the play drawn straight from history, who extrapolates to a national context:

> England still holds fast to a vision about herself. And though in the present moment she is always falling short of this vision, in her sleep, she sees herself transformed into an ever-growing magnificence, into an ever-reaching powerful tenderness. And though England will not exist in that perfected 'morrow of which she dreams, nor smell her own new morning, her brilliance lies in the fact that she still dreams. (*Beat.*) I am part of that dream (114–15).

In her own unique way, Naomi Wallace is part of that dream, too. The utopian urge that animates so many of her plays also lies at the bottom of *The Inland Sea*, like pirate's treasure waiting for salvage and distribution.

Notes

1. The original production of *The Inland Sea* was directed by Dominic Dromgoole and presented by the Oxford Stage Company at Wilton's Music Hall in London in April 2002. As dramaturg for that production, I was involved in the play's development, during the rehearsal period and earlier during a staged reading of the play in October 2001 at the University of Iowa, where I head the graduate playwriting program from which Wallace received an MFA in playwriting in 1993. My observations in this essay are based in part on my experience as dramaturg.
2. Information about Capability Brown is available from a wide range of sources. In the list of books that she consulted for background research for the play, Wallace includes the following: Ann Bermingham, *Landscape and Ideology: the English Rustic Tradition, 1740–1860* (University of California Press, 1986); Thomas Hinde, *Capability Brown: the Story of a Master Gardener* (London: Hutchinson, 1986); Edward Hymas, *Capability Brown and Humphrey Repton* (Johns Hopkins University Press, 1989); and Dorothy Stroud, *Capability Brown* (London: Faber and Faber, 1975).

10
Slip's Bluff

Neil Chudgar

Early in Naomi Wallace's *The Inland Sea*, Asquith Brown interrupts a flirtatious conversation between Slip, a shipbuilder hired to dig, and the rural woman Hesp. The conversation is about dancing; Asquith, uninvited, takes hold of Hesp and starts to dance with her. As they dance, Asquith turns his attention to Slip: "Have you had a read of Burke's *Enquiry into the Origins of our Ideas of the Sublime and Beautiful*?" Slip, who cannot read, tries to bluff: "Course I have." Asquith, cruelly, asks Slip what he thinks of it: "I think, sir, that it is about one man's ideas...of love." Asquith, still dancing, pounces: "Love? Nonsense. It's about the sublime. Read in conjunction with Hogarth's *Analysis of Beauty*, it might give a man an idea or two" (Wallace 2002, 36).[1] Asquith knows whereof he speaks: Edmund Burke, later a profound theorist of conservative politics, and William Hogarth, already a famous painter, provided the foundation of aesthetic theory that underlay the sweeping revisions of the English landscape that Wallace's play dramatizes. But Slip's bluff—that Burke's *Enquiry* is, "about one man's ideas...of love"—is closer to the truth than Asquith knows. Indeed, *The Inland Sea* requires us to understand that aesthetics, its most ordinary modern manifestations, *derives* from certain men's ideas of love.

In his *Analysis*, published in 1753, Hogarth identifies beauty with the gentle curve and recurve of a serpentine line. Hogarth's famous "line of beauty." The aesthetic system that stems from it is nationalistic, explicitly English, opposed to the rigid geometries favored by decadent Continental sensibilities. It is also emphatically masculine, deriving almost directly from the delight a red-blooded English boy might derive—as Hogarth recounts he did himself—from observing the forms of women. Here, Hogarth locates the "line of beauty" in the curling edge of a piece of ribbon:

> I never can forget my frequent strong attention to it, when I was very young, and that its beguiling movement gave me the same kind of sensation then, which I since have felt at seeing a country-dance...particularly when my eye eagerly pursued a favorite dancer, through all the windings of the figure (34).

This fluid movement of sensation from one object to another, from the beauty of a ribbon's edge to the beauty of a woman at a country-dance, is the conceptual lubricant of Hogarth's aesthetic theory. It sets aesthetics free from its bondage to any theoretical criteria and makes beauty the mere index of somebody's feelings.

Hogarth's feelings are no secret. Beauty, he maintains, derives primarily from the "fitness" of an object to the purposes for which it is formed.[2] In this, Hogarth merely iterates for the eighteenth century an aesthetic doctrine familiar from Socrates to Crate & Barrel—the notion, much repeated, that form should follow function. Hogarth's aesthetic theory departs from others in this vein, however, because it wanders from function to gender: the paradigm of the beautiful, for him, is the body of a woman—especially when it is coerced into a particular shape by a corset. The purest example of the "line of beauty," Hogarth instructs, is "every whale-bone of a good stay." His argument vividly diagrams the point: "if a line...were to be drawn, or brought from the top of the lacing of the stay behind, round the body, and down to the bottom peak of the stomacher; it would form such a perfect, precise, serpentine line" (1997, 49). Hogarth concludes that the contour of such a caress, from the middle of a woman's back to the middle of her belly, proves "how much the form of a woman's body surpasses in beauty that of a man" (49).

The eighteenth-century landscape architect Lancelot "Capability" Brown imposed the gently curving "line of beauty" from Hogarth's theory of painting onto the topography of England itself—and, with it, the sexual and ethical commitments of Hogarth's aesthetics. In *The Inland Sea*, Wallace invents Asquith Brown, Lancelot's brother and assistant, to give those commitments a voice and a body. While he dances with Hesp, Asquith smoothly suggests that the changes he is making in the landscape will produce "spaces of grace," as he calls them, landscapes that will undulate gracefully, "into the distance. Just as the body should. That's right. That's nice. Turn, and circle and sweep. No straight lines." Asquith has mastered the metonymic operation of Hogarth's aesthetics: hills undulate *just as* bodies should; ribbons are beautiful *just as* dancing women's bodies are. As Asquith dances and theorizes with Hesp in his arms, Wallace tells us, Slip (who knows a thing or two about aesthetics) "*looks away in disgust*" (37).

In 1757—four years after Hogarth, three years before the time of Wallace's play—Edmund Burke moved beyond Hogarth's *Analysis of Beauty* to theorize the Sublime, a masculine counterpart to Hogarth's Beautiful. For Burke, the Sublime is a quality of an object that inspires terror, which means a fear of harm; and all that increases this terror adds to sublimity—obscurity, blackness, power, roughness.[3] Beauty, on the other hand, is a quality of an object that makes it beautiful. "By beauty," Burke writes, "I mean, that quality or those qualities in bodies by which they cause love... by which I mean that satisfaction which arises to the mind upon contemplating any thing beautiful" (1968, 91). Is this definition circular? Absolutely. Despite Asquith's scornful correction, Slip is precisely correct: Burke's theory of beauty really *is* about "one man's ideas... of love."

And Burke's ideas of love are specific and emphatic. Hogarth only smuggled a gender theory of beauty into an allegedly functional aesthetics: Burke, more candid, elaborately rejects the notion of "fitness" as a cause of beauty. In so doing, he obliquely accuses Hogarth (as bullies love to do) of being confused about sexual propriety. If "fitness" to a purpose causes beauty, Burke argues, then by Hogarth's own reasoning, *anything* "fit" must be beautiful. This unassailable logic leaves Hogarth's theory in an awkward position, which Burke eagerly exploits. "To call strength by the name of beauty," he argues, "to have but one denomination for the qualities of a Venus and Hercules, so totally different in almost all respects, is surely a strange confusion of ideas" (106). From that point on, Burke's aesthetics performs its own sexual commitments with astonishing gusto. We learn about the beauties of, for instance, "a delicate smooth skin," of the way women, "learn to lisp, to totter in their walk, to counterfeit weakness" (because "Beauty in distress is the most affecting beauty"), of "the softer virtues" of "feminine partiality" (108–11). We learn that beautiful objects are small and smooth (113–14). "Observe that part of a beautiful woman," Burke eagerly exhorts us, "where she is perhaps the most beautiful, about the neck and breasts; the smoothness; the softness; the easy and insensible swell" (115). "The beauty of women," Burke says, "is considerably owing to their weakness, or delicacy, and is even enhanced by their timidity" (116). Gentle pastels are more beautiful than stronger colors; a beautiful face, "must be expressive of such gentle and amiable qualities, as correspond with the softness, smoothness, and delicacy of the outward form" (117–18). "All bodies that are pleasant to the touch," finally, "are so by the slightness of the resistance they make." The beautiful, for Burke, is soft, round, and weak; the beautiful is easy to touch. Thus, what is beautiful is loveable—if what you love is soft, and round, and weak, and does not resist (much) when you touch it.

Under the influence of Hogarth and Burke, landscape architects of the later eighteenth century tried to make the English landscape beautiful by making it something an English man could love (or should) by making its surface resemble the curved outside of an English woman's body. In Wallace's play, Lancelot and Asquith have been hired to produce just such a transformation on a nobleman's estate. When they are finished, the brothers confidently predict, this piece of property will be composed of lines of beauty, the sissy formalities of parterre and hedge absorbed into the loveable bosom of gently swelling hills: "Not a fountain or terrace or balustrade left to be seen," Lancelot declares, "A truly English garden." "And the new trees," Asquith adds, "softening the hard edges in the distance" (10).

By the end of this scene, Lancelot has left his brother to superintend the present landscaping project. The responsibility comes with a strange admonition: "Remember, my brother," Lancelot says, "whatever you create out there, as far as the eye can see, is the story of who you are...in here." The stage directions instruct the actor playing Lancelot to, "thump...Asquith's chest gently" (12). What strikes me about this moment—and about the play more generally—is what it implies about the relationship between 'out there' and 'in here': between the landscape and people's insides. Taking an idea or two from Burke and Hogarth, we can imagine what Lancelot Brown believes that relationship to be: if you create beautiful curving hills *out there*, in the landscape, you're telling the story of what you love *in here*. That's how, in the play, Brown can give his brother technical advice about landscaping, marriage, and masturbation as though they were interchangeable activities, each of which can be mastered *just as* the others can. The metonymic relationship of beloved and beautiful that derives from eighteenth-century aesthetic theory—the easy conceptual slips between a length of ribbon, a dancing body, a woman's waist, the soft upheaving of an artificial hill—makes every judgment of beauty a declaration of love.

In our histories of taste, Brown's landscapes often appear as a watershed in the inexorable progress of aesthetic modernity:

> He observed that Nature, distorted by great labour and expense, had lost its power of pleasing...Under his guidance a total change in the fashion of gardens took place, and...the English garden became the universal fashion. Under the great leader Brown...we were taught that Nature was to be our only model (Repton 1840, 327).

And so, in many quarters, Nature remains: "artificial," after all, is still a term of abuse. But the vogue for Nature doesn't come cheap. Artifice may be costly, but it takes far more "labour and expense" to conceal it. Wallace's play tells a story about that labor and reckons up that expense. In *The Inland Sea*, we learn that the beauty of eighteenth-century British landscapes—a kind of 'natural' beauty very much in fashion even now—is an effect of power. The paradox of eighteenth-century aesthetics is that the gentle curve and recurve of beauty, the surfaces that Hogarth and Burke and "Capability" Brown found most loveable, had to be produced by violence. It takes vast power to move immense volumes of soil and plants and animals and water, which do not *want* to be moved, into configurations that, curving smoothly, leave no trace of their own manufacture. This was Brown's project: mobilizing labor and capital to erase the visible traces of human artifice—parterres, allées, fountains, hedges—from the gardens of country estates, and producing in their place new and beautiful landscapes that appeared not to have been produced at all.

Artifice moves in straight lines; nature, we're told, has curves. In the play, Lancelot declares that, "Deep, sustained pleasure cannot be found in a straight line of motion...You have got to be more firm. Brutal even. You've got to—curve it to the left. Curve it to the right. Even if it doesn't like it" (67). That sort of forcible curvature sometimes bends matter past its breaking point. When matter breaks, there's often pain as the insides of things spill out, leaving only their surfaces behind. Emptying out the insides of things is sometimes an accident; but for those who love certain perfect surfaces, it's a principle. Hogarth, in his *Analysis*, instructs his reader to learn about beauty by eviscerating things, reducing them to pure surface. "Let every object," he writes,

> be imagined to have its inward contents scoop'd out...as to have nothing of it left but a thin shell, exactly corresponding both in its inner and outer surface, to the shape of the object itself...The imagination will naturally enter into the vacant space within this shell, and there at once...view the whole from within (1997, 21).

To achieve what's beautiful, it seems, we must hollow out the objects we encounter, then enter into the empty space where the insides were and fill up the vacant skins of things with our imagination. That is in aesthetic theory: in real life, however, scooping out the "inward contents" of objects is a messier business.

There are moments, which any viewer of the play will remember quite vividly, when *The Inland Sea* brings "inward contents" into acute dramatic significance: when Hesp pushes her hand into Asquith's guts, when the soldier Nutley cuts into his arm to expose the bone inside. This violent play of human insides and outsides rhymes with the violent revolutions of the landscape. The deranged vagrant Leafeater discovers the little girl he once murdered both *in here*, as a pile of buried bones, and *out there*, singing and talking in the world, at once. Meanwhile, the Brown brothers employ the labor of Slip and other diggers to overturn the ground, bringing its hidden insides to light on the way to perfecting its outward surface. In these ways, the play exposes the bloody or dirty innards that come out when powerful men hollow out the world's objects to produce the surfaces of things that they can love.

For Wallace, such forcible beautification is always unsuccessful, however violently it may be coerced, however plangently it may be desired. At the end of the play, some land has been overturned by forced labor; some trees have been planted and others have died; a vast lake has flooded the village where Hesp and her neighbors once lived. Much has been hollowed out, but nothing has been perfected. Asquith has failed to produce a beauty he can love. Hesp tells him, "You have turned this land inside out, but nothing has disturbed the surface" (111). The aesthetics of eighteenth-century landscape, which wants us to hollow out the "inward contents" of things to make them lovable, is purely theoretical. In lived practice, in the world of actual bodies with actual contents, there is no way to perfect the relationship between insides and outsides, between contents and surfaces. Even at the bitter end, Asquith still believes that, if he only tried hard enough, he could still bring insides and outsides into beautiful harmony. If only he'd allowed Hesp to split him open and empty him out, leaving nothing of him but a new and better surface, everything might have been different. "Such was the power," he says, "I thought I'd split in two...I yearned for it. That I would never be again who I was. But I couldn't" (111). He couldn't because no one can. It's impossible to make the surface *out there* match the fullness of what's *in here*.

The Inland Sea is a play about eighteenth-century British landscape architecture. That means it is a play about how power produces beauty, and why. I think, as Slip suggests, that it is about one man's ideas of love. But this is a love that hollows out the insides of its objects to make their surfaces loveable, a love that removes forests across continents and drowns whole villages for the view. This kind of love brings power to bear on the world and its bodies, and that's what makes it dangerous. We might expect to find such tragic manifestations of landscape-altering power in the Middle East of Wallace's play *The Fever Chart*, where the surface of the earth itself explodes, but that same kind of power tightens the corset on a lady's belly and heaves up the gentle hills of a country-house lawn. There is secret violence in the aesthetics of eighteenth-century landscape, which carefully hides the power that the love of it brings to bear. The tragedy of *The Inland Sea* comes from the perilous notion that beauty, out there, ever *could* harmonize with the love we want to feel (gently thump your chest) in here. Even today, we often believe that our internal desires have some claim on the world's objects—that *making things beautiful*, whatever that means to us, is *a priori* a worthy aim. That notion is a fantasy, as common as it is pernicious. Wallace invites us to imagine what the world would look like if beauty had nothing to do with love at all—if we relinquished our claims on the inward contents of things, and let surfaces be.

Notes

1. All subsequent quotations from the play, cited by page number only, are from this same edition: Naomi Wallace, *The Inland Sea* (London: Faber and Faber, 2002).
2. Hogarth's theory carefully skirts the objects that might turn aesthetics queer. Although his discussion of the beauty of "fitness" closely follows Socrates' in Xenophon's *Memorabilia*, Hogarth replaces a pair of Socrates' uncomfortable

illustrations with his own safer ones, silently changing a beautiful wrestler and sprinter to a beautiful war-horse and racehorse (1997, 26).
3. *The Inland Sea* provides a perverse instance of the Burkean sublime in the Jamaican sailor Jayfort—obscure, black, and powerful. Not for nothing does Jayfort recite Milton, the great poet of the terrifying sublime.

11
Journeys into the Heart of Whiteness: A Labor Historian Looks at the Work of Naomi Wallace

Peter Rachleff

The plays of Naomi Wallace constitute a form of historical study. Her diligent research includes reading widely in labor history literature, engaging labor historians in conversations, and delving into critical race theory, particularly through the work of James Baldwin.[1] Her refusal to traffic in historical stereotypes and tropes, along with her use of imagination, ghosts, magical realism, and poetic language, has enabled her to create dramatic work that challenges audiences to see workers not only as the products of the historical development of structures of class, race, gender, and sexuality, and the interaction of these structures with each other, but also as the possible architects of new social realities. Her theatre encourages us to think critically about how the power wielded by class, race, gender, and sexuality has shaped our history and how it is shaping our own lives today.[2]

Wallace's rich, complex work offers the opportunity for many types of investigation. I restrict myself here to the topic of greatest interest to me as an historian, a teacher, and an activist—how the forces of class, race, gender, and sexuality in US history have combined to create *whiteness*. Forty years of historical reading, scholarship, teaching, and activism have convinced me that *whiteness* has been the critical glue that has held US society together as we have become the dominant economic and political power in the world.³ At the heart of the construction and reproduction of hegemony, *whiteness* has also shown itself to be fragile, unstable, rife with contradictions, and even susceptible to explosions, which threaten the very social order that it has supported. It is a potent site for personal and social transformation. Wallace's work offers us a journey into this foundational ethic: the making—and the possible unmaking—of this historic *whiteness*.

Making Whiteness in the United States

In the pre–Civil War era, industrialization confronted white workingmen with multiple dimensions of downward mobility. Journeymen found their path to the independent status of a master artisan blocked by the emergence of factories. While one journeyman shoemaker out of two reached self-employment in the era of the American Revolution, only one in twelve achieved similar status by the Civil War. With access to property ownership and economic independence at risk, white workers in state after state, North and South, in the 1830s and 1840s demanded the revision of voting rules to eliminate property qualifications and to put race and gender qualifications in their place. At the same time, the application of a division of labor, mechanized technologies, and a reorganization of production deskilled much work and turned artisans into unskilled laborers. A newly centralized authority, manifest in time clocks, schedules, work rules, and fines, undercut workers' freedoms on the job. The economic insecurities brought on by downturns in business cycles, layoffs, and outright discharges in one's later years jeopardized the status of male workers as family-supporting breadwinners. Their gendered assumptions about being patriarchs—heads of their own households—were in jeopardy as well.⁴

In the United States, the industrial revolution took place within a society in which racially based slavery was already a key economic institution. As white workers sought to make sense of the threats to their independence, their expected socioeconomic-political roles, and their public and private identities, they compared themselves to African-American slaves. Even as they knew that only black men and women could be slaves, they feared they were becoming *like* slaves. Such a comparison was encouraged by employers, politicians, newspaper editors, ministers, and purveyors of popular culture, who then mollified white workers with expressions of kinship, solidarity, shared racial identity, and offers of privilege (such as access to jobs, housing, schools for their children, citizenship and the vote, and the low-paid labor of black household servants).[5]

Although the 75 years of the industrial revolution—roughly 1820 to 1895—were marked by working-class resistance and protest, from the formation of unions, cooperatives, and independent political parties to strikes and protests, *whiteness* undermined organizations and movements and mitigated their effectiveness and power. While workers did occasionally organize together across racial boundaries, white workers frequently organized separately and sought to protect their own layers of privilege. They also directed their anger and vented their frustrations at African-Americans, the Chinese, or Mexicans, sometimes in paroxysms of violence. *Whiteness* became a template that shaped the relationships between native-born white workers and the increasingly motley mix of immigrant workers, shaping in turn their relationships with workers of color, on the one hand, and their employers, on the other. Their disidentification with workers of color and their identification with their own employers were two sides of the same coin.[6]

Thus, *whiteness* was an implicit bargain, forged in relationships among whites across class. It also circulated within and through working-class organizations, institutions, and cultural activities, from volunteer fire companies and mutual benefit societies to trade unions and minstrel shows. In these popular culture forms, working-class whites were given permission to play at being 'black,' a *blackness* shaped by the projections of their repressed desires and fantasies. *Whiteness* was also performed and reinforced in the private space of workers' homes, where men and women adopted and adapted roles of domination and subordination, of patriarchy and power. Race and masculinity, particularly heteronormative masculinity, became linked.[7]

Although this *whiteness* was potent, it was also fragile, as it developed within a capitalism whose primary constant has been change rather than stability. From the industrial revolution through the rise of mass production and, now, deindustrialization and globalization, US capitalism has evolved through substantial reorganizations of work processes, the introduction of new technologies, and the emergence and disappearance of entire industries. From the depressions of the 1870s and 1890s to the Great Depression of the 1930s and the Great Recession of our own era, and through the accelerated economic growth of world wars, the Cold War, and the many smaller wars and "police actions" that have demanded weapons, military machinery, uniforms, and more, US capitalism has experienced economically intense busts and booms. Each of these shifts put at risk the cross-class bargains that underpinned *whiteness*, as they demonstrated that the privileges, identities, and class and racial relationships which rested on these bargains could be destabilized, even erased, in the interests of more pressing items on the elite's agenda, from increased profits and global competitiveness to the appeasement of global opinion during the Cold War.[8]

The very possibility of such shifts revealed the fragility of *whiteness*. Most white workers have sensed, at most times, that as economic circumstances changed, the social contract they had entered into with their immediate employers and with the leaders of the United States' social and political structures, the bargain around which they had organized their lives and constructed their identities, could be dissolved. To be sure, this sense has not always been conscious. Often inchoate, this awareness infused white working-class culture with an edge, a tension, a barely suppressed anger and cynicism. In moments of crisis, this could give way to radically unexpected behaviors, from interracial love and labor solidarity, on the one hand, to race riots and brutality, on the other. *Whiteness* remained a site of both privilege and internal repression, in interaction with constructions of masculinity and femininity, of class as well as race. Working women and men were compelled by their circumstances—and pressured themselves—to behave, to belong, to identify with their employers and leaders and to disidentify with those below them on the social ladder, even if they worked alongside them. For individuals and groups, this situation rippled with instability and insecurity, as many were only a lay-off, a plant closing, a technological innovation, or an injury away from a plunge in socioeconomic-political status. Such a plunge might even be marked by the loss of *whiteness* and its privileges.[9]

This is the state of *whiteness* today as much as it was in 1963 or 1913 or 1863. Its power and its fragility continue to percolate below the surface of identities and relationships. Its crackling tensions haunt relationships between workers and the elite, among white workers, between white workers and workers of color, between working-class men and women, between native born and immigrant workers, and between US workers and workers elsewhere in the world. To dwell in the dialectical tensions between the power and the fragility of *whiteness* is uncomfortable and dangerous, but the world we have inherited and remade for ourselves gives us no choice. We have only the choice of whether we do so consciously or unconsciously.[10]

Wallace's plays ask her witnesses to track her characters' engagement with the possibilities of personal transformation that is grounded in the historical construction, unfolding, and possible shattering of *whiteness*. In this essay, I explore three of her plays—*Slaughter City, Things of Dry Hours,* and *The Hard Weather Boating Party* and discuss how each offers a particular lens through which to view the heart of *whiteness*. Like the *whiteness* that has structured US society, Wallace's central white characters in these plays manifest both power and fragility, driven by these dialectical tensions. Whether each is transformed in the final analysis is less important than our consciousness of the possibilities of both personal and social transformation.

Slaughter City

Inspired by meatpacking strikes in mid-1980s Austin, Minnesota, and early 1990s Louisville, Kentucky, *Slaughter City* also evokes historic labor struggles. The range of characters includes black and white workers, men and women, layers of management, and three ghostly figures unbound by time: "Textile Worker," who was in her mother's womb during the 1911 Triangle Shirtwaist Factory fire and "survived" her mother's deadly leap; "Sausage Man," who grinds sausage in an organ-grinder-like device, referencing both the artisanal roots of butchering and capitalism's chewing up of workers; and "Cod," hired since the strike, of indeterminate age and gender with a personal history as both a striker and a scab in different historical moments. The play's various characters interact on both intimate and symbolic levels as they struggle to determine labor–management relations following the defeat of a strike. In the process, they re-enact the history of capitalist development and class conflict in the United States and confront the historical structures of race as well as gender (Wallace 2001).[11]

The play reflects the dynamics brilliantly theorized in a book that greatly influenced my generation of labor historians—Carter Goodrich's *The Frontier of Control*. Goodrich argued that every workplace could be understood as having an invisible but tacitly recognized line drawn where management's authority ceased and workers' authority began. This line moved frequently, depending on a range of factors—how much the work process relied on the skills and knowledge of the workers; how well-organized the workers were; how effectively management could divide workers by race, ethnicity, nationality, language, and gender; and how effectively management could manipulate workers by different sorts of payment systems. Major historical events—the organization of a union, for instance, or the experience of a strike—could substantially shift this line and the power it represented. *Slaughter City* makes tangible for its audiences Goodrich's analysis of the construction—and the instability—of power in an industrial workplace (Goodrich 1920).

When the play opens, the workers have just been defeated in a bitter strike. Discouragement, fear, and suspicion are rife. Strikebreakers ("scabs") had been hired and some workers had crossed their own picket lines and returned to work, but management has not yet been able to reconstruct its power on the kill floor of the plant. As workers and managers renegotiate their relationships, Sausage Man, Cod, and Textile Worker bring their historical experiences and roles into the mix. Critical to this conflict is the young white worker Brandon. It is through his *whiteness* that the play's key power dynamics get worked out. His work assignment

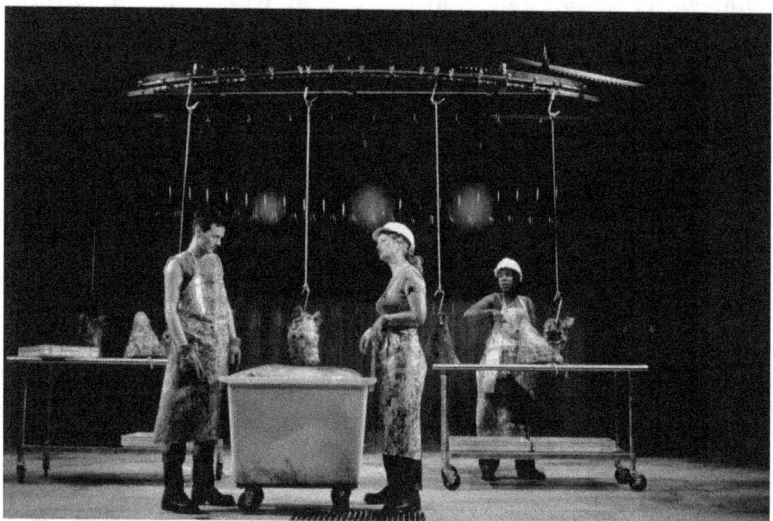

Figure 11.1 Sharon Scruggs (Cod), Judith Hawking (Maggot), and Starla Benford (Roach) in the 1996 American Repertory Theatre production of *Slaughter City*. Director: Ron Daniels. Photo: Richard Feldman. Courtesy of American Repertory Theatre].

makes him central to the setting of the pace of work and, therefore, the locating of the frontier of control for all of the workers. He also symbolizes the privileges and challenges of the white workforce as a whole. He has climbed the job ladder on the kill floor itself, from head boner to scalder to bung dropper to splitter, and he just might be headed into an office or even management job.

While Brandon's racial position has given him privileges above those of other workers, it is also a source of instability and tension in his life. With his higher wages has come intensified pressure to keep moving up the internal job ladder at the plant. We wonder whether Brandon will operate from his position of privilege and alienate himself from the other workers or develop solidarity with them. Wallace reveals other factors that complicate his character: he has been scarred, physically and emotionally, by an abusive father and by his work in the packing plant; he is illiterate and has learned survival skills to hide his illiteracy; and he has a smoldering passion for Roach, an African-American woman worker ten years older than him. His path towards (or away from) class solidarity and personal transformation is played out on the field of this potentially fatal attraction. Wallace constructs Roach as a character with sufficient self-respect and agency that she will not fall for any forms of conventional seduction on Brandon's part. The performance and subversion of power relationships—and therefore *whiteness*—is at the very heart of the passion play between Brandon and Roach.

This volatile relationship reaches a crossroads in Act 1 Scene 9, which takes place on the kill floor of the slaughterhouse and begins, as Wallace writes, with:

> *Brandon alone after everyone has gone home. A makeshift, bloody bandage on his hand, he stands on a work scaffold, then jumps down and clears the space for his "dance." He places his small cassette player in the center of the space and then begins to run, jump, and dance around the stage. The feeling is one of a body taking complete control over the space around it.* (221)

He proceeds to cut down a wrapped carcass of meat hanging from the ceiling and to enact an elaborate, graphic, and stylized seduction, circling the carcass as he strips off his shirt, reciting and singing to it, using his knife to cut away its wrapper, tossing the knife aside to kiss and nip at it, and eventually pushing his arm up inside the meat in an act of possessive penetration that Wallace describes as "both sensual and frightening." Unbeknownst to Brandon, Roach has been watching this whole 'show' from the shadows and comes forward at the moment of his climax:

> Roach picks up the knife. She comes up behind him, takes him by the hair and holds the knife to his throat. She is in complete control.
> ROACH: Oh, but that's not enough, my cherub. No. This piece of meat wants your sweet face inside her, your whole head inside her.
> She crushes his face into the carcass, then turns him on his back so she's straddling him, knife still at his throat. (222)

Driven by her own ambivalent desire, Roach has intervened in Brandon's performance of desire and taken power over him. Brandon yields to her and in yielding he, in effect, wrestles with his own privileged position and begins to be transformed. This is hardly an act of abstract solidarity or generosity (although it is also both); it is a way of emancipating himself from the strictures of *whiteness* and its normative masculinity. That emancipation continues in Act 2 Scene 7 when Roach, again unnoticed (except by the audience), watches Brandon in the women's locker room as he takes off his clothes and puts on a woman's work dress, trying on the opposite gender. Roach emerges and intervenes, assuming the aggressive 'male' role, ripping off his dress just as he ripped the wrapper from the meat in the earlier scene. The two of them dance and gradually move towards a defiant kiss that takes the form of Roach placing a sharp knife in her mouth and inviting him to take it from her mouth with his.

This act of mutual desire propels Brandon's journey through *whiteness*, away from *whiteness*, and into transformation, but his journey and our witnessing of it remains rocky, difficult, painful, and, as written by Wallace, feverish and unstable. His explosive romance with Roach is conditioned by the dangers of the workplace. Over the course of the play, he is injured, rendered unconscious, overcome by blood poisoning, hospitalized, even subjected to electroshock treatment, and out of control. Finally, he dies in the industrial accident that pushes the play to its climax. In that final moment, the workers, incited by Brandon's death and led by Cod, have taken control of the plant and locked themselves in, even as a fire is breaking out. Brandon's personal transformation has set the stage for the workers' engagement with the whole history of capitalism. And when Cod shouts "Fire!" as the closing line of the play, we are reminded of our own presence, our own role, in this narrative.

Things of Dry Hours

Inspired by Robin D. G. Kelley's *Hammer and Hoe: Alabama Communists During the Great Depression*, *Things of Dry Hours* asks its audience to wrestle with the complexity of black–white relationships on the political left and, particularly in the southern working class, in the 1930s. The Great Depression provoked a crisis of *whiteness* for white workers: as profit margins plummeted, the paternalism of employers and the privileges it had bestowed melted away. Some white workers expressed their frustrations through crude explosions of violence against African-Americans; others sought and offered a new solidarity and even a new intimacy across racial boundaries. And in some instances, amidst great tension, both responses emerged and coexisted.[12]

Things of Dry Hours takes place in a small cabin near a railroad line in Birmingham, Alabama and revolves around the relationships of its three occupants. Tice Hogan is an unemployed African-American steelworker, an activist in the local Communist Party, a Sunday school teacher, and the owner of two books: the Bible and *The Communist Manifesto*. His widowed daughter, Cali, lives with him and contributes to the family's survival by taking in white people's laundry. Corbin Teel is an Iowa-born white worker who moved to Birmingham, got work in a foundry, and claims to have killed a foreman there and to need a place to hide out. Narrative uncertainty surrounds the action. Is Corbin Teel who he says he is? If he is, can Tice Hogan educate and radicalize him? Can Corbin, whoever he is, reawaken Cali's apparently lost passion for life?

While *Things of Dry Hours* is rooted in the historically specific context of Alabama in the 1930s, it asks its audience to wrestle with over-arching questions about race and, particularly, *whiteness*, which remain relevant today. Can black and white workers overcome a history of separation and suspicion to build the organizations and movements necessary to change society? Can intimate relationships transcend racial boundaries? Can white workers confront the ways their own identities have been constructed through *whiteness* and embark on a personal transformation that is linked to social transformation?

While the possibilities of Cali's transformation is at the heart of *Things of Dry Hours*, I want to focus on the character of Corbin Teel because his transformation helps us to think about the dialectic of power and fragility that shapes the deep historical structure of *whiteness*. Corbin enters the play midway through its fourth scene, after Wallace has introduced us to Tice and Cali, their personal histories, and their relationship. Through them, Wallace has established *blackness* as the core, the foundation, and the framework for the play. This is, importantly, not a *blackness* that has been fabricated by white projections and fantasies, but a *blackness* produced by the lived experiences of African-Americans. This play takes place in their cabin where they have struggled to make a life for themselves and from which they have struggled to change society.

Corbin arrives with a knock on the door. He claims to be on the run, having killed a foreman in a fight at the foundry, and that "a fellow" sent him to the Hogans because they "were with the party" and would hide him out. Tice and Cali are immediately apprehensive. Tice says: "You're of a white persuasion so we can't be in the same house" (13). But Corbin invokes the power that he possesses even in their home, threatening to turn himself in and to tell the police that, "you, Tice Hogan, put me up to attacking the foreman." Everyone knows that the word of a white man, even a "disheveled and dirty" white man accused of murder, would be taken over that of a black man.

And so begins the complex interactions among Corbin, Tice, and Cali, in a space created by blackness but negotiated through the historical structure of *whiteness*. Corbin acts as if his *whiteness* gives him sufficient power to get what he wants from Tice (information about the Communist Party's membership) and from Cali (sex), but he is limited by their control over their own space, their own identities, and, especially, their relationship with each other. Not only is his power limited, but it also rests on a fragile foundation. He has been rendered vulnerable by the employers who have commanded him to spy on the Hogans or to lose his own freedom, by his illiteracy and bodily scars, and by his developing passion for Cali. While Tice seeks to transform Corbin into a Communist, other, even deeper, layers of transformation appear possible as the three-way relationship between Corbin, Cali, and Tice unfolds over the course of the play.

A sequence at the opening of Act 2 demonstrates how Wallace can shock her audience into confronting the possibility of subverting the historical structure of *whiteness*. It starts innocently with Cali folding sheets. Corbin offers to help her and their interaction quickly turns seductive, with the sheets being used in a role-playing game that goes from playful to serious. He wraps her in a sheet like a Greek goddess; a moment later, he holds the sheet so that he looks like a Ku

Klux Klansman, and then she wraps him in it so he looks like a girl. She takes black shoe polish and applies it to his face, invoking the racist tradition of blackface minstrelsy, and then 'whites up' her face with oatmeal. "Now you gonna kiss this girl or what?" asks Corbin playfully. Though clad in white, Corbin plays the black female to Cali's white male, yielding to her assumption of the physical and symbolic power of *whiteness*—until she threatens to rape him. "I see the lust in your eyes, bitch. I smell the sex on your breath," she says and then grabs between Corbin's legs to feel 'her' wetness. This is too much for him: he breaks free, throws off his sheet, unbuckles his pants, and stands over Cali ready to rape her. The violent yet erotic encounter ends in a tense standoff (Wallace 2007a, 52–58).

In the next scene, Wallace deepens her deconstruction of *whiteness* in a remarkable three-way exchange. "Your problem," Tice tells Corbin, "is you are not, after all, who you think you are." He shifts into teaching mode (and Wallace's writing becomes didactic), as he explains that race is a construction, that not all slaves in world history have been black, and that Corbin "became a white man only 'cause I was said to be colored… What I'm saying is, white is not how you're born, it's what you're paid." Echoing James Baldwin, Tice tells Corbin, "You have a ticket in your pocket which is now sewn to your ass. And that ticket says you get privileges" (63). When Tice insists that "property is privilege" and that the shirt on Corbin's back is one sign of his ticket, Corbin strips off his clothes and stands naked before Tice and Cali (and the audience) as if to prove he is "a man with nothing," without the property of *whiteness*. In front of her father, Corbin appeals to Cali right then and there to accept him, to want him "as I wasn't meant to be," even to touch him, but she can only stare at him in silence and then leave the room. The audience is left to wonder if Corbin has shed *whiteness* and become 'a new man,' and if so, how that will change the relationships among the three characters.

Over the remaining four scenes, *Things of Dry Hours* tumbles towards a reckoning with the possibilities of this transformation. As they prepare for Corbin to leave their household, father and daughter both claim to have kindled a flame in him and debate whether his attraction to Cali is simple lust or sincere affection. Before he goes, Corbin craves a consummating kiss from Cali, but when he moves in close to her, she raises her hand to her mouth so that her palm catches his kiss, rendering it erotic and immaculate all at once. Corbin reveals himself to Tice as a company stooge, demands information about the Party, and leaves, only to return two scenes later fatally wounded by the corporate cabal he served, seeking sanctuary just as he did in the beginning of the play. By now, Corbin's struggle with his *whiteness*, even if not successful for him, has awakened a new desire in Cali:

> I'm talking about the kind of desire that wakes you when it's still dark and you go outside and even the ground at your feet is asleep. But then you listen real hard and you hear the world waking up, leaves talking about things you forgot, insects making a quarrel, and then a little piece of morning comes to rest on your neck. That kind of desire. That everything out there's a gift. (89)

As Corbin is dying in her arms, she unbuttons his shirt, touches him tenderly, kisses him, and takes his hand and places it on parts of her body—thigh, elbow, breast bone—introducing him to the *history* of her body: "Here is where I cut myself as a child. Here, where I burned when the fields caught fire...And this is where you knocked on the door." As Corbin breathes his last, Cali finally, irrevocably, lets him in. For Wallace, personal transformation is, literally, embodied; it takes place through the body, on the body, in the body. While it is deeply, intimately, personal, it also simultaneously references the social body.

The Hard Weather Boating Party

Inspired by the environmental degradation of the Rubbertown manufacturing district in Wallace's hometown of Louisville, Kentucky, *The Hard Weather Boating Party* offers a window into the human costs of economic 'progress' and the difficulties of seeking justice when the collective vehicles of unions have been stripped of their power. The Rubbertown complex began with the construction of an oil refinery by Standard Oil of Kentucky in 1918. Additional refineries were added in the mid-twentieth century and later torn down and replaced by petroleum terminals and a railroad tie manufacturer, a B. F. Goodrich synthetic rubber plant, a Union Carbide plant, and other chemical plants producing vinyl fluoride, urea-formaldehyde resins, and acrylic plastics. Union Carbide's responsibility for the world's deadliest industrial disaster—in Bhopal, India in 1984—heightened local awareness of its historical presence in Rubbertown. The district remains a major source of manufacturing jobs—and deadly pollution, fatal accidents, and widespread disease among workers and residents. Wallace wrote her play on commission for the Actors Theatre of Louisville's Humana Festival of New American Plays; it premiered there in March 2009, just half a dozen miles from its actual setting.[13]

The Hard Weather Boating Party centers on three dying men—one white, one Latino, and one African-American—who are planning to murder the CEO of the Rubbertown company that has poisoned them. Staddon Vance is a white man in his 50s who has climbed—or been elevated—from his initial position within the workforce to a supervisory position in middle management. Coyle Forester, a black man in his 40s, and Lex Nadal, a Latino in his early 20s who sometimes speaks Spanish, are both blue-collar workers. All three are dying from repeated exposure to contamination, and they occasionally spit up horrible phlegm, which shines with an iridescent blue light. Although they are "almost strangers" to each other, they have come together because, says Vance, "There are some things you can't do alone. You need. The company of other men" (347).

They gather to plan their crime in "a sparse, run down Motel 6, or a dream Motel 6 had about itself" (339). The script indicates that the motel room has a foot-long crack in the floor that opens wider as the play progresses. And the room is missing its mirror, which leaves the characters with no way to see themselves other than through each other. "Tonight we are equals," says Staddon Vance. They are united by their illness and their shared fate, but also divided by their experiences of privilege, hostility, and alienation—the results of the historical workings of race, class, and gender, of *whiteness*. The play asks us to consider the depths of the divisions among working people and whether a shared fate can provide the basis for collective action, the merging of identities, and personal and social transformation.

Act 1 is hardly encouraging about their prospects for success, let alone a sense of solidarity or shared identity. They spend the time getting acquainted, sizing each other up, talking about women and sex, and going over their plan and their chances of getting away with it. To kill time and build trust, they play a game of 'Truth or Dare,' which leads to self-abusive, homoerotic, and emasculating moments. These men are not only divided by race and racial objectification, but they are also active agents in performing identities grounded in misogyny and a large dose of self-denigration.

The second act takes place later that night when they meet back at the motel after their attack on Chelton Steff, the CEO of

Amalgamated Synthetics, "King of Rubbertown." They broke into his home, kicked him around, tied him up, demanded ransom, and left him for dead, but everything did not go according to plan. They came away with no money, they triggered a security alarm, and when they heard the police sirens, Coyle and Lex fled the scene, leaving Staddon to complete the murder. But, as Staddon eventually confesses, when he put the gun to the CEO's head, he could not kill the capitalist, explaining: "He deserved to die. But in that moment I hated him too much. Killing a man with that kind of hate inside you is a kind of touching. I didn't want to touch him. So I shot him in the leg" (381).

Staddon's admission triggers a crisis in the shaky alliance of the three men. The dialogue suggests that, perhaps, at the critical moment, despite his claim of hatred, Staddon recognized his shared racial identity with the CEO. We learn that both of them wear socks to bed, a habit racialized as "white," and that Staddon was the secretary for an organization in which Chelton Steff was a leading member, the "Morgan's Men Association," named for the Confederate General who led a famous Civil War raid through Kentucky into Ohio. The dialogue also raises the possibility that his hesitation might have been an expression of his class privilege as a supervisor, or, as Lex prefers to call him, a "zookeeper." Making sense of the role of racial and class position in Staddon's behavior becomes even more complicated when he reveals that he had allowed himself to be exposed to carcinogenic chemicals at the plant in an effort to be like Coyle, Lex, and the other Rubbertown workers.

> STADDON: I saw. I saw your faces over the years. You went in to those buildings and you went in whole. You went in strong like a thousand blocks of ice, hard and clear and useful. Whole crowds of you. I was outside that crowd. I was outside that. Power.
> LEX: Because you're the goddamn zookeeper. You count our peas.
> COYLE: So you wanted to join us?
> STADDON: Yes.
> LEX: So you'd be like us?
> STADDON: Yes.
> COYLE: Well if that isn't the most distorted, disgusting, sentimental piece of solidarity bullshit I have ever heard. Well, I got news for you, Staddon Vance. You are not like us (384).

Vance's self-destructive behavior reflects the fragility of his *whiteness*. The "price of the ticket," to recall James Baldwin, was his isolation and alienation from the workforce that he supervised, on the one hand, and, on the other, from the higher, inner circles of management, whose denizens forever looked down on him because of his working class origins. Vance's effort to transcend this lack of identity leads him to expose himself to the same hazards faced by the workers and then to recruit them for a collective revenge. However, in the heat of the moment, his interaction with Chelton Steff only dragged him more deeply into the quagmires of his racial and class positions. His failure to follow through on his commitment to his coconspirators threatens to alienate him from them all the more, but, in the dramatic economy of the play, all is not lost.

Although Staddon Vance's attempt at solidarity, shared identity, and effective collective action has failed, the play suggests that transformation—social as well as personal—is still thinkable and may be even attainable. The men know they are doomed. If the cops do not barge in at any moment and shoot them dead, the poison inside them will kill them nearly as soon. They begin to discuss good-byes, to their loved ones, to each other, to lives of unfulfilled dreams and expectations, and this leads to transcendent moments for each man, two of which involve Vance stepping outside of his own *whiteness*.

When Vance tells Coyle and Lex that he has no one at home to say good-bye to, no children, no son, Lex says, "I'll be your son. If you want to say good-bye to someone" (377). And this leads to a complicated role-playing sequence in which Lex-the-son accuses Vance-the-father of beating him, his wife, and his daughter. "You never loved us," he charges. Vance denies these claims at first but then yields to Lex's fiction and makes it his own, apologizing for his limitations as the father he never actually was. Vance's alienation is compound: he had no son and his fantasy 'son' here is alienated from him, a victim of neglect or abuse; nevertheless, there is a connection in this enactment—fleeting perhaps, and fueled by Lex's anger with Vance for violating their pact—that suggests the possibility of personal transformation.

This leads to a similar role-play in which Vance takes a turn as the stand-in for an absent loved one. When Coyle despairs that he cannot remember the kiss of his wife Coralee, Vance says, "I can make you remember her the way you want to remember her," and then gets him to close his eyes before stepping in, taking Coyle's face in his hand, and kissing him on the lips. "It was her...It was her!" Coyle insists to Lex, who watches in disbelief. This is an act not of minstrelsy but of surrogacy, generosity, and love. When Lex presses

Vance for an explanation, he responds: "Maybe this kind of poisoning, it leaves behind in us...an opening...Capacity where there wasn't before" (387).

That capacity is in full evidence in the third moment of transformation, a stunning tableau that stems from Lex's boyhood dream of one day owning a classic speed boat—"with craft, chrome hardware, mahogany sides"—just like the ones he saw racing up and down the Ohio River as a kid (362). During this final sequence in the play, Vance convinces Coyle to repay his generosity by relieving his suffering and shooting him in the head. The gun misfires multiple times until Lex finally grabs it and pulls the trigger. Vance slumps over dead, and a moment later, as a terrible storm approaches outside, they prop him up between them as they pray side by side "to whatever's got an ear wide enough to take us in":

> There is an ear-splitting burst of lightning and crash of thunder and suddenly the floor of the motel room cracks open and the hull of a boat breaks up through the floor behind the praying men...It is a beautiful, classic, 1960s speedboat, with wood sides. It seems timeless (390).

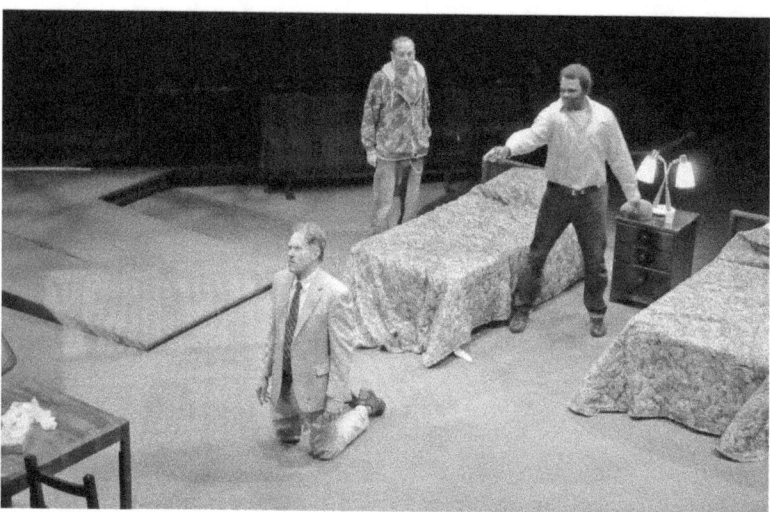

Figure 11.2 Michael Cullen (Staddon Vance, kneeling) Jesse L. Perez (Lex), Kevin Jackson (Coyle, with gun) in the 2009 Actors Theatre of Louisville production of *The Hard Weather Boating Party*. Director: Jo Bonney. Photo: Harlan Taylor. Courtesy of Actors Theatre of Louisville].

The play ends on this timeless note, with Lex and Coyle transfixed with wonder, uncertain if they're dead or alive, but sure of one thing: "It's our boat."

There is no escaping the consequences of environmental degradation like Rubbertown's, but there is a possibility of transcending the human degradation that has been part and parcel of it. Staddon Vance's struggle with his *whiteness*, its power and its fragility, its promotions and its isolation and alienation, has led him to commit suicide several times over, but it has also led him to transform himself through his relationships with Lex Nadal and Coyle Forester, to struggle to be present with them and for them, and for himself. Scarred by the histories of racism, sexism, homophobia, and self-hatred, bearing the burden of *whiteness*, both its objects and its instruments, these 'ordinary' workers—whether they like each other or not—manage to see each other and to see themselves through each other, to feel each other's pain and anguish, and to begin to construct a new solidarity, a new humanity.

Journey into—and through—The Heart of Whiteness

These three plays—and much of the rest of Wallace's plays, screenplays, and poems—offer marvelous lenses through which to observe the intersections of race, class, gender, and sexuality, particularly the ways these intersections have produced in the United States what labor historians and others have termed *whiteness*. In each play, a character defined by his *whiteness*—Brandon in *Slaughter City*, Corbin in *Things of Dry Hours*, Staddon in *The Hard Weather Boating Party*—dies in the final moments, but these deaths become potential sources of transformation for others and perhaps for a wider social transformation in the structures and strictures of *whiteness*.

Historically, the combination of power and fragility that constitutes *whiteness* has found expression in the sexual abuse of slaves, the torture and lynching of black men, the burning and pillage of black communities from Rosewood, Florida, and Tulsa, Oklahoma, to Chicago, Illinois, and the dropping of the atomic bomb on the Japanese cities of Hiroshima and Nagasaki. This same combination can be seen in intimate personal relationships, the Underground Railroad, the Bonus Army of 1932, workplace slowdowns and sit-down strikes, general strikes, and the civil rights movement. Out of these dialectics have emerged experiences, stories, and visions of personal and social transformation. The more conscious human beings have been of these dynamics, the more the arc of history has leaned towards breakthroughs, which have moved us all forward in our humanity. Art plays a vital role in raising this consciousness. Naomi Wallace's work provides us with lenses through which we can see—and become more conscious of—the complexities, contradictions, and possibilities of this central construction of our history.

Notes

1. At the end of her published plays, Wallace provides a bibliography of sources, which are often the most insightful and provocative available work on the given subject. Wallace has also sought out such historians as David Roediger, Howard Zinn, Robin Kelley, Tera Hunter, Joe W. Trotter, Jr., Marcus Rediker, and me for in-depth conversations. See also James Baldwin, *The Price of the Ticket: Collected Nonfiction, 1948–1985* (New York: St. Martin's, 1985).
2. My eyes were opened on these questions by Michel-Rolph Trouillot, *Silencing the Past: Power and the Production of History* (Boston: Beacon Press, 1997), and Harry Elam, Jr., *The Past As Present in the Drama of August Wilson* (Ann Arbor: University of Michigan Press, 2004).
3. David Roediger's *The Wages of Whiteness: Race and the Making of the American Working Class* (New York and London: Verso, 1991) initiated this paradigm shift among labor historians. Also, see his edited collection, David Roediger *Black on White: Black Writers on What It Means to Be White* (New York: Schocken, 1999).
4. See Alan Dawley, *Class and Community: The Industrial Revolution in Lynn* (Cambridge: Harvard University Press, 1976) and Bruce Laurie, *Artisans into Workers* (Urbana: University of Illinois Press, 1997).
5. See David Roediger, *The Wages of Whiteness*, quoted in Theodore Allen, *The Making of the White Race* vol. I and II (New York: Verso, 1994 and 1997) and Alexander Saxton, *The Rise and Fall of the White Republic* (New York: Verso, 2003).
6. See Alexander Saxton, *Indispensable Enemy: Labor and the Anti-Chinese Movement in California* (Berkeley: University of California Press, 1975); Neil Foley, *The White Scourge: Mexicans, Blacks, and Poor Whites in Texas Cotton Culture* (Berkeley: University of California Press, 1999); and Iver Bernstein, *The New York City Draft Riots* (New York: Oxford University Press, 1990).
7. See George Lipsitz, *The Possessive Investment in Whiteness* (Philadelphia: Temple University Press, 1998); Cheryl Harris, "Whiteness as Property," in *Critical Race Theory*, ed. Kimberlé Crenshaw et al (New York: The New Press, 1995, 276–91); and Eric Lott, *Love and Theft: Blackface Minstrelsy and the American Working Class* (New York: Oxford, 1995).

8. See Douglas Dowd, *The Twisted Dream: Capitalist Development in the United States Since 1776* (Cambridge: Winthrop Publishers, 1977); David F. Noble, *Forces of Production: A Social History of Industrial Automation* (New York: Oxford University Press, 1986); and Barry Bluestone, *The Deindustrialization of America* (New York: Basic Books, 1984).
9. See George Lipsitz, *Rainbow at Midnight: Class and Culture in the 1940s* (Urbana: University of Illinois Press, 1994); Jeremy Brecher, *Strike! The True History of Mass Insurrections in U.S. History* (Boston: South End Press, 1999); and Stanley Aronowitz, *False Promises: The Shaping of American Working Class Consciousness* (Durham: Duke University Press, 1991).
10. Among the valuable memoirs and personal narratives situated at these crossroads, these stand out: Mark Naison, *White Boy: A Memoir* (Philadelphia: Temple University Press, 2002); Thandeka, *Learning to Be White: Money, Race, and God in America* (New York: Continuum, 1999); Bérubé, Allen and Florence Bérubé, "Sunset Trailer Park," in *White Trash: Race and Class in America*, ed. Matt Wray and Annalee Newitz (New York: Routledge, 1997, 15–41); Tim Wise, *White Like Me: Reflections on Race from a Privileged Son* (New York: Soft Skull, 2011); and Robert Jenson, *The Heart of Whiteness: Confronting Race, Racism, and White Privilege* (San Francisco: City Lights, 2005). Also, see Naomi Wallace's film *Lawn Dogs* (Strand Releasing, 1997).
11. This and all further quotations from *Slaughter City* come from the edition published in Naomi Wallace, *In the Heart of America and Other Plays* (New York: TCG, 2001). In her bibliography, Wallace cites my book, Peter Rachleff, *Hard-Pressed in the Heartland: The Hormel Strike and the Future of the Labor Movement* (Boston: South End Press, 1993).
12. This and all further quotations from the play come from Naomi Wallace, *Things of Dry Hours* (London: Faber and Faber, 2007). Also see Robin D. G. Kelley, *Hammer and Hoe: Alabama Communists During the Great Depression* (Chapel Hill: University of North Carolina Press, 1990); Theodore Rosengarten, *All God's Dangers: The Life of Nate Shaw* (Chicago: University of Chicago Press, 2000); Nell Painter, *The Narrative of Hosea Hudson: The Life and Times of a Black Radical* (New York: W. W. Norton, 2002); Tera Hunter, *To 'joy My Freedom: Southern Black Women's Lives and Labors After the Civil War* (Cambridge: Harvard University Press, 1998); and Joe W. Trotter, Jr., *Black Milwaukee: The Making of an Industrial Proletariat* (Urbana: University of Illinois Press, 1985). Kelley, Hunter, Trotter, and I were all involved in the play's first production in Pittsburgh in April 2004, engaging in conversations with Wallace, director Israel Hicks, and the cast.
13. This and all further quotations from *The Hard Weather Boating Party* are from the edition found in Hansel, Adrien-Alice and Amy Wegener (eds.), *Humana Festival 2009: The Complete Plays* (New York: Playscripts, 2009). See "Rubbertown: The Louisville Area's Largest Source of Industrial Emissions" by the West Jefferson County Community Task Force, "History of Rubbertown" in the October 10, 2006 *Louisville Courier Journal*; and West Jefferson County Community Task Force, "Health Consultation:

Rubbertown Industrial Area, Jefferson County, Kentucky" by the United States Department of Health and Human Services (Public Health Service: Atlanta, Georgia, August 3, 2006). A Google search for "Rubbertown" in September 2012—more than three years *after* the play's 2009 premiere in Louisville—turned up several stories of deadly accidents in 2011 and 2012.

12
Unbearable Intimacies: Occupation, Utopia, and Creative Destruction in *The Fever Chart*

Adam John Waterman

The Middle East offers perhaps the ideal site from which to consider the political and aesthetic commitments of Naomi Wallace's theatre. As the critic Shannon Baley has argued, one of the signal characteristics of Wallace's work has been its engagement with "apocalypses [that appear]...on the edge of utopia...[places] where death and desire coexist, where bodies can be expanded, become fluid, and new horizons can be seen from what is possible" (Baley 2004, 238–9). Coupled with the ambitions of empire, fantasies of apocalypse and utopia have played an inordinate part in the history of the modern Middle East, from the crusader ambitions of Napoleon's armies to the missionary work of Protestant reformers and the 'modernizing' projects of Zionist colonialism. Imperial designs upon the greater Middle East have been long underwritten by an explicit sense of millennial purpose, one that identifies the greater Middle East—and Palestine, in particular—as the physical site upon which humanity will meet its eschatological reckoning (Boyer 1994).[1] This dream locates utopia as that which emerges only at the end of secular history, the negation of which intervention in the Middle East is ultimately meant to hasten.

In her celebrated triptych *The Fever Chart*, Wallace has dramatized the cost of this misplaced utopianism through a meditation on the dialectics of creative destruction. The three short plays that make up *The Fever Chart* focus upon everyday life in Palestine and Iraq, exemplary sites through which to explore the materiality of invasion and occupation as they underwrite the reproduction—and perpetual reconstruction—of the modern Middle East. Occupation, here, is to be understood as a mode of social relations that begets and sustains a particular state of injury; but in Wallace's rendering, it is also a condition through which to imagine new forms of sociality, new connections between people, and new types of social organization.[2] Throughout her work on the Middle East, Wallace is extraordinarily attentive to the ways in which partition, as one of the primary techniques of occupation, has produced not just new points of disconnection between peoples, but also the implicit fact of alliance, of communion beyond borders. Drawing upon the social, psychic, and cultural detritus of occupation, *The Fever Chart* develops a prophetic, three-part mediation on the creative potentiality that inheres within the destructive actuality of occupation. This potentiality undermines the will to utopia that expresses itself through occupation, pointing to the formative and transformative power of the partial, the gestural, and the performative in the movement for the full de-colonization of the Middle East.

Moving between Palestine and Iraq, sites of incommensurable social and political histories made similar through the imposition of empire, the question of partition as articulation is echoed in the structure of *The Fever Chart*. Articulation, here, should be understood as the uneven and often incoherent process by which relationships are established between disparate elements of the social and cultural field, a process that David Kazanjian has likened to the integration of limbs and motor processes in the human body (2003). The body, by the same token, should be understood not as a coherent, discrete, clearly bounded figure, but as an assemblage that exists in multifarious, prosthetic, and parasitic relationships to other objects-qua-assemblages in the world, a necessarily incomplete figure that is nevertheless always in the process of becoming (Puar 2012). *The Fever Chart* might be read as one instantiation of such a figure. Despite clear thematic overlaps, the plays that make up *The Fever Chart* never cohere into a purposeful whole; rather, they are grafted onto each other in ways that suggest the heterogeneity of those imperial practices that have shaped the Middle East, as well as the irreducible diversity—social and cultural, religious, and ethnic—that characterizes the region and its peoples.

At the same time, the figure of uneasy assemblage presents Wallace with a thematic that she develops through meditations upon those forms of Divine agency through which, in the Judeo-Christian tradition, Creation is manifest: sight, breath, and word. Creation, in *The Fever Chart*, describes the process of assemblage, itself reflected in the prophetic tenor of Wallace's text. Punning on the word "vision," the subtitle of the play, *Three Visions of the Middle East*, evokes both prophetic and prosaic forms of sight, as well as the modes of visual surveillance that accompany and enable occupation. At the same time, "vision" might be read as an ethical injunction, a command to the audience that they 'see' a Middle East that has been hidden in plain sight. Sight, in *The Fever Chart*, is the precondition for creation, just as God's sight, in the first of the Genesis stories of Creation, is that which enables and evaluates its manifestation.

Surveillance, Vision, Recognition: *A State of Innocence*

The layered significance of sight for *The Fever Chart* is suggested in the stage directions that open the first of the plays, *A State of Innocence*. Wallace describes the character of Um Hisham, a middle-aged Palestinian woman, "methodically" wrapping her head in a scarf: "She adjusts it until it's right...She is then ready for the vision to begin" (Wallace 2009a, 7).[3] Refashioning the hijab as a prophetic mantle, Wallace establishes Um Hisham as the agent of vision, reversing the Orientalist convention whereby 'the Arab'—and Arab women, in particular—are forever the object of the colonizing gaze. Indeed, Um Hisham's gaze is directed to Yuval, the character of the young Israeli soldier with whom she shares the stage. Although Yuval has been on stage since the opening of the play, his appearance is explicitly framed by a marked instance of seeing, as if his presence depends upon this moment of recognition. In this brief opening gesture, *A State of Innocence* begins to negotiate the uneven social and cultural terrains in which the characters are situated and how these militate against witnessing as an act of encounter. As Wallace writes in an explanatory note, "Characters often do not look directly at one another. It is as though they can see one another without eye contact" (6). Eschewing eye contact, sight here becomes a seemingly disembodied process, one that

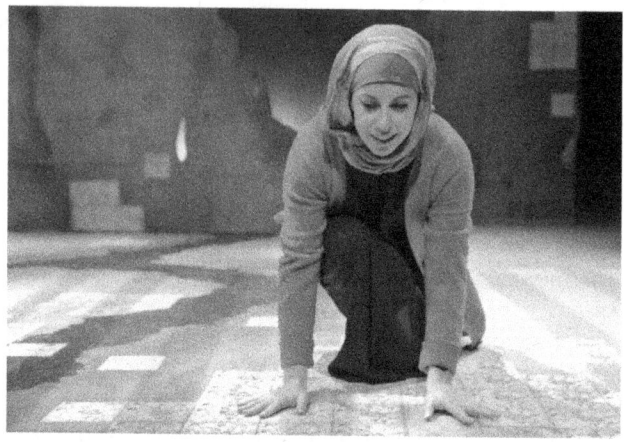

Figure 12.1 Lisa Caruccio Came (Um Hisham Qishta) in the 2010 Pilot Theatre (UK) production of *A State of Innocence*, the first play in *The Fever Chart: Three Visions of the Middle East*. Director: Katie Posner and Marcus Romer. Photo: Toby Farrow. Courtesy of Pilot Theatre.

suggests the optic registers in which Yuval and his counterpart Shlomo move, insofar as their sight is articulated to the panoptic mode of visuality that underwrites the regime of occupation. Projecting their capacity for sight through a carceral register that equates vision and visibility with the aptitude for control, Shlomo and Yuval are abstracted from the realm of everyday intimacies, becoming identical with the deliberately incoherent assemblage of the Israeli security state.[4]

An architect, the character of Shlomo seems to be modeled upon Shlomo Gur-Gerzovsky, the Israeli architect credited with developing *homa umigdal*, the tower-and-stockade construction that provided cover for Zionist colonists during the 1936–1939 Arab revolt in Mandatory Palestine. Enabling the defensive projection of sight over space, *homa umigdal* was, "an observation point, an all-seeing eye that cannot see itself" (Rotbard 2003, 47). Turning the visual register into a highly charged field of colonial power, *homa umigdal* produced a mode of seeing that was static, fixed, objectified, and alienated, while rendering visuality crucial to the materialization of utopian fantasies. "Believing is seeing," Shlomo intones, "like building." To the extent that Zionist colonialism has depended upon an aggressive strategy of architectural occupation, Wallace's likening of seeing to building establishes the visual as one of the material vectors of occupation, as well as a site of struggle over any future sociality. Where Yuval and Shlomo participate throughout the play in the modes of abstracted surveillance that subtend the occupation, Um Hisham is identified with sight as an embodied, physical process, one that works to establish relations between people. Within the play, the characters are trapped together in the ghostly remains of the Rafah Zoo (destroyed, in actuality, by Israeli forces in 2004). Shlomo sees the ruins as an opportunity to erect new systems of surveillance. Yuval is obsessed with minutiae, tending to the remains of the zoo and cleaning its broken cages. Um Hisham, by contrast, sees the ruins for the tragedy they are, and as she looks about the stage, she attempts to assemble the space from memory. Where the panoptic gaze is always partial, insofar as it functions by presenting specific applications of surveillance (Yuval) as general instances of power's capacity for control (Shlomo), only Um Hisham embodies what the panoptic hopes to project: a vision that is total, encompassing. Her vision is integrative, holistic, dynamic, organized around witnessing as an act of articulation; it is the substance of an embodied relation that transcends the alienating disciplinary procedures of the Zionist state and evokes the possibility of a post-Zionist polity.

The Social Body and Its Prosthetics:
Between This Breath and You

In the second of the three plays, Wallace explores articulation and assemblage through a far more direct mode of embodiment, the literal grafting of organs onto bodies. Circling around the character of Tanya, an Ashkenazi Israeli woman whose life was saved by a critical lung transplant, *Between This Breath and You* finds Wallace playing upon the trope of breath as a creative emanation. "All the world is condensed into the fuel of oxygen, sliding in and out of my chest like the hands of God, working me, working my clay into a form that has no material existence, but is as solid and palpable as this flesh" (51). Having received her lungs from Ahmed, a young Palestinian boy who was killed by the Israeli Defense Force, Tanya's survival depends upon the physical remainder of Palestinian life, even as she denies the compatibility of her body with Ahmed's organs. "Had your son's lungs been inside me," she tells his father, Mourid, "I am sure...that I would have rejected them" (46). Confronted by her dependence upon Ahmed's organs, Tanya receives new insight into her dreams of suffocation, now less a recollection of her cystic fibrosis than an image of her body as a disparate, potentially incompatible collection of parts.

Presenting Tanya as disabled, Wallace renders her as a sort of corporeal assemblage, at once countering Zionist projections of the robust, reproductive capacity of the Israeli body, while establishing the dependency of that body upon its relation to its abjected others (Puar 2013). Where in *A State of Innocence* the visual techniques of occupation provided Shlomo and Yuval with the capacity for a disembodied, macroscopic relationship to everyday intimacies, here, medical intervention offers a macroscopic grafting to forms of state power designed to produce a hyper-reproductive, able-bodied, Ashkenazi society. Wallace's rendering of occupation thus resonates with Elizabeth Povinelli's characterization of "the child in the broom closet" in Ursula K. Le Guin's short story, "The Ones Who Walk Away From Omelas," where the misery of a small child confined to a closet is the condition that enables the unmediated happiness of a utopian society. "[T]heir well-being is part of a larger mode of corporeal embodiment in which her carnal misery is a vital organ," Povinelli writes, "[T]he usefulness of the child is inseparable from the distension of her body through the bodies of the citizens of Omelas. And these are not metaphors. She and they are not *like* a shared body; they are a shared body" (2011, 4). Ahmed's lungs, from this perspective, are both a site of occupation and a means of animation, insofar as they enable the expansionist capacity of the Zionist state through its conscription to the sustenance of Israeli life. They are distinct parts of what Povinelli refers to as a "mutual enfleshment" in which different parts are subjected to different degrees of vulnerability, different intensities of pleasure.

Here, Wallace returns to the figure of assemblage as a means of conceptualizing occupation as a world-making project, one whose creative potentiality is sublimated through the violent imposition of social hierarchies based upon instrumentalized projections of religious-cum-racial difference. Triangulating the interactions of Tanya and Mourid with interjections from Sami, a Mizrahi Jew of Moroccan descent, Wallace draws attention to the myriad social distinctions that exist within and between Israeli and Palestinian societies. As a Jew, Sami is afforded civic recognition under Israeli law, even as his North African heritage bars him from full participation in Israel's social and cultural life. At the same time, his status as a Jewish Israeli citizen works to complicate his identity as Arab, rendering him suspect in the eyes of fellow Arab Palestinians. Where Mourid is presented as well educated and reasonably affluent, Sami is unmistakably of the working class; he is a janitor whose frustrated dreams of education now find expression through incoherent philosophical reveries. Manifest in uneasy banter between the characters, the play disrupts essentialized constructions of difference that inhere in the opposition of Jew and Arab, Israeli and Palestinian, suggesting the multiple modes of differentiation and disarticulation that inhere in life under conditions of occupation, the ways in which occupation establishes identity-in-difference as a means of preventing the realization of a new social assemblage.

Tanya's uneasiness breathing here serves as an image of society forged in and through occupation, an evocation of the body politic reduced to an unlikely collection of organs. But while Tanya's representation as assemblage is initially signaled through her dependence upon Ahmed and his lungs, Wallace complicates the singularity of this figure by underscoring her prosthetic dependence on Mourid, her inability to breathe absent his instruction. Tanya's reliance upon Mourid is further reflected in Mourid's dependence upon Tanya as an aide memoire, a living shrine holding a *memento mori* of his son. "You like that idea: a piece of Ahmed inside me...[I]t gives your entire being a shape and a focus you would not have otherwise. Otherwise you'd be just a bag of liquid grief—we could pick you up, poke a hole in the bottom, and you'd just spill away" (49–50). The image of Mourid as a "bag of liquid grief" gives shape to the inconsolability of melancholy, the loss of self that occurs through pathological attachment to, and identification with, a lost object. No longer a body in melancholic grief, Mourid is himself reduced to the form of an organ, here suggestive of nothing so much as the bladder. Mirroring Tanya, Mourid is not so much a singular, integrated body, but a part dependent upon its articulation to other parts, yet ultimately unable to sublate those dependencies into a meaningful sense of wholeness.

By evoking the shape of the bladder, the description of Mourid as a bag of liquid grief works to constellate the myriad instances of the excremental that occur throughout the play, beginning with Sami's opening monologue on the Dead Sea. "It's not the salt that makes you float," he tells Mourid, "but the shit, shit, shit...It hisses, shushes, sighs in my ears like some alien lullaby" (28). The excrementally debased goes on to become, in Sami's account, the substance through which human creation expresses itself, the matter from which the human comes into being. "We leave everything behind on [the floor] our hair, our skin, our drippings and droolings, our lint, our nefarious discards, our shameful discords. With what this mop gathers I could build, particle by particle, out of abandoned parts, an entirely new human being." Meditating upon the intimacy of the excremental as expressed in the co-mingling of "our nefarious discards [and] our shameful discords," upon the "human floor," Sami goes on to describe the creative potentiality that inheres in his mop. "A mop is an extension of Divine power, a gatherer of the slough; a mop is, in short, a functional God" (29). Where the biblical account of creation finds the human formed from the dust of the earth, granted life through the Divine force of God's breath, here Wallace presents creation as the assemblage of the excremental, brought together by a powerful force that is nonetheless unholy. The mop is not God but rather a functional equivalent, one that mocks the capacity for creation that is the exclusive province of the Divine. In so doing, Wallace distinguishes between creation as a capacity of the human, and Creation as bound to divine emanation. "I can build a human being," Sami tells her, "but I cannot build a life."

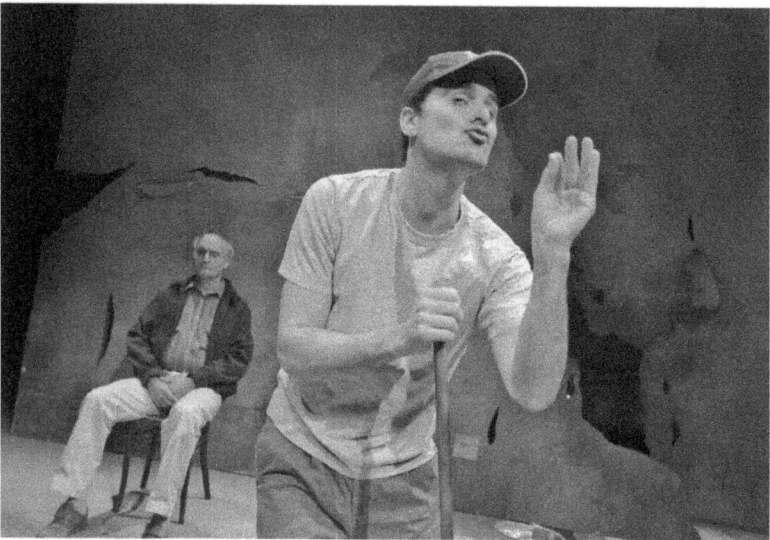

Figure 12.2 Sidney Kean (Mourid) and Daniel Rabin (Sami) in the 2010 Pilot Theatre (UK) production of *Between This Breath and You,* the second play in *The Fever Chart: Three Visions of the Middle East.* Director: Katie Posner and Marcus Romer. Photo: Toby Farrow. Courtesy of Pilot Theatre.

Distinguishing between the assembly of a human being and the animation of life, Sami posits a difference between those weak powers of creation afforded humans and the Divine capacity of Creation *ex nihilo*. Even as Wallace celebrates human creativity as one consequence of our physical vulnerability, the play underscores the fragility of human creation, its inherent incoherence and imperfection. In *The Fever Chart*, the human capacity for creation is not to be valorized *tout court*, but rather only inasmuch as creation serves to mitigate the vulnerability of the physical body. By evaluating human creativity with respect to its consequences for the body, Wallace is able to hold onto a sense of the occupation as a creative force, while critiquing its dialectical manifestation as the destruction of sociality and the promotion of physical pain. In *Between This Breath and You*, creation is most directly manifest, and valorized, in the prosthetic relationship between Tanya and Mourid, as each of their bodily singularities are expressed through their dependency upon the other. The play closes with Tanya breathing in time with Mourid's instructions, and Tanya manifesting, through her breath, the life force of Mourid's son, each serving as an extension of, and support for, the other. As such, their relationship works to inhibit the manifestation of both the physical and emotional distress brought on by the occupation.

Creative Destruction and the Posthuman Horizon: *The Retreating World*

In the final of the three plays, the prosthetic character of social relations is projected upon language itself, as Wallace plays upon St. John's account of Creation through the agency of the Word. Unlike in the previous two works, in *The Retreating World* Wallace allows the destructive capacity of human creativity to come to the fore, as she explores the impact of sanctions as a mode of erasure visited upon the people of Iraq. To the extent that both serve, within the context of the often incoherent assemblage that is US empire, to effect the attenuation if not outright abrogation of specific forms of national sovereignty, the sanctions regime might be likened to the regime of direct occupation; yet they are distinguished, at least in part, by the physical absence of the invading force. Indeed, *The Retreating World* is haunted by absences; it strikes a far more dramatically elegiac tone than its companions, as the relations that constitute the social dissolve into nothingness, as does the language through which the world is constituted and made meaningful. Insofar as the world is accessible only through language, it offers a prosthesis through which the subject engages in the constitution of the world. In *The Retreating World* that prosthesis is removed, thus undermining the social basis of subjectivity, itself.

This point is underscored by the format of the play. Presented as a monologue, the play focuses entirely on the character of Ali, for whom all other characters exist only as evanescent traces of memory. Ali's actions, as much as his dialogue, establish the devaluation of language as the prosthetic through which the social is constituted; he first appears on stage balancing a book on his head. "Nowadays you can pick up a book like this for next to nothing," he tells the audience, "Whole libraries, years and years of reading, set out by the side of the road. For sale. For next to nothing" (57). No longer the ideological nexus through which the social comes to be, here, the possibility of literature is evoked to highlight its devaluation into a mere object of commodity value. No longer a transcendent signifier of authorship or readerly engagement, the value of the book inheres now only in its status as an object for sale; as such, it is all but worthless, inasmuch as its value as an object for sale inheres in the transcendence of its commodity status. Transfigured by the loss of its aura, the book becomes mere matter, a thing whose value inheres in its mutability, its capacity to become other things. Just as Ahmed's lung was no mere metaphor, here, the fungibility of the book as commodity is made literal: it is transubstantiated. First kicking the book like a football, Ali next holds the book up to his face as a mask. "Books can be used for many things besides reading," Ali instructs the audience, "For exercising the ankles and toes...[or] to create a man with a bookish face."

By its very opacity, both for the audience and for Ali, the book-mask suggests the devaluation of language as a vehicle of sociality. It represents language as obscured and obscuring, a disguise through which one thing becomes another. "[T]his is a book on bird 'fancying' as they say in the north of England. It took me ages to understand, even though I am fluent in English...But this was not English. This was north of English and about pigeons and doves" (58). The language of the book, in this instance, is obscured by its idiomatic traces, as well as the relative unintelligibility of its subject. "One suspects, after fifty pages or so, that in fact it is not a book about keeping birds as a hobby, but something far more...important. Like how to keep your love, or swindle your friends. Or find inner peace" (58). No longer a privileged lens through which the social comes to know itself, language here is nothing more than a collection of signifiers, leached of the social conventions that mediated their relationship to the signified. Ali's description of the book and its contents thereby establishes an analogy between language, the book collections that have been discarded as worthless, and the collection of pigeons that he once kept.

The dissolution of any standard of value is evoked, hauntingly, at the end of this passage, where Ali recommends that no one ever name a pigeon after a member of the family or a friend. "For two reasons: pigeons have short lives—and when a pigeon named after an uncle dies, this can be disconcerting. And second: these times are dangerous for pigeons—they can be caught and eaten...[C]annibalism can put you off a hobby" (58). By itself, the notion that one might call an animal by the given name of a family member seems to suggest a near cataclysmic erosion of the social, insofar as the sovereignty that inheres in the proper name of an individual—the condition of that individual's interpellation within the social—has been evacuated to the extent that it might be applied to an inherently non-social form of life. From this perspective, the declension of value implicit in this passage might be understood to evoke the conditions of life in a society trapped within what Frantz Fanon referred to as the, "zone of non-being," that, "place most far from the light that, in a theistic system, radiates reality" (Gordon 2005, 3). While at the end of the previous two plays, Wallace has offered the audience moments of mutual recognition that evoke the emergence of a new, singular body, here, the sanctions regime would seem only to effect the declension of the self into an agglomeration of organs, a non-body that coheres to no recognizable ego ideal.

Late in the play, this non-body momentarily takes the shape of Ali's friend Samir, hit by an anti-tank missile fired by US troops near the end of the first Gulf War. "I could not. I could not recognize. My friend Samir. A piece of his spine stuck upright in the sand. His left hand blown so high in the air it was still falling" (66). Like the social formation that was Iraq, in this passage, Samir becomes a collection of parts, his disintegration echoed by the fragmented sentences that compose Ali's dialogue. Cast as a broken body scattered in pieces on the ground, there is little doubt that Wallace means this figure to register the grotesquerie of war. Nonetheless, in its monstrosity, this figure offers an idiosyncratically hopeful close to *The Retreating World* as well as a hermeneutic through which to reconsider the earlier sections of the play. Turning again to the subject of pigeons, Ali informs the audience that he only just sold his last bird: "Tomorrow I will sell the cage. The day after that I will have nothing to sell. But I keep track of the buyers, and who the buyers sell to. I go to their homes and ask for the bones....I boil the bones, and keep them in a bucket" (67). Crossing the stage, Ali picks up the bucket and begins to shake it. As the bucket rattles, he offers it to the audience: "These are the bones of those who have died, from the avenue of palms, from the land of dates. I have come here to give them to you for safekeeping...Catch them. If you can." Ali throws the contents of the bucket into the air, scattering hundreds of white feathers over the audience.

The image of bones transformed into feathers stands out as one possibly hopeful end, despite its resonance with liberal constructions of secular redemption that figure justice as the future realization of sensual beauty (Scarry 2001). Yet, to the extent that Wallace's larger work privileges the rhizomorphic and multiple over the singular and sovereign, the plays in *The Fever Chart* exceed this normative frame, proceeding instead from a place in which the beautiful cohabitates with the monstrous, participating in what Elizabeth Povinelli has described as the capacitation of new worlds and new forms of life (2013). Indeed, by articulating the bones of the nominally human with the bones of the nominally animal, in this final image, Wallace subtly refuses the taxonomies of difference that subtend distinctions between human and animal forms of life—and thus, implicitly, distinctions based upon constructions of racial or sexual or sectarian difference—rejecting the modes of sovereignty that they presume and enable.[5] In *The Retreating World*, the animal and the human do not become one inasmuch as they dwell together, remaining multiple, refusing the interpellation which would seek to manage their difference by subsuming it within a normative state-social formation. The declension of signification evoked by *The Retreating World* suggests not so much the unraveling of the social as the passage into a different form of life, a way of living and cohabiting that, as Povinelli indicates, is not defined by its finitude, but rather by circuits of relationality which might be exhausted though not extinguished. This closing image thus harkens back to earlier works in *The Fever Chart*, destabilizing the unities they portend and the normative juridical frames through which they are to be constructed, frames that seek to regulate, if not arrest, the potentialities that inhere within the play of desire. In marking the simultaneity of the human and the animal, the living and the dead, the feathers offer an image of creativity unbound, of new landscapes and sensualities that are always already taking shape; of creativity as a force beyond sovereignty or agency; of resistance as often inchoate and illegible and sociality as a condition that is still yet to be realized.

Notes

1. On the history of Protestant Reformism and Zionism in relation to fantasies of apocalypse, see Ussama Makdisi, *Faith Misplaced: The Broken Promise of US-Arab Relations, 1820–2001* (New York: PublicAffairs, 2010); and Hilton Obenzinger, *American Palestine: Melville, Twain, and the Holy Land Mania* (Princeton: Princeton University Press, 1999).
2. On invasion and occupation as a structure of social relations, see Patrick Wolfe, *Settler Colonialism and the Transformation of Anthropology: The Politics and Poetics of an Ethnographic Event* (London and New York: Cassell, 1999).
3. All subsequent quotations from the play, cited by page number only, are from this same edition: Naomi Wallace, *The Fever Chart: Three Visions of the Middle East* (New York: Theatre Communications Group, 2009).
4. On societies of control and their distinction from disciplinary societies see Gilles Deleuze, "Society of Control," *L'Autre Journal* 1 (May 1990); on the legacy of security states and neoliberal governmentality, see Paul Amar, *The Security Archipelago: Human-Security States, Sexuality Politics, and the End of Neoliberalism* (Durham: Duke University Press, 2013).
5. My point here is informed by Nadia Dropkin's work on pigeon fancying and human/animal sensualities. See Nadia Dropkin, "Skyscapes of Abdeen, Cairo: Pigeons, Men, and Alternate Socialities," Sexual Sovereignties Conference at the American University of Beirut, Beirut, Lebanon, March 14, 2013. To be clear, Dropkin's work concentrates on pigeon fancying in the working-class Abdeen neighborhood of downtown Cairo, yet her points about human/animal socialities resonate across a range of spaces and practices.

13

To Girl or Not to Girl

Erica Stevens Abbitt

Transgressions and Innovations

Naomi Wallace—the award-winning Kentucky-born playwright, poet, scriptwriter, political activist, and educator—presents an interesting conundrum to those seeking to understand the attraction of her plays to two generations of cutting-edge directors, performers, designers, dramaturgs, and spectators. What makes her work so popular with a new generation of theatre spectators and practitioners, yet marked as "outsider" art, rebuffed by commercial main stages of West End and Broadway? Why, despite decades of honors, awards, and advocacy, is the work of Naomi Wallace so often labeled "alternative" or "political"? In Britain, where she has been based since 1997, Wallace has had her work produced at regional theatres and London stages from the Bush Theatre to the Trafalgar Studios and the National. In 2012, she became the first living American playwright to have a play accepted into the permanent repertory of France's national theatre, *La Comédie-Française*. But in her native country, Wallace's plays examining power, homophobia, racism, sexuality, and war seem destined to be produced at university, off-Broadway, and regional theatres, while response to her work by mainstream American critics has ranged from lukewarm acknowledgment of her innovative style to downright hostility towards her political content.[1] Why does mainstream recognition of Wallace's work lag so strongly behind her accolades by granting bodies, and impassioned advocacy by fellow practitioners?

Does this have anything to do with issues beyond the left-wing sensibility of her work or its unusual mixture of poetic language and realist situations?

As a scholar and practitioner who has explored Wallace's works for over a decade, I am interested in an aspect of her work that is often overlooked: her use of child labor. While other scholars have explored the importance of child and teenage characters in her plays, few have explored how young laboring bodies—particularly female bodies—shape the reception of Wallace's complex and often provocative work. Could it be that the affect created by youthful actors is an important factor in Wallace's dramaturgy? I'm intrigued by this question and the way it connects to Wallace's trademark interaction between circulations of meaning and feeling with the most down-to-earth, mundane, and practical elements of everyday life. Should young actors—particularly child actors and especially *female* child actors—be used for Wallace's provocative and often erotically charged work? "To girl or not to girl?"—that is my question.

A Performative Mandate for Change

In her writing about theatre, as well as in her work for the stage, Wallace has explicitly outlined a project of transgression. She has sustained a life-long commitment to political action, organizing fellow artists to participate with her in such initiatives as the "Free Mumia Abu-Jamal" event (1999), an evening of play-reading on the subject of Iraq for "Artists Network of Refuse and Resist!" (2001), a post 9/11 antiwar event—with Trevor Griffiths and Harold Pinter—and a series of exchanges between British, American, and Palestinian theatre practitioners. In a 2003 article entitled "Strange Times," Wallace set out her deliberately provocative agenda for theatre:

> Today it is, once again, war and empire. And it is with these monstrosities that we should engage in one form or another. What would Euripides, Marlowe or Brecht have done? They would have made these times strange, to use a Brechtian formula, so that an audience could see their society anew and possibly act on those new visions. Why settle for a lesser goal?[2]

This political goal to awaken spectators to the invisible circulations of power seems strongly linked to a focus on laboring bodies.

In a 2004 interview with Connie Julian for *The Revolutionary Worker*, Wallace explained her fascination with the way in which work marks bodies, and how this dynamic reveals a system of oppression: "[F]or most of the people in this world who must labor with their bodies still, how the body is damaged through labor intimately affects how you function in the rest of your life...The damage bodies receive is intimately connected with the quality of our lives." Wallace insists that labor is quite literally, "written on the body": "It's interconnected, what happens outside in the world, how we labor, and what happens inside us and in our relationship with others" (Julian 2004, 9). In this interview, Julian makes an interesting connection between Wallace's transgressive agenda, her focus on labor, and her interest in youth:

> CJ: I've noticed that some of the wise and the brave people in your work are very young, even children, like the young girl Morse in *One Flea Spare* and Devon in *Lawn Dogs*. What are you doing with these characters?
>
> NW: I often see in children a force for refusing to accept the notion that things cannot change. And while some people call it naive, I think there's a courage in the youth that our culture certainly does not value and actively represses. We are an extremely anti-youth culture that sets out to basically pathologize being young, being a teenager. Especially young people who are not privileged, looking at them as a problem, a pathology to be taken care of, to be drugged, rather than a source of incredible energy, creativity and talent. Also, children are expected to be a certain way, and I like the unexpectedness of how children really are if you watch them. So that's why I often use children. Sometimes children just don't go by the rules, they often have a natural inclination not to, which we as adults have often lost. (2004, 5)

Apart from writing youthful characters, Wallace has also written plays for young audiences with her partner Bruce McLeod, including *The Girl Who Fell Through a Hole in Her Jumper* and *In the Sweat* (produced at the 1997 National Theatre Festival for Youth and directed by David Gothard).[3] In addition, she has issued what might be seen as a political manifesto for young theatre practitioners. Her 2008 article for *American Theatre* entitled "On Writing as Transgression" (reprinted in this anthology) is a plea to theatre educators to encourage subversion in young playwrights, who have the potential to transform the theatrical landscape and the social order:

> I am not calling for a condescending theatre or a "preach to the converted" theatre but a welcoming, vigorous, inquisitive and brutal theatre. If we encourage our students to dig, they will find the body, in all its intimacy and vulnerability, under the garbage of mainstream political rhetoric (2008, 102).

But one could argue that Wallace's provocative agenda goes beyond the creation of plays for youthful spectators and political manifestos for young writers. Perhaps the most transgressive act of all in Wallace's work is the use of young laboring bodies in the live theatrical arena.

Girl Ghosts and 'Boys-To-Men'

Wallace's plays are recognized for two recurring types of roles designed for young actors. The first is the vibrant, dangerous, endangered young male on the cusp of adulthood. These young men are often warriors (soldiers, urban warriors, or questing boys) who rehearse the erotics of death and violence—on the Texas border (*The War Boys*), in a military hospital (*Birdy*), on the battlefields of Desert Storm (*In the Heart of America*), on the Gaza strip (*A State of Innocence*), in a dead-end town in Depression-era Kentucky (*The Trestle at Pope Lick Creek*), and in war-torn Iraq (*The Retreating World*). Handsome, powerful, angry, and volatile, these young men are also vulnerable, terrified of their own power, self-reflexive, and open to change. These characters draw spectators into a troubled and complicated empathy: hoping they survive; praying that they are stopped before they can do more harm. Certainly, these 'boys-to-men,' whether American, Israeli, or Iraqi, resonate with recurring images in everyday media and computer games of young males in trouble, at war, in jeopardy: returning from battles broken or completely destroyed. They manifest a jazzed and jagged sexuality, an unexpected boyish charm, and a rich energy as they flirt with life, death, and unexpectedly (or perhaps inevitably) with each other. They also share certain core characteristics: resourcefulness, imagination, humor, drive, yearning, and a powerful desire to connect with a world that dissolves the moment they reach out to touch it. These young male outcasts and soldiers exemplify promise while they prophesy destruction. They are the 'dead men walking' of war and empire: ghosts of a generation marked for extinction, rendered all the more poignant for their fury and love of violence, as they dance on the site where they will all too soon be contained by prison or the grave.

The second recurring youthful figure in Wallace's work is more truly a child. This is a prepubescent or teen-age "ghost girl" who stands at the center of the narrative: the tiny, prescient Morse in the Restoration drama *One Flea Spare*; the rebellious tomboy Pace in *The Trestle at Pope Lick Creek*; the 11-year-old village girl Bliss in *The Inland Sea*, set in eighteenth-century Britain; and the precocious Devon in Wallace's award-winning independent film, *Lawn Dogs*, set in suburban Kentucky. This character evokes a cultural tradition of feisty, magical girlhood from *Harriet the Spy* and *Pippi Longstocking* to manga and Disney heroines, although, unlike these prototypes, she does not fully triumph over death and disaster. This uncanny girl is essentially a revenant—a flickering ghost haunting the scene of her destruction.[4] Surrounded by adults supposedly charged with her care, this "flying girl" walks through time and space, giving spectators a moving reminder of how often youthful promise is erased before its time.

These 'boys-to-men' and ghostly girls reflect Wallace's fascination with the consumption of the bodies of young people in a political system that 'eats' its children alive in factories, desert wars, prisons, and the dead-end towns of America's exurbia. Wallace's use of youthful characters in plays exploring commodification, race, class, gender, and sexuality has been insightfully critiqued in the work of Kim Solga, Claudia Barnett, Gwendolyn Hale, and other feminist scholars.[5] The relevance of her manifesto to contemporary theatre arts curricula has been well documented in the writings of Amy Steiger (2011, 21–32), and in the progressive classroom practice of university educators such as Susan Harris Smith.[6] Wallace herself, in a series of workshops and residencies in the United States, Britain, and Egypt, has continued to encourage youthful theatre practitioners to represent their vigorous opposition to the political status quo.[7] Strangely, however, little has been made of her use of the sweat equity of child and teenage actors in her productions.

Young Laboring Bodies

How important are child and teenage actors to Wallace's mandate of transgression? Do her plays 'work' better if young adults are cast in the roles of teenagers and children in her plays? Are there risks as well as advantages in the use of child and teenage performers in her highly charged, erotic, political dramas?

It could be argued, for example, that Wallace's 'boys-to-men' could benefit from being performed by age-appropriate teenage male actors, able to represent the potent mixture of testosterone-fueled violence and the aching vulnerability of the very young. In a similar fashion, the feisty ghost girls in Wallace's plays seem to call for 'underage' female actors able to represent the complex amalgam of naiveté, anger, eroticism, cruelty, victimization, and agency so cleverly embodied in these characters. Yet concerns about youth, exploitation, expertise, and just plain convenience seem to haunt the casting practices connected to some of Wallace's key works, particularly where females are concerned, so that young women are cast in the roles of ghost girls instead of age-appropriate performers.[8]

Over the past 15 years, I've witnessed several productions of *One Flea Spare* and *The Trestle at Pope Lick Creek* in which young-looking women in their 20s (and beyond) have been cast to play the girl child at the center of the play. This practice raises several questions. If we do not trust (or train) our teenage actors to perform challenging and complex roles in the theatre workplace, what does this say about our attitude toward young people in general?[9] Why would courageous theatre directors, presumably attracted to Wallace's work because of its political content and innovative style, hesitate when it comes to casting a child or teenage girl performer in the role of a girl?

"Never Work With Animals or Children"

Scholarship on the issue of girlhood and theatrical representation can be strangely tentative in tone, even within the feminist critique of performance.[10] Perhaps this is due to the emotive and highly contested terms used in such analysis, where the descriptor "girl" can seem dismissive or derisive. There seems to be a profound ambivalence on the subject. Indeed, many of the most productive insights on the issue of girlhood and performance can be found in current writings exploring new trends in psychology, sociology, film studies, fandom, and cultural politics.[11] Recent studies linking labor, affect, and performance offer useful insights when looking at the 'sticky' question of child labor on stage, particularly when girls are involved.

One such work is *Stage Fright, Animals and Other Theatrical Problems* by Nicholas Ridout. In this analysis of the hidden aspects of theatrical reception, Ridout suggests that the laughter raised by

W. C. Fields famous quip "never work with animals or children" is caused by anxiety, not amusement. He is fascinated by the disruptive potential of children (and animals) on stage, linking these tiny performers to a dynamic that undermines the apparatus of realism. In a witty chapter entitled "Mouse in the House," Ridout recounts his observations when attending a production of *The Caretaker* in which a mouse wandered out on stage, making the spectators (as well as the performers) distinctly edgy: "We know what we expect to see on stage...So when we get something else, it appears as an anomaly, and a worrying one at that" (2006, 97). Ridout points out that this anxiety towards animals and children on stage has several sources: the humanitarian concern that the child or animal performer is being exploited and the deeper, darker anxiety (perhaps at an unconscious level) that the spectator is complicit in this abuse, taking a dangerous pleasure in a position of power over a diminutive subject. There is also the worry that the audience member may be in danger:

> Bringing in an animal here is courting disaster. We'll have them in our homes, so long as they have been properly trained, but in the super-artifice of the theatre, we fear that even the best-trained creatures could run amok at any moment, and spoil everything, especially since we know, don't we, that they would really rather be anywhere but here (2006, 98).

These tiny, dangerous, attractive performers excite sympathy and fear at the same time. Spectators find it hard to turn away, and this interest—whether protective or prurient—has the power to make them feel uncomfortable. They prefer their theatrical reality contained. Child actors threaten the whole infrastructure of performance, even when (or perhaps *especially* when) they succeed in terms of artistry:

> The precocious child is uncanny and (on stage at least) unpleasant, because of its knowing, or non-knowing-enough imitation of the imitations of its adult colleagues. They tend to appear as mini-adults and some of our unease at their appearance seems to arise out of a sense that they are learning, and displaying, and displaying too much too young (2006, 99).

According to Ridout, these small creatures that bite undermine the theatrical applecart. They, "illuminate...the reality of theatrical employment itself," making spectators uncomfortably aware of the labor involved in producing the illusion onstage (2006, 100).

Children and animals have an extraordinary ability to awaken the audience's awareness of theatre as *work* and of performance as fiction. Ridout's "mouse in the house" is a powerful agent—a tiny creature whose run across the stage has the power to undermine a whole economy of representation. Wandering uncontained into theatrical fiction, the animal (and child) performer becomes the unwitting ally of radical theatre—a tiny Brecht, a pocket postmodernist, puncturing for once and all the shaky truth claims of theatre.

"Uncanny" Child Labor: Girls in the Plays of Naomi Wallace

Ridout's critique of children and animals provides (at least for me) an unexpected point of access to the phenomenon of Wallace's ghost girls. In *Stage Fright,* Ridout characterizes child and animal performers as *agent provocateurs,* although he sees these tiny interlopers as operating almost entirely by accident. This begs the question: what powerful effects might such tiny laboring bodies produce if they were deliberately deployed? What happens when child actors are strategically used as destabilizing agents in transgressive theatrical productions? How would this work in plays of Naomi Wallace in which the role of a female child—and the virtuoso performance of a girl actor—are central to the power dynamics of the play?

One of the trademark "ghost girl" roles in the plays of Naomi Wallace is the rebellious teenage Pace in the Depression-era drama *The Trestle at Pope Lick Creek*. Pace Creagan is a17-year-old tomboy who dares the 15-year-old "mama's boy" Dalton to join her in a bid to outrun a train rushing through their dead-end Kentucky town. Though the character appears to be a lively teen, bubbling over with energy, she is soon revealed as the ghost of a girl destroyed by the train's, "one hundred and fifty-three tons [of]...cold, lip-smackin' steel" (Wallace 2001, 285). The young female actor playing this role must perform in an extraordinary scene where she appears as a vision to the frightened teenage boy Dalton, bringing him to a climax in a "touchless" sexual encounter when she informs him that she has penetrated his body. Perhaps for this reason, the uncanny role of Pace is often played by a young-looking female actor in her 20s, despite the fact that the sex scene between the teenagers involves no nudity, no touching, and no offensive language. My own experience

To Girl or Not to Girl 177

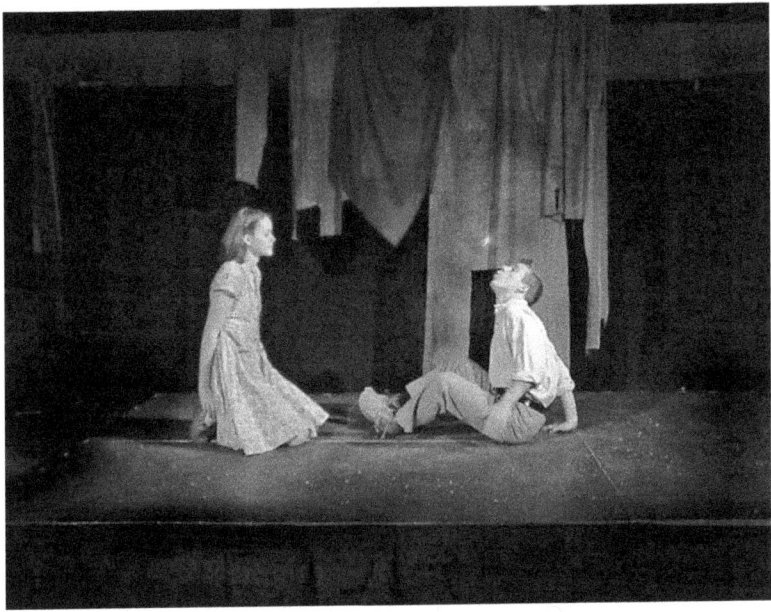

Figure 13.1 Lauren Shannon (Pace) and Ben McGinley (Dalton) in the 2011 Rogoff Theatre Company production of *The Trestle at Pope Lick Creek*. Director: Braden LuBell. Photo: Elizabeth Cocco. Courtesy of Braden LuBell.

of seeing the play in three separate productions in a span of nine years (once in Britain and twice in the United States) suggests that there is more to the casting practice of substituting an adult for a teenager than the desire to protect a female minor from exploitation, sexual or otherwise.[12]

Although one could argue that the actor playing Pace is made vulnerable to the objectifying gaze of the audience in a disturbing enactment of youthful sexuality, Wallace has designed the stage dynamics so that the two youthful actors (male and female) are protected by a dream-like, almost visionary framework, poetic language, and a carefully-choreographed interchange in which the eroticism is described, not seen. This tactic of 'tricking sight' (well known to feminist practitioners and theorists) avoids arousing the spectators and victimizing the youthful performers.

So why isn't a child or teenage actor used in this central role? Certainly, using an adult to perform the role of Pace (the white trash girl on the edge of adulthood) changes the economy of production, both in terms of the power relations in the play, and in terms of the actor–audience relationship. A young female adult imitating an adolescent tomboy (in a time-honored tradition of soubrettes and sexy ingénues from Gigi to Gidget) does not 'play' girl in the same way as a female child on the brink of sexual knowingness and death. Spectators will be much more comfortable in their seats when a young woman plays the role of a girl in scenes involving sexual initiation and a ghostly return from the grave, but is their comfort important? Could it be that casting a girl in this role gives a child entirely too much ability to provoke and disturb: that a powerful child playing a powerful character is a proposition entirely too radical for all concerned, from spectators to director, cast and crew?

The question of "to girl or not to girl" is also central to the casting practices surrounding the character of 12-year-old Morse in Wallace's plague drama, *One Flea Spare*. Like Pace, this lively girlish character appears to be brimming with promise but is eventually revealed as marked (if not entirely claimed) by death. The character has playful scenes, where she makes fun of the aristocrats and their home, into which she has insinuated her tiny, trickster presence. She is a witness to adult games of violence and sexual intrigue between the master of the house, a sailor, and the aristocratic mistress, whom Morse eventually delivers from the plague with a knife. At the end of the play, this articulate and eerie girl stands alone on the stage, warning the spectators about the tendency of adults to hurt the children left in their care: "So beware. Because I loved them, and they have marked me" (Wallace 2001, 74).

The technical challenges of this role are many. The young practitioner playing Morse must deal with lengthy, dense, and poetic text. The role requires vocal dexterity, sustained concentration, physical stamina, and the ability to interact well with adult co-workers. And, of course, there is the ever-present issue of child labor and exploitation, particularly in the scenes involving erotic content and references to bodily functions, from urination to sexual ecstasy. However, as in *The Trestle at Pope Lick Creek*, Wallace has carefully framed the action to avoid victimizing the child worker in the theatrical workplace. When Morse doffs the magnificent aristocratic dress she purloined and reveals a childish body in camiknickers, the effect is humorous rather than erotic, more Tom Sawyer than 'Pretty Baby.' When the girl allows the guard who polices the house to suck her toe in exchange for food, his clumsy attempts to possess her take on a slapstick quality, as she slips away, laughing. In the erotic scenes between the sailor and the wounded aristocratic woman, the actual sexual contact is (once again) invisible. The woman cries out in an operatic aria of longing and release, but the child standing next to the couple sees nothing of the man's hand beneath the woman's dress, and neither do the spectators who overlook this ghostly encounter.

The role of Morse has certainly been performed by child actors, the most noteworthy being 13-year-old Mischa Barton, best known for her adult role in the television series *The O.C.* Barton began her professional stage career at age nine with the New York production of Tony Kushner's *Slavs*. She starred in the 1997 off-Broadway production of *One Flea Spare* and also performed the role of the "uncanny" girl in Wallace's film *Lawn Dogs*. Even Ben Brantley, who heartily disliked *One Flea Spare* and thought most of the actors moved like "uncomfortable pieces of furniture," noted the young Barton's appeal and skill in this production (Brantley 1997). In an online interview, Barton notes that when she played challenging stage roles as a child she enjoyed the experience of being treated as an equal by adult co-workers (Freidson 2005).[13]

Another child actor, Natasha Greenblatt, was 13 when she performed the role of Morse for the 1998 Canadian premiere of *One*

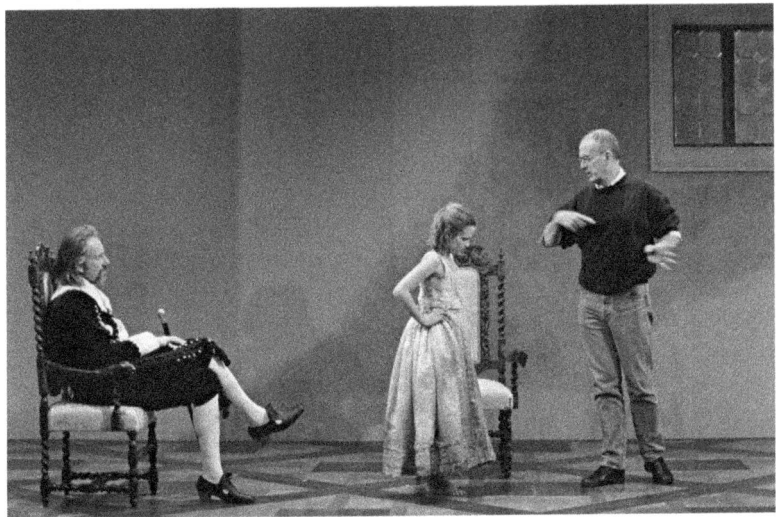

Figure 13.2 Jon De Vries (William Snelgrave) and Mischa Barton (Morse) in rehearsal with director Ron Daniels for the 1997 Public Theater production of *One Flea Spare*. Photo © Michal Daniel, 2007.

Flea Spare at Nightwood Theatre in Toronto. Greenblatt has very specific memories of the working conditions of this production. As a child with a strong literary bent and several years of experience on stage and television, she found the text interesting and easy to learn, despite its complexity. She loved her costumes (particularly the bloomers!) and remembers vividly the sense of being in the middle of an intriguing adult narrative that she enjoyed, but did not quite understand. Greenblatt relished the role of Morse, which director Alisa Palmer described as, "one small entity who embodies a lot of worlds" (Connolly 1998).

> She's an awesome character. She was powerful…especially for someone who, even as I age, often gets called to play young parts…I've been called "cute." I've been infantilized…so getting to play someone who was dangerous, who had a dark side, who could do good and bad things, who had control and agency—it was definitely fun and empowering.[14]

While Greenblatt acknowledges the challenges of finding the right child actor for such a difficult role, from her viewpoint today as an adult actor, activist, and playwright, she feels that child actors should be given more credit:

> I think we often underestimate children—especially someone in their young teens. They *want* to be asked to go somewhere a bit beyond their reach. They're dying for things that are dark, that are challenging. Those things exist in their lives.[15]

In 2011, when the Eclipse Theatre in Chicago presented a season exclusively devoted to plays by Naomi Wallace, director Anish Jethmalani cast 15-year-old Elizabeth Stenholt (who trained at the Goodman Theatre) in the role he described as the "most central stoic" figure in the play (Cisneros 2011). In this small-scale, fairly realist, and painterly production for an intimate 62-seat house, Stenholt's Morse was a focal point of energy and movement, contrasting sharply with the gravid adults who surrounded her in the kitchen/prison space. Reviewers noted Stenholt's ability to sustain this arduous role and remarked on the interesting dynamics between her character and the ravaged, compelling aristocratic woman who pleads with the angelic child to take her life.[16]

For the 2012 premiere of *One Flea Spare* (*Une puce, épargnez-la*) at the *Comédie-Française*, however, director Anne-Laure Liégeois chose an adult actor to embody the 'uncanny' child at the center of this provocative drama. Liégeois' postmodern rendering of Wallace's play rejected all vestiges of American realism. Opting for surrealist evocations of seventeenth-century painting and theatre, Liégeois placed her actors in a vast, dimly-lit space where walls and windows suddenly proliferated and statues of dead birds appeared as if by magic. Julie Sicard, the lithe 30-something actor playing the role of the 12-year-old Morse, wandered doll-like into the middle of this nightmare landscape, evoking the Velázquez portrait of the Spanish Infanta: a tiny icon of power in a golden robe staring out at the spectators.[17]

The result was visually stunning, but vastly different from North American productions of this piece that reflect the visceral, red-blooded clash between material realities and poetic vision. As one of the spectators in the company's *Théâtre-Éphémère*, I made an interesting personal discovery about affect and labor as I watched the play unfold. Though the critic at *Le Figaro* contended that it was appropriate for a woman to portray a girl in an historical era when children were treated as miniature adults (Héliot 2012), I was not convinced. Like Ridout, I became increasingly disturbed by the gap between the fictional world on stage and the realities of the actors presenting it. This time, however, it was not the presence of something unexpected (like a tiny animal inadvertently scurrying across the stage) that bothered me; it was the reverse. The production was seamless, the acting superb, but (for me, at least) something was lacking. I missed the mouse.

Child Labor/Adult Affect

The question of the mouse continues to haunt me, even as I try to rationalize the casting choices concerning girls in Naomi Wallace's works. A range of factors impact the casting of a girl in the role of Pace or Morse. The director's vision is one; the casting policies and institutional structure of a theatre company are others. The standards of training and relative lack of experience of child performers might also be factors. Child labor laws, which differ from country to country, trade association, and union rules in such bodies as the Alliance of Canadian Cinema, Television, and Radio Artists (ACTRA) or British and American Equity might also influence the decision. But the issue is not just a matter of practicality or theatre training. If directors and producers hesitated to cast female children in adult dramas because of anxieties about their performance abilities, the casting practices for blockbuster musicals and Shakespearean classics in the West End and Broadway would be vastly different. A closer look at the issues surrounding this practice suggests that there may be more here than meets the eye.

In my opinion, the question of "to girl or not to girl" in the works of Naomi Wallace goes straight to the heart of her radical enterprise. Ridout's critique implies that the problem with child and animal performers goes beyond the potential for exploitation. It also involves the anxiety of spectators, who worry that they may perpetuate abuse. I believe that Wallace has made productive use of this anxiety, using child actors to play ghost girls in narratives that remind audience members of their complicity in a machinery of state that destroys the young. If only on an unconscious level, this strategy evokes guilt and resentment, goading spectators into an awareness of their passivity in the face of systemic oppression. Indeed, Wallace's innovative use of child performers is almost *too* effective. It disturbs at a level that is hard to articulate, even for critics. It speaks to social taboos, and the (unspoken) rules that govern the collaboration of adults with children in modern society. Wallace's use of female child labor on stage involves too much democracy, too much intimacy, too much power-sharing; it is too close for comfort in every way. In a 2012 television interview in France, Wallace stated: "When I go to theatre I think it should do two things: change me in some way, and give me the courage to be a more dangerous citizen" (Baudeau 2012). This remark and the experience of watching *Une puce, épargnez-la* in Paris made me realize that the question of "to girl or not to girl" in Wallace's work is not simply a matter of convenience, aesthetics, training, or ethics. There is more at stake here, whether we are conscious of it or not.

Labor, Affect, and Negotiation

The argument of this essay is not that directors should be denied artistic freedom in casting youthful roles or that Wallace's work relies solely on the use of child actors for impact and efficacy. However, I would like to propose two ideas. The first is that the strategic deployment of child actors in Wallace's plays is often overlooked.[18] The second is that the response of spectators to female children on stage is an extremely important element in Wallace's plays, which are deftly constructed to evoke a complicated mixture of thought and feeling.[19] Wallace's plays may range widely in their geographical and historical settings, but they are connected by a focus on systematic victimization of youth in a social order in which adults cannot (or will not) protect them. The use of child actors in ghost girl roles is an integral part of the theatrical operation, designed by Wallace to awaken audience members to the role they play in endangering the youngest members of the body politic.

Is this tactic productive? Erin Hurley's *Theatre and Feeling*, a thoughtful study on labor and affect on stage, goes to a core question about the social value of theatre: "Should it contribute to a moral or pedagogical programme? Is it there to make us feel more alive?" (2010, 3). To answer this, Hurley engages directly with Ridout's insights on child and animal performers, noting that, for him, "theatre is an affect machine—both by design and, most provocatively for Ridout, by mistake." In live performance, "we become disquieted by our position as consumers of others' labour" (2010, 8). Hurley believes that this discomfort can be extremely useful. She links the labor of performing children and animals to the product it engenders: the thoughts and feelings of the spectators.

According to Hurley, "feeling work" is an important form of stage labor, which she connects to Jill Dolan's concept of constructing social affiliations in *Utopia and Performance: Finding Hope at the Theater* (2005) and Sara Ahmed's provocative critique of the way feelings produce value by generating human exchange in *The Cultural Politics of Emotion* (2004). She explores a workplace dynamic involving the exchange between actors and spectators: "If emotion is made in the relationship between the stage and the audience (the stimulus and receiver, if you will) it cannot simply be projected by actors and caught as the same emotion by the audience. The theatre's emotional labour, then is, in part a negotiation" (2010, 20). This analysis of stage labor as a circulation of affect—a conversation produced by sweat equity—suggests that Ridout's accidental "mouse in the house" and Wallace's ghost girls are members of a cadre of theatrical 'others' who play an important role in cultural production. They are agents of change. They serve as a resource in the 'mousetrap' of theatre, where the "aha!" moment (or "feeling-work") must be produced through a skilled negotiation with the live audience. Using adults to do the work of children, it follows, is simply a less efficient way of realizing the possibilities of Wallace's plays, undermining the algorithm of her dramaturgy, finely calculated to elicit maximum response. This possibility is worth considering when casting her plays, watching them, responding to them, teaching them—and considering their potential effect on audience members.

Hard Work/Child's Play

The use of child labor *as* transgression *for* transgression is unique in Wallace's work. While other radical dramatists, from Brecht to Kushner and Churchill, may use child labor in their ground-breaking plays, Wallace's reliance on the skill of child actors is unusual, and so is her promotion of these workers to positions of extraordinary responsibility on the shop floor. The effects of this deployment of child labor can be powerful, even startling. Being an audience member at a Naomi Wallace play can be hard work. The language may be beautiful, the plots intriguing, and the characters (especially the young ones) accessible and compelling, but the "feeling work" is demanding. Spectators lulled by poetic speeches and playful children are led into complicated and painful negotiations, and the insights they gain from these are not necessarily pleasant.

In examining the use of child actors in roles designed for girls, but often played by adults, I do not make a claim for children as more authentic performers of youth. (Indeed, as Ridout's analysis suggests, child actors trouble the shaky edifice of twentieth-century realism, and a good thing, too!). I do, however, support the concept that female child labor is integral to Wallace's political project. Any long-time observer of Wallace's plays in production soon becomes aware of her deft manipulation of this subversive, insinuating 'push-pull' dynamic of attraction and repulsion. Wallace's deliberate use of young characters who transgress and actors who are 'too young' to be on stage sets up a productive disturbance that facilitates the emotional labor described by Hurley. This innovative technique creates a dynamic interchange between spectators and actors. The girls who serve on the production team are part of this equation. Not to use them, one could argue, is to undermine the economy of representation deliberately set up by Wallace to attract, disturb, challenge, and transform.

Youthful Appeal

When exploring the connection between youth and transgression in the works of Naomi Wallace, it is seductive to focus on the appeal of her works to a new generation of practitioners and theatregoers rather than on her use of child labor. Caitlin McLeod, the youthful director of the 2011 British premiere of Wallace's *And I And Silence*, finds that Wallace's plays have a special resonance with young artists because they break away from the constraints of naturalism and offer an alternate view of society.[20] She echoes Greenblatt's assertion that young artists and audiences like to be challenged and believes that they respond well to a theatrical aesthetic that mixes the familiar and the strange:

> I think it's the same sort of excitement that you get when you're in the middle of a demonstration. You feel that even if it's just for this moment, and even if I go home and I feel that I'm conforming to everything that I'm shouting about right now, for that moment, there is a connection to the other people on the team as well. And with an audience, you have that feeling of right here, right now, we talking about something. Either I loathe it or it's something that needs to be changed, or something that we don't usually talk about, or characters that we don't usually see.[21]

It is clear that Wallace hails youth in her project of social transformation and theatrical revitalization. This hailing is important. It is provocative. It may even be transformational. But I believe that it is not her appeal to youthful audiences, but her use of child labor that makes Wallace's work truly transgressive. When the tactic works, even when it elicits hostility, it generates strong feeling, critical awareness, and the type of productive conversation that is the *raison d'être* of theatre.

Scandalous Bodies in a Critique of Use

Wallace's body of work can be viewed as an extended meditation on labor. It's not necessary to be a Marxist to understand that her plays explore the operations of power in the capitalist world: the erosion of the human body through our system of monetary exchange, and the exploitation of the working class, racial, and sexual 'other.' It is not only activists who acknowledge that Wallace's work for theatre has a social agenda. It is not essential to stake a claim as a feminist, queer or postmodern theorist in order to show that her use of (scandalous) speaking bodies is theatrically effective. Many scholars and practitioners have acknowledged these components of her work, but few have focused on her use of child labor—particularly the work of girls—as part of this radical project. I hope, with this exploration, to encourage an ongoing conversation on the subject.

In an era where youthful activists are demanding inclusion in global power structures, Naomi Wallace is willing to collaborate with child and teenage artists on the ground floor of production. This reveals an unusual amount of respect for the labor of youth: an attitude that deserves fuller attention, particularly in the context of Wallace's revolutionary mandate. In a volume such as this, which sets up a dialogue between different points of view, the question of "to girl or not to girl" was introduced to set up its own productive disquiet. While I believe it is valuable to explore Naomi Wallace's works in terms of aesthetic innovation, I hope to see this critique of labor, gender, age, and affect extended even further into theatre training and performative practices, giving greater recognition to the productive, troubling power of laboring child bodies in Wallace's continuing project of transgression, and social change.

Notes

1. Negative reviews of Wallace's work typically disparage her leftist leanings and complex language. Ben Brantley's *New York Times* review of *One Flea Spare* at the Public Theater (1997) dismissed the play as, "carved in stone." J. Cooper Robb derisively titled his review of Wallace's *In the Heart of America* at Philadelphia's InterAct Theatre (2004) as "Gulf Bore." Charles Isherwood's *New York Times* review of *Things of Dry Hours* at the New York Theatre Workshop (2009) called the play a "Marxist gospel" and described it as, "static, lifeless and achingly literary."
2. Wallace's article "Strange Times" (*The Guardian* 2003) is reprinted in this anthology.
3. Both of these plays for youth have been produced in Britain. The first is published in the United States as *The Girl Who Fell Through the Hole in Her Sweater*.
4. See Claudia Barnett's critique of girl ghosts in "Dialectic and the Drama of Naomi Wallace" and "Judith Thompson's Ghosts: The Revenants that Haunt the Plays" as well as my own writings on girlhood and ghosting.
5. Also contributing to this feminist critique is Shannon Baley, whose article "Death and Desire" (*Modern Drama* 2004) is reprinted in this anthology.

6. Susan Harris Smith, noted scholar and professor of English at the University of Pittsburgh led a senior seminar on the works of Naomi Wallace, linking them to aspects of contemporary performance explored in her undergraduate curriculum.
7. This advocacy includes support of two emerging playwrights from the University of Iowa Playwrights Workshop, Kevin Artigue and Joshua Casteel. Artigue's *People of the Ditch* critiques American military involvement in Afghanistan. Casteel, a divinity student who served as an army interrogator in Abu Ghraib, died of cancer in 2012. His play *Returns*, based on his war experiences, was directed in Iowa in 2007 by British director David Gothard, a contributor to this volume. See http://news-releases.uiowa.edu/2011/may/050311playfest_people.html and http://news-releases.uiowa.edu/2007/february/020207returns-casteel.html.
8. See Beth Cleary's essay in this text for further considerations of sexuality and youthful performance in the works of Naomi Wallace.
9. I originally asked this question in my *Theatre Journal* review of the 2002 production of *The Trestle at Pope Lick Creek* at the Aurora Theatre, Berkeley.
10. This was the subject of my doctoral dissertation, "Resisting Bodies: Promise and Change in the Feminist Representation of Girls in the Performative Arena" (UCLA, 2003).
11. See writings on girlhood, grrl, and girl studies by Michelle Fine, Mary Kearney, Sherrie Inness, Lisa Soccio, Carol Gilligan, and Mary Pipher.
12. These three productions of *The Trestle at Pope Lick Creek* were at the Aurora Theatre, Berkeley (2002), Southwark Theatre, London (2003), and the Eclipse Theatre, Chicago (2011).
13. Ironically, as a child star, Barton was featured as the character "Mouse" in the film *Lost and Delirious*, adapted for the screen from Susan Swan's novel *The Wives of Bath* by Canadian playwright, Judith Thompson.
14. Natasha Greenblatt, interview by Erica Stevens Abbitt, June 2012.
15. Ibid.
16. The role of Darcy in this production was performed by Susan Monts-Bologna.
17. Velázquez's most famous painting, *Las Meninas* (The Maids of Honor) features a tiny Spanish princess in elaborate dress, posing with her girlish attendant in a court filled with shadowy male figures, including the painter himself.
18. See the writings of Jo Machon and Beth Cleary, also in this volume, which chronicle the experience of working with university students in Naomi Wallace's plays.
19. See "The Dramaturgy of Rehearsal" by Lindsay Cummings, also in this volume.
20. She also notes that the play, originally commissioned by Clean Break (a company dedicated to theatre for and about the imprisoned), had a positive response when performed for an audience of young female offenders.
21. Caitlin McLeod, telephone interview by Erica Stevens Abbitt, June 2011.

Part II

Collaborators

Dominic Dromgoole

Standing on Your Head

Dominic Dromgoole has been Artistic Director of Shakespeare's Globe since 2006. His initiatives there include commissioning new work, starting a touring operation, creating the 2012 Globe to Globe Festival, and opening a new indoor playhouse lit by candlelight. As Artistic Director of London's Bush Theatre (1990–1996), he played a pivotal role in Wallace's early career when he directed the world premieres of In the Heart of America *(1994) and* One Flea Spare *(1995). He also directed the world premiere of Wallace's* The Inland Sea *(2002) while Artistic Director of the Oxford Stage Company (1999–2005). A regular contributor to the* Sunday Times, *he is also the author of* The Full Room *(2000) and* Will and Me: How Shakespeare Took Over My Life *(2006).*

* * *

When we did *In the Heart of America* at the Bush in 1994, there was a wonderful actor in the cast named Richard Dormer who played Craver, the white soldier from Kentucky. We were all floundering a bit as to how to play it because the dialogue has this lilt and rhythm to it, and if you go overstiff and rhetorical on it, it sounds daft, and if you try to naturalize and mumble it, it gets equally daft. We were doing the scene where Craver is standing on his head, and Richard came down from that in an acrobatic maneuver, down and up and then straight into the next line with a certain degree of poise that unlocked a whole way of playing for us.

There is a special elegance in Naomi's writing, a reserve, a deliberate or held quality in the way she uses language. There is a sort of sprung wit within it that you have to observe from moment to moment—a bit like Jane Austen—a specific music that sits alongside truth. It is not an artificial music. It is not about being fake or rhetorical. There is something quite mischievous and subversive in Naomi's writing, an intense and pure formality, and within that, humor and eroticism and danger. So there needs to be a balance. When actors discover that and feel comfortable playing it, they are off and running. Before they find that pitch and poise, it can be agony because there are a thousand ways that you can get it wrong—by making it overly naturalistic or overly stylized or whatever. When you find the particular rhythm and balance that it requires it is massively enjoyable to perform—like Shakespeare in a way. There is a constant, uneasy dynamic in Shakespeare between humanity and metrical form. You can veer too far towards metrical form and you can veer too far towards humanity. You have to strike the balance between character and cadence.

The older you get the more you realize that you have to talk to an audience—in any art form but in theatre more than any other. You need to build a conversation with a particular audience. Shakespeare, for 21 years between 1592 and 1613, had a constant ongoing conversation with a singular audience who were always pushing him, inclining him to be bolder and to experiment. They were enthusiastic for his jumps and they always wanted him to jump. Popular audiences are much bolder than academics, much bolder than critics, much bolder than other members of your own art form, all of whom will stultify or kill you in some way. But a popular audience will always push you in a healthy direction.

That sort of thing is not available to Naomi now, of course. There's no Globe of our day, and in any case, the form in which she's chosen to tell her stories, the purity of the voice, makes for a wonderful and beautiful sculptural event, but it does not make for a popular, broadly accessible event. I think Naomi would be perfectly capable of writing something *for* a popular audience in a mature, grown-up, radical style politically consistent with her own beliefs. But there is something about the singularity of her voice that is always calling her back to fidelity to itself. She's astute. It's a choice she's making. She knows what she is doing.

If a playwright is lucky, he finds his own audience. But it is almost impossible for a writer to get into a regular relationship with an audience these days because they have to walk such a fractured path through their careers. They are made to think, "I'll start out in a little out-of-town fringe venue. And then I'll get a few readings around town. And then I'll get into a more subsidized Royal Court-y venue. And then I'll get into a relationship with the National. And then I'll have some plays on in the West End. And then I'll write a couple movies...and then I'll retire." They lose the vital sense of an ongoing discussion with a group of people—it could be small, it doesn't have to be huge—who are going to help them grow their art and their writing not in isolation but in a free and open conversation. That conversation is the purpose of writing, in a sense.

Sarah Kane was working at the Bush when Naomi was writing her plays there, and they got to know each other at that time. Sarah Kane is never going to have her plays on in the commercial theatre, but without any particular popular success, she has had an immense effect on the culture and how people write plays. I think it is the same with Naomi. There is a deliberate quality and a lyricism in the way she writes: a gravity and a spectral sense that will have an enormous impact on how people write plays for a long time.

Ron Daniels

Naomi Is Inside My Head

Ron Daniels *is an internationally acclaimed director of opera and classical and contemporary theatre. A native of Brazil, he was a founding member of Teatro Oficina in São Paulo. He directed for the Royal Shakespeare Company for fifteen 15 years and was named an Honorary Associate Director of the RSC. In the United States, he has directed numerous plays as Associate Artistic Director of the American Repertory Theatre in Cambridge, MA, and as an independent artist. His L.A. Opera production of* Il Postino *starring Plácido Domingo opened in Los Angeles in 2012 and has been seen in Paris and Vienna. In 1996, he directed world-premiere and U.S.-premiere productions of* Slaughter City *for the RSC in London and the American Repertory Theatre and the New York premiere of* One Flea Spare *at the Public Theatre. His first feature-length film, a version of Wallace's* The War Boys, *was released in 2009.*

* * *

Naomi is inside my head. It's probably the same for all of us, but from the first time I read one of her plays, I seemed to understand what she was saying and be affected by it in some instinctive and mysterious way. As if I recognized within me the words she spoke. As if these were my own words.

Of course, this has to do with feeling in sympathy with the way she sees the world and feeling an unbounded admiration for her fighting spirit, for her passionate and unflinching support of the outsider and the oppressed, and for the way that her politics is not merely a collection of abstract ideas, but something deeply personal, experienced in the flesh. And through the flesh. The human body as the locus of political engagement.

She is a poet. However, she is a poet of the stage, and as a poet her dramaturgy is free flowing. It takes narrative leaps that are breathtaking and often exhilarating and even scary for a director and actors, but which can make unexpected demands on an audience—and as Naomi does not try to please or pander, this may seem arrogant and even threatening. For her, as a true poet, words matter. Not in the mere reproduction of banal, everyday speech, but in carefully controlled and precise rhythms and structures that lead to deep resonance and meaning.

The worlds Naomi creates are haunting, at times unsettling, and quite unorthodox. Perhaps what is most original about her is precisely this courageous and often even shocking unorthodoxy, where not only values but also expected roles, including sexual roles, are questioned and reversed. Characters cross the line and find themselves in landscapes they have never been in before but which they somehow recognize, to misquote a line of George's in *The War Boys*. Invariably, her female characters are strong, self-assured, and assertive for all their insecurity—empowered agents of their own lives. Even if they have to dress and pass as men, like Cod in *Slaughter City*. Tough young men are obsessed with forbidding older women like Roach in *Slaughter City* or Marta in *The War Boys*. Often these young men are mutilated or they mutilate themselves and so, in some way, they become 'feminized'—Brandon in *Slaughter City* who has been silenced by having his mouth sewn up, though he may only have dreamed this; David in *The War Boys*, who self destructively shoots staples into his own hand; and Bunce in *One Flea Spare*, who has a constantly bleeding vagina-like wound in his side into which Mrs. Snelgrave inserts her finger. Children show more wisdom, are more understanding, and more caring than grown ups: on my first trip to Louisville I came across Naomi's youngest daughter Tegan—she could have been no more than four or five at the time—her hair cropped short and disheveled, and totally naked feeding a little wounded bird with the thin end of a spoon. I imagine Nadira, Caitlin, and Tegan—Naomi's beautiful daughters—could not have but been the prototypes to Morse in *One Flea Spare*, Cat in *The War Boys,* and Devon in *Lawn Dogs*.

Inspired by real people, by historical events, or simply drawn from her imagination, Naomi has the ability to reveal the deepest and most complex secrets of her characters in a way that we can identify with and relate to from within our own experience. And yet these characters are always the reflection of a larger social and political battleground.

It took us many years to raise the financing for the film version of *The War Boys*, the story of three young vigilantes on the border between the United States and Mexico. There are two parallel narratives in the film: one, a 'Latino'/vigilante-on-the-border story line (Greg comes to realize that he is no different from the Mexican illegals he chases back across the border) and the other, a 'gay' narrative (David and George discover that they are in love with each other and that that love makes them outsiders, as vulnerable as the fleeing illegal immigrants). Financing would have been much easier had we cut the gay story line and concentrated solely on the issue of illegal immigration: this was indeed specifically proposed to us by several potential sources of finance. The point of the film, however—and we were adamant about this—was precisely that the 'political' and the deeply 'personal' narratives were intertwined, reflected each other, and were equally important.

Her plays are far from being political tracts. At times they involve painful journeys of self-discovery, unsentimental and yet profoundly moving, lyrical in unexpected and even harsh ways, bold and vibrant, journeys that are challenging and often incredibly lonely—think of Cod in *Slaughter City* describing herself as a limpet, stuck to a rock. A feeling of otherness pervades her work—and perhaps this is a feeling that she shares, in spite of her wonderful family life and an army of comrades and admirers. Once when we were in New York together, maybe walking on a rainy night in Washington Square, Naomi described how she always felt as if she never was "where it was all happening." I think that was the way she described it. Or maybe it was that she always felt that she was always "elsewhere," and never "at the center of things."

I suppose we could say that Naomi's characters, the struggles they endure and the images that result from these struggles, are what I would call 'supra realistic'—real, yes, but magically, yet through their specificity, given a larger than life reality and resonating well beyond themselves. They are born out of her resolute desire not only to reflect the world as she sees it, but also how she would like it to be, and her urgent, passionate need to change it. To some, these situations and images may appear excessive and far-fetched, even frightening. But they are the true and familiar landscape through which Naomi wanders, alone.

I've loved every occasion I've had to wander in that landscape by her side.

It feels very much like home.

Riccardo Hernandez

Designing Wallace

Riccardo Hernandez *is an eminent American scenic designer for theatre, opera, and musical theatre. His designs have been seen on Broadway, at the Public Theater and other major New York theatres, at dozens of resident theatres and opera companies around the United States, and abroad at the Royal National Theatre and the Royal Court in London, the Avignon Festival, and the Det Norske Teatret in Oslo. He has designed scenery for three Wallace plays:* One Flea Spare *at the Public Theater in 1997,* The Trestle at Pope Lick Creek *at New York Theater Workshop in 1999, and* Things of Dry Hours *at Baltimore's Center Stage in 2007. He is also a lecturer at Princeton University.*

* * *

American set designers tend not to like the term 'scenography,' but it's a much better word for what I do than 'set design.' When I design, my aim is to discover and articulate a suggestive, nonimitative place that can only exist in performance time. It is a poem rather than an illustration. Rather than a set, it is what Strindberg described as a space "where anything can happen, everything is possible and probable. Time and place do not exist." It creates its own logic and invites us to dream, to transcend our daily routines, especially at a time when our lives are so encumbered by an ailing economic system and a political cynicism that burdens us with deep mistrust.

I am baffled when today's theatre critics say they are confused because the 'set designer' has not been specific enough in portraying 'location.' The theatre of Shakespeare relied on *no* scenery.

Ingmar Bergman's production of *Long Day's Journey into Night* dispensed with O'Neill's iconic home and turned the stage into a ritualistic platform with no walls. Today's great theatre artists—Ariane Mnouchkine, Romeo Castellucci, Angelica Liddell, Robert Woodruff, Arthur Nauzyciel, and Naomi Wallace—keep luring us back to a performance-audience connection with barely nothing at their disposal.

The first time I heard Naomi's name I was designing Suzan-Lori Parks' *The America Play* at the Public in 1994. I remember George Wolfe kept saying that he had just read this amazing play. He really went on and on about it. Then Ron Daniels called me about working on *One Flea Spare*, and I realized this was the play George Wolfe had told me about. So I was very excited to do it. With *One Flea Spare* at the Public in 1996, we had to create a space that wasn't entirely real—a space that allowed Naomi's language to resonate. The problem was the specifics of location. We did a façade of the seventeenth-century house outside, and then took it away to reveal the kitchen. And that's what designers need to do with Naomi's work: create an outside and then open it up to reveal the inside. I'd love to try this particular set again sometime in order to solve the problem of suggesting the inside and how the characters are trapped, surrounded by the world outside, using less, not more.

I tried to do this again with *The Trestle at Pope Lick Creek* at the New York Theatre Workshop in 1999. We had to go further than creating minute details and making it 'real.' I created a set that had no walls and used the industrial texture of New York Theatre Workshop's brick walls to create my own "blasted heath." Again, it was not a specific setting, but a space that allowed for a metaphysical journey, illustrating the philosophy summed up in a beautiful passage of *The Dramatic Imagination* in which Robert Edmond Jones quotes Walt Whitman: "I seek less to display any theme or thought and more to bring you into the atmosphere of the theme or thought—there to pursue your own flight."

The unseen trestle towering over the two teenagers in a small Depression-era town in Kentucky and a prison-like room looking out onto a street in Restoration London ask the audience to use their imagination to see and hear something that is not real. This is the kind of simplicity Robert Edmond Jones called for—but it can be scary.

When I first started working with Naomi in 1996, I was not as fearless as I am now. As I got older, I no longer felt the need to blow people away with theatrical trickery and a plethora of moving scenic elements. I came to believe in removing everything that is not absolutely necessary. I always return to the fact that "less is more."

When I was working on *Things of Dry Hours* in 2007, I happened to be in London, so the director Kwame Kwei-Armah and I took the train up to Yorkshire to meet with Naomi. We were in her environment: her home, her landscape. It was very moving. We had the kind of conversation that you live for, where we talked about all kinds of issues besides the play. We were trying to get a sense of direction, a word, or an image that might open up something and answer the question: what is the space that you need to create for these words? In this play, as in all Naomi's works, there is a fascination with the unknown, a need to discover and to decipher.

More and more, as I get older, and more fearless, this is my approach. When I teach at Princeton, I make my students look at the space of the play, but I ask them to consider the inside of a play to find a visual vocabulary that will serve this idea. This is very hard for them. Students are daunted by what they *think* is necessary. They get caught up with details instead of going deeper into the theatrical event. I want them to look differently at the process—not to try to illustrate, not to focus on the minutiae of everyday life, but to create a space for the work to grow.

I keep remembering Artaud and his search for a new language of theatre not because he was crazy, but because he felt modern theatre had arrived at a dead end and needed to be blown open. Naomi's plays do this. They make us think about the world in all its complexity. They pose major questions. There is an almost mythic quality to her work that invites us to take a leap of faith. This can be terrifying—it certainly seems to scare some critics! —and it also can be uplifting. I believe this is what you need to keep in mind when designing her plays. You need to surrender to the ambiguity.

Jessica Dromgoole

In the Fields of Naomi Wallace

Jessica Dromgoole is a producer and director of radio dramas who joined the BBC as New Writing Coordinator for Drama, Entertainment and Children's Programmes in 1991. Prior to that, she was for three years the Artistic Director of Finborough Theatre, which premiered Wallace's The War Boys *in 1993. That same year, she directed* In the Fields of Aceldama *for the London New Play Festival. Her many projects for the BBC include co-creating the popular science-fiction series* Planet B, *co-directing a serial adaptation of* A Tale of Two Cities, *and producing Katie Hims's* Lost Property: The Year My Mother Went Missing, *for which she won the first ever BBC Audio Drama Award for Best Audio Drama.*

* * *

The London New Play Festival, where I first came across Naomi's work, was—like so many ad hoc, unsubsidized festivals—the coming together, for a noisy moment, of people on the way up, people on the way down, and people standing still. People on the way down were often the best company, and the people standing still could be navigated around. Naomi and I were on our way up, me to the nearest hilltop and Naomi to the stars.

Scripts came in from all over, and were carefully and rigorously appraised by an oddball panel of unpaid and, in some cases, completely unqualified readers, before the festival director chose the program. *In the Fields of Aceldama* arrived quite late in the process, and was a thing of wonder. Poetic, ugly, beautiful, difficult, culturally a little out of reach, but with an impressive visceral confidence that the

Festival desperately lacked; it also had the dubious cachet of being unpronounceable (quite the thing since *Dancing at Lughnasa*) and a little holier-theatre-than-thou touch, which delighted the more exclusive on the panel. Notions of Naomi began to form.

It's a fragmented piece that comes at the story of a brutalized Kentucky family of three: Henry, a bald and inarticulate smallholder who collects moles and dreams of heroic conflict; his wife Mattie, the daughter of a Basque immigrant, who emotionally and sexually controls the games the family plays; and their daughter Annie, both product and first hand critic of this household, who has died, aged 17, thrown from her horse, just as she was about to kiss her first boy. The fragmentation spins out from Henry and Mattie mourning the loss of their child and trying to look forward, and, in short, frayed, organically woven sequences takes in their courtship, the tight and unregulated violence of family life, and Annie's death. Love and hatred, pride and guilt mingle inextricably in the memory storm that structures the play, and a host of taboos are smashed and subverted along the way. In many ways, it probably isn't a play. It's a work of literature made up of stage tropes, traditional and revolutionary.

A few of the festival readers shied away from it—it was printed in various fonts to an extraordinary and unknown template on a dot matrix printer (the very latest thing in 1993) and had 'controlling writer' written all over it. Extensive notes on design, warnings of what not to do, and a huge amount of directing and acting decisions were written into it. It read like the transcript of a carefully notated collaboration, where all the collaborators were Naomi. Many of the directors working at the festival were keenly identifying scripts they could 'really do something with'—a phrase that makes one's heart and stomach sink even without meeting them. *In the Fields of Aceldama* sat on the table, thousands of miles from its creator, in clear-eyed nerveless defiance of that impulse. Ideas of who Naomi Wallace was—based on nothing but the script and a cursory cover letter—became entrenched.

I was very taken with it. I've always been an avid consumer of dirt-poor-white-trash fiction. I'm a comfortable, sheltered, educated middle-class woman who thrills at ugliness in fiction, and is appalled by it in life. I argued for the play, championed it through a few hurdles, some reasonable and some inane, and found that I was being asked to direct it. I was delighted, and very frightened. As always. Some of the adrenalin I get entering into a production that features this great 'other' is fear of the reality behind it. And Naomi wasn't going to come to Britain until the last couple of days of the rehearsal, so we were alone with it. By the time she arrived, I told myself, we'd all be speaking fluent Naomi.

The cast took a while to get together. Ian Bailey and Maureen Purkis were fantastic, nailing their accents, and allowing the dialogue to do the work, without elaboration or judgment. The girl playing Annie got freaked by it and walked after five days. Anna Clarkson came in late, game for everything that came her way. Her gameness and spirit of adventure never quite left the stage ('look what I'm taking on!' was writ large in her performance), but it was a small price to pay. In fact, a lot of people loved her. We worked the play hard, delving into its darkness, loving its poetry, trying to breathe easily in the world of it, nervous always that Naomi would arrive, fresh from her trailer park, and be appalled at our efforts, smash up the set and quite possibly glass us all.

And yet, and yet...Under scrutiny, the scattergun challenges were sometimes hard to accommodate together. As much attention was paid to the frisson of unshaven armpits as to the idle threat of incestuous sexual conquest. The soundscape of occasional helicopter blades and Henry's desire to fight for America were a strange cultural distraction for British actors. Mattie's fierce love of Annie, her sexual control of Henry, her violent jealousy of Annie and Henry, the breaking of a dead woman's toes all struck sound notes with the cast, belonged together, while the delousing felt like a deliberate stomach-turner, part of another play. It never occurred to us that this play was anything other than complete. The controlling writer behind the dot matrices cowed us. Made us earnest. Made the production earnest, humorless theatre than thou.

Finally, the day came when Naomi was due. The day of a dress rehearsal as it happened. A way for the actors and me to show her everything we'd got in one hit. And then to take whatever she wanted to give back. We were feeling very nervous, but very brave. We loved the play, loved what we'd been doing together, and our fascination with the alien Naomi Wallace had become unbearable. And in she came. She looked lovely. Young, smart, super educated, middle class, and friendly. She was relieved that the actors were so specific with their accents and full of praise for their work. She was fond, and flirtatious, and funny.

And for the first time, for the very first time, it occurred to us that we'd been working on an apprentice piece. A play full of the heart and poetry and brutality and political fire and moral skew that would fill out in her later work, but an immature piece, crammed slightly too full of challenge and shock, perhaps a touch repetitive where repetition wasn't needed, perhaps a touch oblique where clarity would have helped. And as soon as that occurred to us, we relaxed, and the play's humanity, and wit, and love—so necessary and thus far so elusive—eased out into the open.

David Gothard

Radical Poetry

David Gothard *is a British theatre director, impresario, and leading advocate for contemporary, interdisciplinary, avant-garde performance around the globe, from Beckett, Terayama, Fo, and Kantor to a new generation of playwrights, including Naomi Wallace. For nine years, he was programmer and then artistic director at Riverside Studios in London. He is a regular guest teacher at Britain's National Film and Television School, the University of London, and the University of Iowa Playwrights Workshop. He is also an Associate aArtist of the Abbey Theatre in Dublin.*

* * *

To me as a director, teacher, and facilitator of contemporary art and performance, the poetical space is a political space—and this space can make theatre revolutionary. One hundred years ago, W. B. Yeats founded the Abbey Theatre, now the National Theatre of Ireland, in revolution. He was motivated by a nation needing poetic drama at its heart to survive and to show its true nature. To my mind, this is what Naomi Wallace does for the American stage, brilliantly bridging a universe from small town to global power and destruction. Theatre cannot be strictly controlled. It needs mistakes and interference. The theatre has a history of embracing its intelligentsia and audience, which it is in danger of losing in an over-commercialized world. The important theatre writer confronts that.

When I first met Naomi, she was essentially a poet. If you don't start out with her poems first, you miss out, because the language that she has invented comes from her seriousness as a poet, her radicalism as a poet, and the fact that she flourished at The Playwrights Workshop at the University of Iowa, a university that has been a crucible for poetry and literature. I taught her there briefly in the early 1900s. She was ready to march on campus in the Doc Martens of the time. There was a spirited fever of feminism. For a moment, women called the tune in educational and intellectual circles, catching up with a world dominated by out-of-date authority and power. Future prize-winning playwrights such as Rebecca Gilman and David Hancock provoked and improvised. Naomi plunged into this generation with an authority balanced by a huge political commitment to her country and the world and a familiarity with the political history of Cuba and Mexico on the one hand and the plight of the Palestinians and the Iraqis on the other. At night, with her growing family, she retreated to a curious stretch of Iowa river that I would visit for its sun-bathing turtles and its nearby redneck bar.

My great practical value for Naomi when she moved to Britain after graduating from Iowa was to get her an agent. I also directed *In the Sweat* (co-written by Naomi and Bruce McLeod) for the Youth Festival at the National Theatre in London in 1998 and *The Fever Chart* for Mill Mountain Theatre in Roanoke, Virginia in 2007. As teachers, Naomi and I have often teamed up, double-checking with each other when the tide seems to be going the wrong way in the institution, theatre, or college, against the individual.

We both shared a connection with a talented young writer named Joshua Casteel, discovered by Naomi as a 29-year-old undergraduate. He was a Midwesterner and a Christian. At 16, he had signed his education expenses away to the United States army with an ideological belief in all that is good about America. His home was in Cedar Rapids where the individual connects with farmstead, fields, and bars to give us an 'ache' that stays with us, a yearning reflected in an American tradition of playwriting from O'Neill to Williams to Shepard—and of course, Wallace herself. Joshua graduated from Army training in Arabic in three months. He was flown into Abu Ghraib as part of the American military cleanup there: a descent into a private hell. He became a conscientious objector and returned as a postgraduate to Iowa to write a brilliant play, *Returns: A Meditation in Post Trauma*.

I directed *Returns* in Iowa as part of Josh's studies and the play went on to be produced in Chicago, Princeton, New York, and Dublin. In a way, it was an apotheosis of a Naomi Wallace education: attention to the detail of the work but with full participation as the final act. The role of a playwright, represented by both Naomi and Joshua, is to communicate with the audience and then go out and *do*. Tragically, in the summer of 2012, Joshua Casteel died of cancer, contaminated from guarding fire dumps in the fields of Baghdad. At that time, Naomi was fighting for the release of Zakaria Zubeidi, cofounder of the Freedom Theatre in Jenin, being held without charge by the Palestinian Authority. Joshua Casteel's final piece of writing, two weeks before his death, warned of the dangers of war contamination for the farmers and inhabitants of Iraq. He had an unfinished commission for a play about Jackson Pollock. I have a letter from Naomi expressing regret: "I wish I'd had permission from Joshua to work on it with him...but of course one couldn't ask such things in the end."

With this elegiac example in mind, I keep returning to the notion of Naomi's plays (and her teaching as well) as a poetical space. And the poetical is always political. Think of Beckett. When I worked with Beckett (during my time at Riverside Studios), one of my tasks would be to open his mail. I would find letters from ordinary people saying, "I'm halfway through my strike as a coal miner, and I couldn't get out of bed in the morning if it wasn't for your work." Visionaries like Beckett and Naomi Wallace communicate to people in a very individual, private way. People find a release from the tedium of theatre in their work. They find a language for which they *yearn*, a language ordinary theatre is not giving them. As a poet, playwright, teacher, and activist, Naomi invites us to find this language and to engage with each other and the world. This is her particular gift to actors, directors, spectators, and other playwrights in these troubled times that call for radical change in theatre and in the world.

Some of the people she has worked with—director Juliano Mer Khamis in Palestine or the soldier-playwright Joshua Casteel—are no longer with us, but the work remains. The revolutionary thread persists.

Ismail Khalidi

Being the "Other": Naomi Wallace and The Middle East

Ismail Khalidi is a poet, actor, and playwright whose plays include Truth Serum Blues, Final Status, *and* Tennis in Nablus, *which premiered at the Alliance Theatre in Atlanta in 2010. He is currently co-editing an anthology of Palestinian plays and, with Naomi Wallace, adapting Ghassan Kanafani's* Return to Haifa *for the stage. He holds an MFA in Dramatic Writing from NYU's Tisch School of the Arts and serves on the board of the Friends of Jenin Freedom Theatre.*

* * *

I first read and then saw *In the Heart of America* as a 21-year-old student. The play entered my life at a moment when, as a Palestinian-American, I found myself alienated, angry, and without hope in a post-9/11 United States overflowing with war, racism, and torture. I was struck by Naomi Wallace's masterful and poetic storytelling. It was revelatory to see an American writer tackle the Middle East and the ever-taboo subject of Palestine with such nuance and imagination and at the same time such a fierce sense of justice and such a firm and courageous grasp on history. To connect the Gulf War with Palestine and Vietnam as well as with racism and homophobia in the United States, as Naomi does so seamlessly in *In the Heart of America*, was to me a subversive act of solidarity and a stroke of genius.

Over the next three years I would come to know Naomi's wider body of work and would be lucky enough to work with her as an actor on a workshop of *21 Positions* at the Playwrights Center in Minneapolis and then, in 2007, on a production of *The Fever*

Chart. Since then, Naomi has been an invaluable mentor, friend, and colleague as I have tried in my own writing to tackle the question of Palestine for American audiences in the face of varying degrees of misunderstanding, censorship, and at times, downright bigotry.

In fact, in many ways it was my initial encounter with Naomi's plays on Palestine and the Middle East that helped push me towards the theatre as a life's work. They helped to instill in me a gnawing hope that there is indeed a place for the question of Palestine in the American theatre, a place that can engage both artistically and politically and that can combine multiple views of history—all the while infused with an instinctive belief in magic and, as she herself says, "a ruthless, carnivalesque sense of hope."

Such hope is imperative when faced with the ongoing injustice in Palestine and even more so in resisting the Orwellian twisting of language and logic employed in mainstream media in order to provide cover for the vilification and erasure of Palestinians and Palestine respectively.

Naomi Wallace is something of an anomaly when it comes to Americans who have written about the Middle East for the stage. One reason is that she vigorously and actively avoids the pith-helmeted gaze so often present in the work of American writers who delve into the Middle East with only their *New York Times* subscription and a surplus of well-meaning liberal guilt to guide them. To do this, Naomi travels and undertakes rigorous research about the region, its people, and politics. But she also possesses a natural aversion to the imperial gaze and in turn an unforced solidarity with the victims of Empire, Power, and Capital. For this reason, there always remains in Naomi's work a poetry that is all her own and which she does not abandon in search of the voice of the elusive 'other.'

In fact, it is precisely because she refuses to differentiate between 'us' and the 'other' in her plays that she is able to write about the Middle East just as intimately as she might delve into a Kentucky night. It is her sensitivity and openness to the particular and the universal that makes her Palestinian characters feel as real as her British or American characters. Wallace understands that, "We are already and always complicit, interconnected and related to the stranger, the Other, the unfamiliar," and so she commits an "act of trespass" in order to better erase those invented borders erected between all of us by the powerful. As she writes in the January 2013 issue of *American Theatre*:

> Mainstream theatre does not generally enter into the lives and bodies of those we consider "strangers." Writing that does not actually violate boundaries, that does not enter into the process of trespass, is often a writing that is safe, consumable and shallow. A theatre that does not challenge its own assumptions, its own ignorance, with curiosity and humility is a contracted theatre, a diminished theatre. (Wallace 2013, 88)

Naomi Wallace does not shy from the politics or the history of her subject(s). This, of course, does not mean her characters are always 'real' in the sense of inhabiting a universe governed by realism. On the contrary, her characters—whether African American, white American, Welsh, Mexican or Palestinian, rich or poor—can all be heightened and thus inhabit worlds full of magic, poetry, and mystery. By infusing the carnivalesque into the real and into the historical and political moments and beings of her work, Naomi allows us all at once to get closer to her characters and to step back in order to better see the bigger picture.

In this way, Naomi's theatre sets new standards by which we judge what we see and hear on stage. It lowers our tolerance for safe and shallow works and makes us suitably cautious of the sentimentality and the didacticism (both real and imagined) often associated with 'political' theatre. The brilliance of Naomi's work on the Middle East and in general is her ability to depict history without lecture and the 'other' without the orientalist gaze. Her writing is itself an act of solidarity with the most vulnerable and downtrodden of humanity, the 'wretched of the earth,' the 'disremembered.' In her capable hands, the dead speak, the living rhyme, and Kentucky is London is Baghdad is Alabama is Palestine.

Dominique Hollier

Translating Wallace

Dominique Hollier *is a Paris-based actor, translator, and dramaturg with credits in film, television, and theatre. She has translated many Naomi Wallace plays into French, including* In the Heart of America, The Trestle at Pope Lick Creek, The Inland Sea, Things of Dry Hours, The Fever Chart, And I and Silence, *as well as* One Flea Spare, *which in 2012 was introduced into the permanent repertoire of the Comédie-Française.*

* * *

Translating for the stage is more like acting than writing. Whether through the voice and body of the actor or the other language of the translator, it's a matter of understanding the essence of the characters and language, making them your own, and delivering them so as to convey in the best possible way the thoughts, feelings, and music of the playwright. It's a matter of showing what the words *do*, rather than what they *are*. I myself am not a writer. I am an actress, and I have always considered my translating work to be very close to that of an actor.

Naomi Wallace's plays are a blessing for actors. I have never met an actor who has read one of her plays and not wanted to be in it. Her characters are always so 'real,' so alive, and concrete. Her plays never present what we call in France a *débat d'idées*. Their power and meaning stem from the bodies and minds of her characters. You don't feel like you are sitting through a lecture about the powerful and the oppressed. It's not a matter of proclaiming "war is wrong and the Israelis should not oppress Palestinians that way," but saying simply, as in *Between This Breath and You*, "my son is still alive in you." Whatever the situation, each play focuses on the humanity of individual characters with clarity and generosity. Any political 'message' derives from there.

I have translated quite a few Wallace plays by now. Naomi has always been incredibly open to my questions, which makes the work all the more interesting. *One Flea Spare* is the first one I read, and I immediately fell in love with her writing, for both its political and poetical qualities, probably because of the unbelievably deft combination of the two. Naomi's words are a pleasure to translate. I try to render them in a way that fits her unique style, so inventive and creative, not ordinary, so that as soon as you start reading (just as in English) you know it's a Naomi Wallace play. Rhymes and songs are always a fun challenge. For example, in *One Flea Spare*, all things related to ships and knots have exotic, evocative names. This called for lots of research and brain wracking in order to find names that convey the same kind of images in French as in English. Plays like *The Fever Chart* or *In the Heart of America* call for a slightly different approach because the language is more contemporary and characters may come from different geographical and social backgrounds. This is more difficult to convey in French, especially if you want to retain the poetical charge.

It is highly significant that *One Flea Spare* (which I have translated as *Une puce, épargnez-la*) has entered the permanent repertory of the Comédie-Française. Very few contemporary playwrights have been voted into the repertory by the committee members of this government-subsidized national theatre. These include Pinter, Tom Stoppard, and Dario Fo. Tennessee Williams has work in the permanent repertory, and Tony Kushner's work has been done by members of the company, but it is not in the permanent repertory. Naomi is the only living American playwright to be granted this honor.

Audiences at the Comédie-Française were often disturbed by *Une puce, épargnez-la*. I mean this in a good way. It was an aesthetically admirable piece of work. People discovering Naomi's work for the first time seemed to be very impressed by the strength and originality of her writing. I think the French public was particularly happy to see such powerful female figures in a play. Some critics spoke of her as "a female contemporary Shakespeare." The press was for the most part very enthusiastic, though some mainstream papers had a more tepid reaction, perhaps due in part to the fact that the play was done in the main house where people are more accustomed to seeing classic plays. Had the play been done in the smaller Studio-Théâtre where more contemporary work is done, reactions would probably have been different. But fact that it was produced in the seven-hundred-seat Théâtre-Éphémère was in itself a major event. It is a mystery to me why it took so long for a French theatre to produce *One Flea Spare*, but the Comédie-Française production signals a growing interest in Naomi's work in France, aided in part by the steady work of her publisher (Editions Théâtrales). The Maison Antoine Vitez (MAV), a subsidized organization dedicated to the translating of plays from all over the world, has been a strong supporter from the beginning, and I have received multiple grants from the MAV for translations of her plays. The "MAV" label on a play usually speaks in favor of it, prompting directors and companies in the subsidized public sector to look into her published plays and inquire about any unpublished work. There have been many public readings at festivals around the country, and audiences always respond strongly and enthusiastically. Many people in the theatre world in France—be it in the Centre National du Theatre (CNT) or reading committees in major public theatres and festivals—recognize her as one of the strongest and most important voices in contemporary theatre.

Raz Shaw

Betting on Naomi and The Boss

Raz Shaw is a prolific director who has worked extensively nationally and internationally for, amongst others, Shakespeare's Globe, Soho Theatre, The Royal Court, The Royal Exchange, The Gate Theatre, The Arcola and Salisbury Playhouse. In 2006 he was awarded the Jerwood Directors Award at the Young Vic. He has directed several Naomi Wallace plays, including the European premiere of Things of Dry Hours *at Manchester Royal Exchange and the Gate Theatre/London.*

* * *

Naomi Wallace has played a huge part in my life.

Before I had even met her, her plays taught me life, love, and humanity. They taught me about the power and beauty of the surprising and the unexpected. They taught me that being a radical doesn't exclude you from having a heart. More to the point, a radical without a heart is not a radical.

Sometime around 2002, I was looking for a play that would speak to me. I thought that would be easy. But so many plays seemed a bit ordinary to me, not striving very hard or saying too much or pushing the envelope far enough. And they didn't seem to be saying what I needed to say at that time. I couldn't even tell you what that was, but I hoped that if I found the right play I would know.

I had heard of Naomi Wallace and had been told by more than one person about the brilliance of *One Flea Spare*. A friend recommended her anthology, and when he pointed out that she had written the screenplay for *Lawn Dogs* I knew I had to read her stuff. *Lawn Dogs* is one of my favorite films of all time. If you haven't seen it, you must. It has beauty, grace, oddness, the power of an underdog, a splash of strange sex, and unique, unconventional relationships: in other words, pure Naomi Wallace.

The last play in the anthology was *The Trestle at Pope Lick Creek*. I got thoroughly lost in it and instantly knew it was the one. When I pitched it to Thea Sharrock, then Artistic Director of Southwark Playhouse, the clearest way I could describe it was like a perfectly formed Bruce Springsteen song. Despite the darkness of the world it is set in, it is unusually and unexpectedly positive. Thea got the play and the Bruce Springsteen reference. (She has taste, so she would.) It remains possibly the most elegant, lyrical, and passionate play that I have ever directed.

In fact, Bruce Springsteen and Naomi Wallace have many things in common. Bruce Springsteen says that he writes about the gap between the American dream and the American reality. So does Naomi Wallace. They both have the genius to find the light and beauty in the harshest and hardest of situations. They know how to make you gasp, laugh, and cry in one heartbeat. And they both believe passionately in the beauty and strength of the human spirit. So on our first meeting, when I was trying to convince her to give me the rights, I hesitatingly asked whether she was a fan, knowing how some people just don't get Bruce and this might blow the deal. Thankfully she was.

Directing *The Trestle at Pope Lick Creek* taught me many things. It taught me the power and beauty of simple, spare theatrical moments. The feather blowing moment in the middle of the play, for instance, says more about the instinctive emotional connection between Pace and Dalton than any words could. Plus it's echoingly transfixing. It showed me how power within a play is driven by walking the fine line between emotional expression and emotional restraint. Spoon-feeding the audience is mostly never interesting and watching an actor cry onstage is often a lot less interesting and powerful than watching an actor/character full of emotion try their darnedest *not* to let it out. A trembly lip moves an audience more than a flood of tears, usually.

Most of all, it taught me that Naomi was a unique talent whose constant desire to tell stories illuminating the heart and soul and political hunger of the disaffected and disabused was often moving and always inspiring. I knew I wouldn't rest until we had worked together on a new play at some point in the future.

After *Trestle*, I directed Naomi's *A State of Innocence* at Theatre 503 in 2005. It is a 40-minute play that sums up everything that is great about Naomi's work: beautiful, eloquent, angry, raw, magical, passionate, elusive, lyrical, and always singular. I also directed the staged reading of *Rawalpindi*, which was commissioned by and for the National Theatre. The play is stuffed full of ideas. In a way, it is über-Naomi. It is wonderfully out there. So out there that it is impossible to ignore it, but at the same time almost impossible to imagine a management producing it, sadly. And in 2007, I directed the British premiere of *Things of Dry Hours*, a play that merges the political and the personal in a wonderfully overt and unashamed way.

Our working relationship is often fiery, sometimes confrontational, but always creative, theatrically thrilling and unique. In 2009, we were asked to team up on a kind of role-reversal project. The new writing theatre company, Paines Plough, approached directors and writers who had worked together a lot and asked the writer to create a short play for that director to perform. The writer would direct it. This would prove to be Naomi's ultimate revenge! It was just ten minutes long and was only going to be seen for one night at The Soho Theatre, but in a way this was some of the best work we've ever done together.

Other people did funny stuff, lighter stuff. Trust Naomi and me not to tow the conventional path. Naomi wanted to write a play based on the three things about me that interested her most—my cancer, my gambling addiction, and my obsession with Bruce Springsteen. We spent many hours, both face to face and on the phone, discussing themes, ideas, and stories. Through research and instinct, Naomi managed to weave those three strands together and make a piece that skates a beautiful path between reality and fantasy and more incredibly somehow manages to get under my skin and jump deep into my psyche.

The play is called *Word's a Slave*. I believe my performance was definitive. Or is that derivative? And my singing was indescribable. And not in a good way. I'll leave the singing to The Boss. Bruce that is, not Naomi. (Though she may well be the other boss!) Naomi's direction was fierce, relentless, and particular, and it produced a rather extraordinary piece of work. Here is a brief excerpt:

> So here I am, holding my breath and dancing the canary, dealing the medicine of the Blackjack God to my right and to my left, and turning my skin over and over and inside out again and again and I'm just

losing and I'm just losing and I'm just losing but then I'm almost winning and I'm almost winning and I'm losing again, I'm losing again, I will not get up from this table I will not get up from this cunting table because it feels too good and I can win again and it feels too good and I will win again.

And then it's silent. The canary stops singing.

Sure it can kill you. The gambling, the praying, whatever you want to call it. The cancer too. But then there's almost nothing in this world that won't. Kill you. But before it does, it'll flash your blood and send a sting of heat 'cross your gums, down your throat and into your gut. It's a kind of sustenance.

Naomi, too, is a kind of sustenance. As I go forward on other projects, from Shakespeare to new writing to comedy, I am aware of the thread that connects the shows I choose to work on: big plays, personal plays, plays about finding your own moral code, theatre that is both accessible and ambitious, theatre that is wild, energetic, sometimes fierce, sometimes left-field, a little bit sexy and often surprisingly positive. Material that is ambitious, passionate, and brave. All these things are embodied in Naomi Wallace's writing, which is why I know we will work together again. Or hope we will. Where else am I going to get my emotional education?

Erin B. Mee

Mindscapes of Palestine

Erin B. Mee *is a theatre scholar, activist, and director who has worked at New York Theatre Workshop, The Public Theater, The Guthrie Theater, the Magic Theatre, and in India. She is the author of* The Theatre of Roots: Redirecting the Modern Indian Stage *(2008), co-editor (with Helene Foley) of* Antigone on the Contemporary World Stage *(2011), and editor of* Drama Contemporary: India *(2001). She is Assistant Professor and Faculty Fellow in the English Department at New York University.*

* * *

When Naomi Wallace and I went to the West Bank in 2011 on a trip organized by New York Theatre Workshop, we met Juliano Mer Khamis, artistic director of The Freedom Theatre (TFT) in Jenin. He explained to us his mission to create a venue to support the Palestinian people in their struggle for liberation with art, poetry, music, film, and theatre. My learning curve on that trip was vertical, and Naomi was one of many guides who helped me navigate and understand the mindscapes of Palestine. We became both friends and colleagues.

Mer Khamis was murdered on April 4, 2011, shortly after our return. Naomi and I mourned his loss by co-writing several letters to the editor of *The Guardian* about The Freedom Theatre; she helped me with a piece I wrote for *TDR*; we cowrote an article (with Ismail Khalidi) about TFT for *American Theater* magazine; and we embarked on editing a collection of Palestinian plays (with Ismail Khalidi) to be published by Theatre Communications Group. When one of TFT's cofounders, Zakaria Zubeidi, began a hunger strike in prison, we wrote and called and organized to get him released—and we sent each other daily messages of support and encouragement.

With Naomi, theatre, politics, and writing are intertwined. She encourages that intertwining in my work, too. When we write together, we pass ideas and paragraphs and sentences back and forth, we brainstorm, we change our minds again and again, and we edit each other's work so that I can no longer tell who has written what. This is the generosity of Naomi's process, an embodied politics that is exemplified in both the style and content of *Twenty-One Positions: A Cartographic Dream of the Middle East*, which she co-wrote with Abdelfattah Abusrour and Lisa Schlesinger.

Twenty-One Positions follows Fawaz, a Palestinian-American man who arrives in the West Bank for his estranged brother's wedding, only to find that his brother has disappeared. Fawaz confronts the realities of Occupation: he is stopped at a checkpoint, rescued by a young girl whose school has disappeared, and thrown in an Israeli prison. He discovers, eventually, that his brother has been shot down by the Israeli military while hang gliding over the Wall to pick a rare single bee orchid for his wife Hala on their wedding day.

Plays that acknowledge the Palestinian point of view usually do so by creating a binary opposition between an Israeli and a Palestinian in 'dialogue' with each other, by giving audiences a single person's experience in a solo performance, or by retelling the events of 1948 from the Palestinian perspective in a historical play. Naomi and her coauthors set *Twenty-One Positions* in the mindscapes of those living under Occupation: Rund, a young girl who fixes a map by eating all the towns that have been taken over or occupied since 1948 and enacts a scene in which pencils "escape" from her schoolbag and are rounded up by soldiers; the architect of the Wall who carefully replants all the flower bulbs that have been displaced by its construction, but not the houses or schools; and Rashid, who sails over the Wall in a homemade glider. This is Palestine as portrayed in *Twenty-One Positions*.

Without denying the political realities—indeed, while calling attention to them—Wallace, Abusrour, and Schlesinger celebrate the strength and complexities of these characters. *Twenty-One Positions* is a surreal exploration of an all-too-real situation and its effect on the dreamscapes of those who live under Occupation. The characters suffer, but they are not victims: they are strong, compassionate, generous, resourceful, creative. They are survivors, and they continue to survive with their humanity intact. Rund lost a sock at a checkpoint because "it didn't hold up to interrogation" and she lost her school when "the Wall came through and round and snatched it," but she has not lost her determination. "I am a bulb," she tells Danny T., master-builder and architect of the Wall. "You are a girl," he tells her. "No," she insists, "I have an underground storage system that allows me to survive under difficult circumstances." Rund's aunt Maryam, who quit school when she couldn't get through the checkpoints to take her exams, went to work for the United Nations and still places her faith in articles of law. "One day," she vows, "I'm going to make those articles believe in us." While everyone is focused on "facts on the ground"—maps, measurements, surveys, and archeological digs designed to prove that the origins of Israelite civilization can be found near Jerusalem—Rashid flies his glider above it all. He sees another world. A world of breeze, movement, freedom, open space. He offers us the possibility of another perspective, another way of life. Rashid tells Hala he will bring her back a gift. That gift is his ability to dream, to fly over the Wall.

This is the Palestine I continue to visit—the country where I collaborate with theatre artists to create new 'intertwinings' of ideas and visions for the future. Encouraged and inspired by Naomi's approach to the world, I try to create new maps of the mind.

Naomi's ultimate message is that this is not the only world. We must redefine the ways we think in order to envision and create a more just world. This viewpoint, her mindscape, her political stance, is not only the subject of her plays; it is embodied in the way she works and in her style of writing.

Jo Bonney

Directing Wallace

Jo Bonney *is a stage director who has worked in theatres in New York, around the United States and internationally with a wide range of contemporary playwrights, including Lynn Nottage, Eve Ensler, Neil LaBute, Suzan-Lori Parks, José Rivera, Charles Fuller, Danny Hoch, and Eric Bogosian. She directed the American premiere of Naomi Wallace's* The Fever Chart *for the Public Theatre Lab in 2008 and the world premiere of* The Hard Weather Boating Party *at the Actors Theatre of Louisville's Humana Festival of New American Plays in 2009. She is the recipient of a 1998 Obie Award for Sustained Excellence in Directing and the editor of* Extreme Exposure: An Anthology of Solo Performance Texts from the Twentieth Century.

* * *

Naomi's plays are very much about language. She gives her characters the gift of eloquence, of a lyrical form of speech, almost as if this is the language in their heart or the language of their imagination let loose. They are wonderful storytellers, as is Naomi. She comes from Kentucky and is part of the extraordinary history of Southern storytelling—although her stories take place all over the world. The characters in *The Fever Chart* and *The Hard Weather Boating Party* are everyday people: an Israeli soldier, a Palestinian mother, Kentucky factory workers, a Moroccan-Israeli who mops hospital floors at night. Some have an education but lack opportunities, others have little formal education, but they all give eloquent expression to the memory of a lost loved one or a vision of a hoped-for future or a longing for a dream unrealized. Naomi allows us to hear these people in a fresh way; a way that cuts through the stereotypes.

The language is delicious to work with, both for the actors and the director, but something I became aware of early in the process of working with Naomi is that although the language is heightened and the circumstances at times fantastical, her work is very grounded. You may have a character delivering an incredibly lyrical, poetic monologue, but this is a character who is speaking of a real incident, of a real moment of loss or pain or joy, so the work asks of you as the director to ground it and to encourage the actors to deliver her language with simplicity. It's a little like the work of José Rivera, who I've collaborated with a number of times. He also often works in a heightened style; some people call it "magic realism," although I tend to shy away from labels like that. The trap is to fall into the idea that you're working with characters who behave outside our everyday reality.

The Fever Chart consists of three short plays. In the first one, *A State of Innocence*, Um Hisham, a Palestinian woman whose daughter has been killed by Israeli bullets, tells of the death of Yuval the Israeli soldier, shot by a Palestinian sniper, and how she cradled him in her arms as he died, something she could not do for her own daughter. It's a long, beautifully detailed speech and I remember that Naomi in the stage directions specifically indicates, "She just tells the story. She doesn't relive it." We had an amazing cast and they were all very emotionally, personally, invested in this material, so part of my job on this particular speech was to support that investment but to watch that it never tipped into a melodramatic reliving of the moment. Um Hisham does not indulge the story emotionally. She's a survivor and must relive this moment everyday, although the greatness of her loss vibrates just under the surface at all times. The words are doing the work. Both *The Fever Chart* and *The Hard Weather Boating Party* are peopled with characters dealing with loss and pain, betrayal and misunderstanding, often suspicious of each other but trying to communicate in difficult circumstances. So one of the unexpected pleasures of directing Naomi's plays was discovering how much humor is them—sometimes black humor, sometimes a wonderful silliness that counters the weight of the situations. There's a lot of room for personal interpretation and physical comedy. It just asks for a very light hand.

Naomi's language and stories are rich, dense. You don't read a play of hers once and grasp the whole of it. The interplay of the characters, the references, the sense of humor, the juxtaposition of the ugly and the beautiful, the real and the surreal are slowly revealed. The tangible world we put our hands on sits very close to the intangible world of dreamscape, metaphor, and the unconscious. The play often does not reveal itself until deep into the process. If you're going to be in a rehearsal room eight hours a day running scenes over and over, you want to work on something that keeps revealing itself and revealing itself and presenting hidden little meanings. The preview period in front of an audience becomes incredibly important: you can see "Oh, they're not getting that. Great, they're getting that. Oh, they think that's funny, but we thought it was serious." It keeps the whole process very alive. And that's the pleasure of working with a playwright like Naomi. She's right there, engaged the entire time.

Abdelfattah Abusrour

Beautiful Resistance

Abdelfattah Abusrour is a writer, actor, and painter who cofounded the Alrowwad Cultural and Theatre Training Society, an independent, community-based center for artistic, cultural, and theatre training for children and youth in Aida Refugee Camp near Bethlehem. For his work with Alrowwad, he was the first Palestinian to be named an Ashoka Fellow. He has been the president of the Palestinian Theatre League since 2009.

* * *

In March 1998, with a group of friends, I founded Alrowwad Cultural and Theatre Training Society (ACTS) in my two-room family house in Aida refugee camp in Bethlehem. The Aida camp was established in 1950 to house refugees from over 40 villages uprooted from their homes from 1947 onwards, one of 59 camps in total in an area rented by the United Nations Relief and Works Agency (UNRWA) for 99 years. It effectively made us visitors and exiles in our country, with no right of return to our homes. The camp is located north of Bethlehem, south of Jerusalem, surrounded by a wall illegally built in 2002, first as barbwire and then converted in 2005 to blocks of cement eight meters high. It is guarded by Israeli snipers and surveillance cameras. Of the six thousand people who live here now, 66 percent are under 18 years old. The camp has no playgrounds or green spaces.

I was born in the Aida refugee camp. I was lucky to get a scholarship to continue my studies in France, where I got my PhD in biological and medical engineering and developed my artistic work as a painter, playwright, and actor. I returned to Palestine after nine years in France thinking that Palestine was only waiting for me to save it!

With some friends I established Alrowwad with a philosophy that I call "Beautiful Resistance" against the ugliness of occupation and its violence. It was our way to provide a place within this rented space where theatre, arts, culture, and education could be a means for children and young people to express themselves in positive, constructive, and nonviolent ways. It was important to help children and young people see the potential for their creativity and the power of the arts in building hope in times of despair. We want to celebrate their successes. We want them to grow up and to think that they can change the world and create miracles without the need to carry a gun and shoot everybody else or explode themselves or burn themselves up in protest. We want them to stay alive.

Although the situation has not changed and Israeli soldiers of occupation still make incursions into our camp, we still believe that the values of justice, freedom, equality, peace, love, and human rights are values we share with all human beings around the world, regardless of color or religion or race or ethnicity. At Alrowwad, despite the difficulties of running programs, we do what we have to do. We have created "friends of Alrowwad"—individuals who support and volunteer on different levels. We tour our mobile programs and shows locally and internationally in order to build bridges and to create an image of Palestine that is not usually shown in the media, representing ourselves to the world as human beings who claim and defend their humanity, not as people born with genes of hatred or violence.

When I first met with Naomi Wallace in 2002 it was after her family had been in Palestine during the Israeli invasion of Bethlehem that spring. Three of her sisters and her mother were visiting at that time in solidarity with the Palestinian people. Her sister Carla and four other people from Louisville, Kentucky, were part of a group of Americans and internationals who stayed with us in Aida Refugee Camp during many days of that siege. Carla Wallace is a great friend of Alrowwad Theatre, and she talked about my work to Naomi, who then came to visit with British director David Gothard. She talked about the idea of bringing American playwrights to connect with Palestinian playwrights, and I worked with her to coordinate this visit.

In September 2002, she came to us with Tony Kushner, Lisa Schlesinger, Kia Corthron, Robert O'Hara, and Betty Shamieh. It was a time of great discovery for all of us. We talked about possible partnerships and how American artists and playwrights could provide support to Palestinian theatres and artists. The six playwrights published a beautiful article in *American Theatre* magazine. My friendship with the playwrights developed, and most of them became supporters of Alrowwad. Some returned to work with us or other Palestinian theatres.

In 2004, Naomi proposed to Lisa Schlesinger and me that the three of us should co-write a play commissioned by the Guthrie Theatre. Of course, we both accepted, even without knowing if it would work. There were so many questions: What were we going to write about? How were we going to write it? Should we have a play that involved Americans and Palestinians? Or Americans of Palestinian origin? Looking around us, we saw a growing apartheid wall of 6–12 meters of cement, rising in the West Bank, taking more land from Palestinians, and clearly not about security – not even according to Israelis themselves. A wall that completely suffocated the Aida refugee camp.

So we started developing ideas and wrote individual scenes and read over what each other wrote and suggested modifications and kept going. There was a great spirit of collaboration in writing our play *Twenty-One Positions*, and by the end we didn't really know who wrote what. No egos, no selfishness, and also no compromises: just real commitment from the three of us to create a play that we were satisfied with.

In the end, we created a play about two American-Palestinian brothers. One decides to come back to his parents' country of origin, Palestine, where he falls in love with his cousin, who is an intelligent, educated engineer, and decides to marry her. The other brother comes to Palestine for his brother's wedding, even though this is the last place he wants to be. He witnesses firsthand what it is like to go through Israeli controls at the airport and at checkpoints and what it is like to live behind a wall. When he arrives, it turns out his brother is missing and even his fiancée does not know where to find him. The journey to find his brother, his meeting with this little girl who sneaks through a hole in the wall to reach her school, his encounter with an Iraqi Jew and with the designer of the wall, all of this influences his vision and his decisions about the future.

The reception of *Twenty-One Positions* varied depending on the audience. Some felt that it was pro-Palestinian because it showed the story from a Palestinian point of view. They wanted a more diplomatic play showing the two points of views, even though both are present to a certain level in the play. Others loved it, of course. But for us, as playwrights, the question remains: since when is theatre about diplomacy and showing the two points of view of oppressor and oppressed? Rapist and victim? An apartheid system and victims of this apartheid system? The Holocaust and Hitler's justification of what he has done? Theatre is about change, about provocation, about asking hard questions, not about compromises and diplomacy or being politically correct. Theatre is about challenging stereotypes and presenting stories of the oppressed.

When you look at Naomi's writing and the passion with which she writes, there is always a focus on showing the humanity behind the characters. It is clear that her plays never compromise. Naomi would be much more produced by American theatres if she followed the stream of politically correct plays. She does not. And that is one of the great strengths of her work.

Naomi Wallace is a great friend, as well as a very interesting playwright and human being. She is sensitive to injustice. She fights for freedom, pushing beyond expected boundaries. Her work is based upon intensive research, very detailed and deep, and it brings us characters that we might never otherwise meet on stage. She is a fine artist of words and feelings who tackles taboo subjects in politics. Whether she brings Palestine or Iraq or other injustices on stage or goes to subjects from centuries ago, she explores systems and challenges power.

I, as a Palestinian, know how much this kind of work is needed and appreciated. I am not a believer in "Art for Art's sake" or in theatre that is detached from life and reality. I believe in theatre that creates a change and irritates and provokes people and asks the hard questions and pushes people to think and analyze and find their own answers. Theatre is not about stereotypes or demonizing the 'other' or propaganda or giving answers and telling people what they want to hear. It is about continuous action. Naomi's theatre in my opinion does all of this. She surprises us with the profound humanity of her characters. She gives breath to an engaged theatre that challenges and irritates and undermines power structures. Theatre needs more writers like Naomi Wallace, who remind us of how human we are in this often inhuman world that we share.

Robin D. G. Kelley

The Facts of Love

Robin D. G. Kelley is the Gary B. Nash Professor of American History at UCLA. He is the author of more half a dozen works of history, including Thelonious Monk: The Life and Times of an Amerian Original *(2009)*, Freedom Dreams: The Black Radical Imagination *(2002), and* Hammer and Hoe: Alabama Communists During the Great Depresssion *(1990), which was the inspiration and basis for* Things of Dry Hours. *His research and teaching interests extend to the history of labor and radical movements in the United States, Africa, and the African Diaspora, as well as intellectual and cultural history, especially music and visual culture. He has held teaching appointments, fellowships, or residencies at Southeastern Massachusetts University, Emory, University of Michigan, Brooklyn College, Dartmouth, NYU, Columbia, USC, and Oxford University.*

* * *

My country loves me. That's why it's killing me. It's killing my father. Those are the facts. Those are the facts of love.

—Dalton Chance, from The Trestle at Pope Lick Creek

"I'm working on a play inspired by your book, *Hammer and Hoe*, and before I proceed I wanted to make sure it was all right with you." It was Naomi Wallace on the other end of the line. The trepidation in her voice was palpable, though it paled in comparison with the combination of sheer terror and excitement that came over me as she spoke. She had read my book about the Communist Party in Alabama during the 1930s and apparently liked it enough to set her next play in that milieu.

I don't remember what I said in response besides "yes, of course, I'm honored." My friend and fellow historian Peter Rachleff had introduced me to her work a couple of years earlier, and it blew me away. After reading *Slaughter City*, one of the great meditations on labor history, love, solidarity, and power, I devoured *In the Heart of America*, Wallace's take on the culture of war through love and memory and ghosts, and then I leapt head first into *One Flea Spare*, her hilarious send-up of ruling class mores and morality. All of her plays appealed to me in part because they are brilliant history—and by brilliant I don't just mean smart but radiant, resplendent, sharp, clear. Besides capturing the naturally poetic language of ordinary people, she takes social context, personal experience, relations of power, memory, desire, and the psyche and folds them all out like a Cubist painting and then reveals the connections between them. The surrealist and magical elements in her plays do not flee reality or escape history, but instead they illuminate the places where material reality and imagination meet—in the unconscious, in the accumulation of suppressed emotions, in those electric moments when human choices and actions are unpredictable. *The Trestle at Pope Lick Creek*, for example, undercuts the myth that Depression-era America was dominated by despair and hopelessness. Despair certainly hung in the air, but Naomi discovers glimmers of hope and action through expressions of desire, sensual connection, honest and direct language, a fierce defiance of symbols of capital (i.e., freight trains and factory bosses). No need for dramatic stories of socialists or fascists to illustrate a feeling for rebellion. Revolution is embodied.

So when she called me that afternoon some 13 years ago, I had already become a devoted fan, despite having not yet seen her work on stage.

Things of Dry Hours is set in Alabama during the 1930s, and it is about Communists, but I wouldn't exactly call it a collaboration. Without any help from me, Naomi had completely absorbed every nuance, every argument, every detail in my book, and grasped what it meant to build a radical, interracial working-class movement in the heart of the Deep South. Violence and even death came with the territory. Black Communists' very survival depended on their invisibility, on leaving few traces behind while waging big fights for social and economic justice and political rights. This is why Party members met in the wee hours behind drawn shades and usually spread their message by planting leaflets in trees in the middle of the night, or dropping them on the ground so the wind could take them away, or hiding them in laundry baskets as they pretended to be domestic workers going into white comrades' homes. Yes, there were shootouts between black sharecroppers and sheriffs, occasional mass demonstrations in downtown Birmingham, lynchings, kidnappings, and high profile court cases involving poor black men falsely accused of raping white women.

I always thought the 'drama' resided in these violent confrontations and public events. But Naomi knew better. She set the entire play inside the home of Tice Hogan, a black Communist elder, who turns his tiny shotgun house into a secret refuge hidden in plain sight. We don't see the violence or the protests or the actual street organizing, but we know it's there. The virtually claustrophobic setting becomes a metaphor for the interior lives of Southern working people—black and white, radical and reactionary. Naomi succeeded in taking three characters and reconstructing the world I found elusive, the complex story of how people struggle to find life, love, meaning, and connection under the incredible circumstances of building a revolutionary movement in the Jim Crow South. This is exactly what great theatre does. It does not dramatize 'facts' but lays bare emotional truths, reveals what bubbles underneath the surface: in this case, Love and Desire. She revealed father–daughter love, in context of building a new society in their heads; comradely love across the color line; sexual agency and terror.

From the very first private reading of *Things of Dry Hours* at the Public Theater to its production in Pittsburgh and later in New York, I had come to see more clearly the limitations of my book and the conventional methods of writing history. Indeed, my journey with Naomi—a journey that continues to this day—has changed my approach to history. In particular, she compelled me to consider 'love,' in all of its dimensions, as a principal force in human history, perhaps *the* principal force. Not long after encountering Naomi Wallace's work, I published a book titled *Freedom Dreams* in which I wrote:

> Freedom and Love may be the most revolutionary ideas available to us, and yet as intellectuals we have failed miserably to grapple with their political and analytical importance. Despite having spent a decade and a half writing about radical social movements, I am only just beginning to see what animated, motivated, and knitted together these gatherings

of aggrieved folks. I have come to realize that once we strip radical social movements down to their bare essence and understand the collective desires of people in motion, Freedom and Love lay at the very heart of the matter (Kelley 2002, 11).

Wallace's revolutionary conception of love, not just in *Things of Dry Hours* but also in all of her plays, resonates with that of Dr. Martin Luther King Jr. who understood love as a constant struggle to build and rebuild community. Making community requires a kind of nakedness: leaving one's armor at the door, opening oneself up to others and giving freely, being vulnerable, speaking truth while allowing others their voice. Love, in other words, is not a thing one can adopt or embrace; it's a process of making community, nourishing relationships, remaking oneself over and over again. But she also reveals love's dark side—the pain, betrayal, violent passions, loss, the social oppressions that blunt, deform, or outright destroy love. Such nakedness in a world governed by power, inequality, racism, sexism, and exploitation means we love at our own risk.

Naomi Wallace continues to raise the stakes, exploring the twin themes of "Freedom and Love" in history with astonishing depth and insight. I had been reading extensively on the history of the prison-industrial complex when Naomi sent me a draft of *And I and Silence*, her poignant story of two women prisoners/ex-cons, one black, one white, who find love and each other behind bars in the era of Jim Crow, but in freedom discover that they are still incarcerated by the hidden bars of race, gender, and class. Her text was more powerful than any of the three dozen books I'd been reading, replete with an array of dizzying statistics and horrific details of prison conditions, draconian laws, and lives destroyed. Why? Because *And I and Silence* asks the question no scholarly text could ask or answer: how do human beings under those conditions muster the capacity to sustain life, imagination, and love?

Finally, her recent work, *The Liquid Plain*, wrestles with the very historical foundations of our modern world: the history of slavery. I cannot fully describe the profound impact this work has had on me, both as a historian and as a descendant of Africans in captivity. First, she understands better than most of my colleagues that the system of slavery and the trans-Atlantic slave trade brought everyone into its bloody fold: Europeans as well as Africans, children as well as adults, women as well as men, the rich as well as the dispossessed. No one was completely free. Nor had captivity turned anyone into a slave. Better than any work of formal history, *The Liquid Plain* captures what historians Peter Linebaugh and Marcus Rediker call the "Revolutionary Atlantic," the kidnapped Africans escaping bondage, the sailors resisting impressment, the laboring women fighting concubinage, the masters and owners and managers wrestling with their own dehumanization (Linebaugh and Rediker 2000). Naomi tells this story in rich, vibrant colors, capturing all of its complexities, contradictions, and cultures in flux.

But none of this fully explains the visceral impact the play had on me. The only thing that comes close is the email I sent to Naomi upon finishing the play, dashed off in that electric, orgasmic moment when my imagination has been kissed and licked and sweetly penetrated by a terror and beauty unimaginable. Let me close with a brief passage:

> I have so much more to say but I'm just trying to come to terms with what happened—both in the text and what happened to me. It's hard to explain but I have never been one to identify with enslaved Africans in an ancestral way, you know, but your play felt very personal... perhaps because of the intimacies between ALL the characters, and it is precisely that intimacy that is missing in most accounts of the Middle Passage... But *The Liquid Plain* did it for me, made me feel for the first time that I/we have inherited the pain and loss of slavery... As you always do, you've penetrated the very heart of American history and its place in the world.

Bruce McLeod

Nettle Soup

Bruce McLeod *is an essayist, playwright, screenwriter, graphic artist, scholar of English Literature, and author of* The Geography of Empire in English Literature 1580–1745 *(1999)*. *He has partnered with Naomi Wallace on numerous projects, including the plays* The Girl Who Fell Through the Hole in Her Jumper *(1994) and* In the Sweat *(1997); screenplays for* Lawn Dogs *(1997),* The War Boys *(2009),* Flying Blind *(2012), and* Cross My Mind *(2014); and raising their three children in the North of England.*

* * *

In the spring, Naomi heads into the field next to our house in Yorkshire to cut off the tender heads of stinging nettles (*Urtica doica*). She makes a great nettle soup. There is just a hint of their painful sting: an added warmth, the memory of the sting, the recoil, the itch and rash. She wears gloves of course when gathering the nettles. My part in this is to grow the onions and the potatoes (wash and peel them) and to resist the temptation to chop down or even spray the invasive nettles (which ironically do best on sites where humans have dumped their detritus, especially fertilizing phosphates).

When it comes to writing and our collaborative projects however, Naomi grasps the nettle time and time again. I am quite gentlemanly about this: I let her agonize. After all, she is THE writer, wins the awards, teaches workshops, gives lectures; she can cope with (deserves?) the pain. While I tend to approach the 'nettle' via visuals and context, a roundabout approach, Naomi has the courage to grasp it. And she doesn't let go. Or the sting doesn't subside. Often just as

I'm falling asleep, problems with a screenplay set aside for the night, Naomi will suddenly suggest a solution or present a question. If I concentrate I can almost hear her mind ticking over although I try not to because that would mean two of us sleepless. I drift off while Naomi returns to the darkened fields to continue searching through the nettles.

If she often suffers from chronic self-doubt about her own writing—usually at the start of a new project—as a co-writer she enjoys sharing the task at hand, although I usually have to 'go first.' Naomi is naturally drawn to collaboration; it gels with her disavowal of literary work being private property, something sacrosanct, the mark (as in territory) of genius. It is one of the reasons she moved from poetry to playwriting, from the solitary to solicitation. Howard Barker has recently stated, "I'm not interested in collaboration. I'm interested in getting people to realize what I'm telling them." But Naomi's interests are always with seeking out the other, to inhabit the literal meaning of to be interested, which derives, as Eric Fromm notes, from the Latin *inter esse*, i.e., "to be among." In this spirit, she has often invited me to add songs or a scene to her plays, showing only gratitude and generosity for such irresponsible intrusions (if they don't work, I can just shrug my shoulders and if they do work, I enjoy Naomi's unhesitating acknowledgment). Naomi takes seriously Brecht's adage that "corruption is our only hope." Her work as well in the collaborative process is all about corruption: the undermining and disestablishing of authority and expectation. Just as her plays often feature a female protagonist and/or an outsider who radically redraws boundaries and initiates decomposure and per/version, collaboration unsettles what it is to be an author and to be in control of one's words.

We have now collaborated on nearly a dozen screenplays and two plays (*The Girl Who Fell Through A Hole In Her Sweater* and *In the Sweat*). After mapping out a very detailed treatment, our *modus operandi* is to pass the text back and forth, usually after ten pages or so. We might reserve certain scenes, but for the most part we just work off what the other has created, follow each other's lead. It is a rally rather than a relay in that we constantly negotiate what the other has written and build upon it. Our only ground rule is that we have the right to change anything the other has written. There are, of course, dark moments when one realizes that a favorite line has disappeared, a particularly brilliant beat has been rewritten, the crushing insights into a character edited beyond recognition. And in these dark moments there can arise feelings of resentment, disbelief (if not mistrust), and even the desire for revenge. Alternatively, one can simply reinsert said line, beat, and insight and hope it passes the censor on a second go-round. But for the most part sulks and appeals are rare; the writing goes so smoothly it is suspicious. It is the read-through when we are in the same room—and when, typically, Naomi reads the script aloud and types our corrections—that debate can get heated, bargains are made, and compromise enforced. Bribery is not out of the question. But one of the pleasures of collaboration is the productive disruption that goes on within a structure of mutual support.

We have learnt, usually due to being at the blunt end of some producer's or director's 'feedback,' that as long as work is first affirmed, any sort of critique and rewrite is palatable. Thus Naomi and I have become adept at praising what the other has achieved before addressing the one or two 'notes' we might have. To compliment is to complement, to engage in a productive combination. As Italo Calvino contends at the conclusion of his *6 Memos for the Next Millennium*: "Who are we, who is each one of us, if not a combinatoria of experiences, information, books we have read, things imagined? Each life is an encyclopaedia..." One has only to invite in or, as Naomi would put it, be hospitable to combination, to being part of a union, for the work to benefit. In our particular combinatoria we have learnt that if we put our individual 'rights' (and perceived slights) on the back burner, the results are often surprising (and hopefully surprisingly good).

And so to return to stinging nettles. If we don't always equally share the 'pain' of writing we have learned to offer each other both respite and resilience. Nettles, as many who've been stung surely know, often grow within spitting distance of the remedy for their sting: doc leaves (*Rumex obtusifolius*). It seems to me that the nettle and the doc leaf, both securely rooted in human sediment, is a fitting metaphor for the way Naomi and I have come to work together. The two together encapsulate our dialectic; it is a combinatoria that hopefully rubs off on what we write.

Part III

Wallace in Her Own Words

Naomi Wallace

Strange Times

This article first appeared in The Guardian *on March 29, 2003. The United States-led invasion of Iraq and the long war that followed began on March 20. At the time, the Menagerie Theatre Company's production of Wallace's* The Retreating World, *a monologue about the effects of sanctions on everyday Iraqis following the Gulf War, was playing at the Latchmere in London.* Things of Dry Hours *premiered in Pittsburgh in 2004.*

* * *

I have no problem with calling myself a political writer. I do, however, have a bone to pick with the question: "Do you consider yourself a political writer?" It suggests, perhaps more insidiously in the United States (especially the south, where I am from) than in Britain, a certain narrowing of vision, a less than "human" exploration of life forces within the writing itself. Perhaps the problem is the very term "political": most often it is used to mean theatre with a left-wing axe to grind. So, among other things, the question carries with it a hackle-raising, almost indiscernible whiff of red-baiting: "Are you now or have you ever been a member of the...?"

Added to this, there is the fairly mainstream notion that ideas and political theory are limiting for writers, if not downright hostile to talent and the "real," and that truth springs from the individual, unencumbered by the blinkers of politicking. Only some superior "individual experience," the tiresome argument goes, can provide the writer with authentic organic matter from which to draw words and images. And yet the fact is that the individual and the cultural values and ideologies of his or her time are intimately and intricately linked.

Think chicken and egg. Why should we divorce these elements from one another?

Instead of asking them about politics, we might ask writers whether they consider themselves engaged. Engaged, for example, with questions of power and its myriad forms; questions of who has it and who doesn't and the reasons why. Questions of what happens to those who struggle with their disempowerment; who we are allowed to touch, what color of skin articulates which desire; what orifices are worthy of worship; which of us is beaten to death for not following the rule book on acceptable sexual conduct—all these are questions intimately connected to our social contracts.

I admit—and this is an unfashionable confession—I write from ideas. I do not start by drawing from the well of authentic experience uncontaminated by the dead carcass of "issues." I write to explore theories. My new play, *Things of Dry Hours*, began when I read the book *Hammer and Hoe* by the brilliant historian and cultural critic Robin D. G. Kelley. It is a history of the Alabama Communist Party during the Great Depression of the 1930s. Built from scratch by working people who had no Euro-American radical political tradition, it was composed largely of blacks, most of whom were semi-literate and religious. It also attracted a handful of whites. What ideas fired the imaginations of these people? What kind of dreams did they dream for another kind of America? In other words, what were the intimate motivations and repercussions of this political movement and social milieu?

But the play is, finally, a love story, and as Kelley and other blazing historians like Peter Rachleff and Howard Zinn have taught me, joining the Communist Party back then was an intensely personal act that had everything to do with love and desire. If one could not feed one's children (and being able to feed one's children is still in itself an act of love), then joining the party and striking for better pay was an act of hope to ensure the family's survival. One of the many Communist Party projects was working against house evictions, which leads again to the question of desire: if you didn't have a roof over your head, if you didn't even have a bed in which to fuck your lover, your personal life took an ugly downturn.

Clearly, the facile opposition between the political and the poetic, as it were, makes no sense. Look at one of the greatest successes in twentieth-century theatre, Tony Kushner's *Angels in America*. It is an intensely political piece dealing with topical issues—but it is also sexy, entertaining, and a deeply personal experience. Politicized theatre is a scarce commodity, whereas writers delving into the human soul, anguished or otherwise, represent the vast majority of playwriting. And the human-soul school of writing has produced an awful lot of bad, bad stuff. Writing that seeks to be oppositional or defamiliarizing, to turn history upside down or tackle pressing social problems, has the virtue of at least attempting to unsettle us, to make us act out.

So who's afraid of the political? Certainly not the great writers of the past, who saw topical political and socioeconomic issues as their subject. Look at the Greek playwrights or Shakespeare. Where would Spenser be without the colonization of Ireland, or Milton without the English civil war? Historically, writers have not been above politics, the consciences of the nation unsullied by the dirt of everyday bickerings. No, they have—to stick with British and American writers—been up to their elbows in the muck and blood of empire building and its repercussions at home.

Which isn't to say that theatre writers, novelists, and poets haven't been just as passionately in support of empire and war as they have been against it. The point is, writers have not and should not now exempt themselves from dealing with the pressing politics of the time. Today it is, once again, war and empire. And it is with these monstrosities that we should engage in one form or another. What would Euripides, Marlowe, or Brecht have done? They would have made these times strange, to use a Brechtian formula, so that an audience could see their society anew and possibly act on those new visions. Why settle for a lesser goal?

It is quiet where I live with my family in Yorkshire, so far from the war. But, writing here alone, it is sustenance to know of a growing community of courageous playwrights who are working—on and, importantly, off the stage—to confront and resist racism and empire. In the United States there is Kia Corthron, Robert O'Hara, Kushner, Lisa Schlesinger, Betty Shamieh, Richard Montoya, and August Wilson; in Britain think of Trevor Griffiths, Edward Bond, Sarah Daniels, Biyi Bandele, April de Angelis, Mark Ravenhill, Gary Mitchell. Political theatre, engaged theatre, whatever damn name you want to call it, is not diminished by ideas of justice or theories of resistance. On the contrary, ideas and theories are the elemental sparks from heaven. We can only pray that these sparks burn a hole through our skulls and stir our hands to writing. And so for today, let us use these sparks to imagine, in every detail, the hundreds of new ghosts that our governments are creating in Iraq. We can make these ghosts real. We can open our doors to them, invite them to sit at our tables. We can talk to them about the theories and ideas that have killed them. And we can make a choice not to let their murder go unrecorded.

Naomi Wallace

Seven Poems

Naomi Wallace started writing poetry when she was in elementary school: "I would bring poems to my teachers in the hopes that they would like me" (Baker 2006, 2000). She received a Master of Fine Arts degree in Poetry from the University of Iowa, and Peterloo Poets of Cornwall published an anthology of her poems titled To Dance a Stony Field *in 1995. "Poetry, for me," she says, "was a necessity for finding and exploring what was not visible, a method for making connections between one thing and another in a way that I was not taught to do in school."*

"Sometimes I will write a poem on an area of interest that is going to become a play," she has said. "It's helpful in that I distill the idea down to like twenty lines and then sometimes parts of that poem will go into the play, although usually it's later cut out" (Stephenson 164). Some of these precursor poems include "Kentucky Soldier in the Saudi Desert on the Eve of War" (In the Heart of America), *"Meat Strike"* (Slaughter City), *"The Trestle at Pope Lick Creek"* (The Trestle at Pope Lick Creek), *"Looking for Karl Marx's Apartment, 28 Dean Street"* (Things of Dry Hours), *and "The Retreating World"* (The Retreating World). *Poems with no direct connection to a particular play often explore themes and imagery that circulate through her dramatic work.*

The selection here concludes with two Wallace poems that have never been published. "The Corner of Turning" has no particular political inflection. "Rolled to Starboard" is a poem she wrote for her daughter.

* * *

Kentucky Soldier in the Saudi Desert on the Eve of War

I can't use the latrines, the smell of clorox
and shit, the flies as big as thumbs on the tin walls. I
walk out to the edge of the camp, take a spoon from
my jacket, dig a hole and squat. As a boy
I did the same on the banks of Harrod's creek
while I watched the minnows shoot from rock to rock.
Once my friends and I kidnapped a black kid,
took him down, blindfolded, to the creek.
In a tin can we caught a crayfish, forced the boy's mouth
open with a stick and stuck the critter inside. The kid
screamed so hard we let loose. He spit
the thing out but it left its claw behind on his tongue. The
crayfish lay on the dry rocks, snapping
its one victorious claw in the quiet air

between us; I crushed it under my boot.
I cover my shit with sand. Behaving like a dog,
I feel more like a man. This time it's Arabs. *First you
hate 'em, then you kill 'em.* The Sergeant tells me:
These are sand-niggers. These are camel-jockeys.
At night I try not to sleep, but the dreams, they start in on
me again: I am breaking open his jaw, jamming the
crayfish in. But this kid does not scream. This kid breaks
my hold, opens his mouth and the critter
I forced in flies out. Its claw goes for my face,
hangs from my eye like an ornament on a dead tree. Then
I wake up. *First you hate 'em, then you kill 'em.* Urine pools
at my thighs. Under my sheets, the smell of cold piss is a
comfort. Tomorrow we go to war.

* * *

Meat Strike

I haul the split, black slabs of beef, then lay
them on a belt. It isn't my job. The guy whose job it is
stands outside the packhouse, all day,
on strike, uptight, calls me a meat-fucking scab. At
5 a.m., when we walk in, I look the other way.

I grew up in the city, never touched a cow alive.
Here I touch them in pieces. I stroke them from the inside out,
where they're wet; it's not right. The meat slaps me
hard when I lift it from the hooks. For balance, I lean my head to
the bone. Once I slipped on the guts, took a dive

with my face in it. I could swear that the bloody slab
made a sound, a sneer, like glass dragging on glass.
At 5 p.m. we go home. The man from whom I took this job until
they break the strike, he spits at me. He misses.
He spits again. He misses again. If I could risk this job

I'd ask him if he's heard it, like I did, the meat
talking to him or when his nose is full of blood and his hair
webbed with fat, if he's ever heard it laugh. We're both shit
without money. The Company rolls the coin into the centre of the
strike and we have no choice but to kill for it.

The third time he spits I get it right on the brow.
I still won't look him in the face. I walk through the gate. If
meat laughs, I'd like to tell him, it's because it's how it's no
longer an animal, but flesh turned the wrong way, turned
inside out, as I am, as we both are now.

* * *

The Trestle at Pope Lick Creek

The train was pulling eight cars at seventy tons apiece.
But not a big train, as trains go, though two of the country boys
thought otherwise, their faces opening out like a kiss
against the engine, one hundred and fifty three tons of indisputable
fact and steel. Their bodies, ridged, with surprise, were flung
from the bridge, falling in a scatter-shot of wool and blood.
What did they say to each other, those two boys, brave on gum
and dime store liquor, before they made the cross? It was a game.
Nothing much to lose and they could lose almost anything twice.
Did they laugh as their fast tennis shoes, red and white
on the rusty ties, flashed in the dark? Did they think they could fly?
Finally, no where else to go. Two hundred feet above a dry creek bed,
night clattering chance and change in their ears, they kept running,
their still new hearts tossing like dice in their chests.

* * *

Looking for Karl Marx's Apartment, 28 Dean Street

A round, blue plaque on the brick wall, two floors up. Below it
now, though certainly not then, a burly restaurant, bright lights
and food fit for kings. The kind you despised. Not the food, but
the kings. Here you lived with your wife in poverty. You
wouldn't go out on the street for weeks

at a time because you'd pawned your coat and shoes.
Three of your children died up there, behind that glass.
And while Engels worked himself to sickness over
an office desk he despised, just to keep your genius afloat,
history-to-be unfolded in the lungs of your children,
the phlegm so thick it could talk. Did they have, still
children then, nothing to lose but their chains?
No. Not them. Not yet. And while your broken wife wept on the
floor of filth behind you, you stared out the window at your
dream of revolution, the blackened city straining and shifting
under its own dead weight, the working women and men drifting
past your gaze like broken shells. How long until their day?
Inevitable. Inevitable it was,
as was the last abrupt noise your eight year old son Edgar made
when you turned away from that vision, just for a moment,
to see him on the bed, clawing open his own throat for air.

* * *

The Retreating World

Through this man you could look at the sky,
his arms raised beside seven hundred other men.
This is documented: he didn't make a sound.
European Parliament, 1991. Members of the committee

recorded the testimony, with blue flowers in
their mouths, and cups of cold coffee: the defeated
troops were surrounding. That morning the soldier
had knelt to lace the shoes of a dead friend.

He'd sucked an orange mint, the smoke from the napalm
making his gums bleed. He'd relieved himself
in the sand while invisible jets broke the black
glass sky across the horizon. He thought three

things—this is not documented—as his column moved
towards the unit to surrender: *I want to put my hands
in a bucket of cold water. I want to smell the back
of my father's neck. I want to tell an astonishing joke

to my friends until they cry for relief.* The commander
of the unit fired, at this one man, an antitank missile.
A missile meant to pierce armour. At one man. The other
Iraqi soldiers, arms still raised, stopped walking.

They looked but could not recognise their severed friend.
A piece of his spine stuck upright in the sand.
His left hand blown so high in the air it was still falling.
Quick surprise flushed the sportive American faces,

as their handsome mouths went slack, eyebrows raised:
the instantaneous disintegration almost like a miracle.
And so their bodies leaned hard towards this wonder
as they opened fire on the rest of the men.

And from the mercurial wounds of the ruined soldiers,
small blue flowers spilled. And when the victors knelt
to examine them, it was noted that the blossoms had no
smell. This is documented. The Parliament of the

Europeans: blood as black as coffee. Cold flowers.
The cry inside an astonishing joke. The jets, the jets
inside an empty cup. The lullaby of currency and order.
The antitank missile. 1991. The hand still falling.

* * *

The Corner of Turning

Each morning I wake and it's yesterday.
I can hear you laugh there.

The white flowers, the red foxtails, the phobias.
In their shadow, the wet black slugs
roll in their hunger, feeding on the green leaves.

I count the trees, the birds, how many times the wind
forgets but I can't clear the path.

Children play in the yard as the sun
warms the tops of their heads and draws
out the sleep still to come through their crowns.

The children don't think it's yesterday.
They know that time is the manner in which we yearn
to be counted: *I am here. I am here.*

And they don't care about the end—there is only
now—a red coat in the grass, a jump rope around a tree.
Your shadow on the garden chair without you.

The clouds above me are the bones of animals.
The sun falls through them. I don't know what I am
doing when I hold out my arms.

* * *

Rolled to Starboard

A girl is a thread, the steam from a tea pot,
a buttercup dipped in blood. Will you be

the astronaut or the astronaut's wife?
The face enclosed in the thick, plastic globe,

the oxygen so fresh your gums bleed.
Floating out there in your silver suit,

the earth is an orange at your feet.
A girl is a splinter, the stick in a lolly-pop.

When you grow up, will the astronaut hit you?
And if so, how many times?

This is the hand that breaks you.
This is the hand that holds the key.

This is the crayon that draws the cord that links you
to the space-ship. The stars have sharp edges,

watch out. You could float out there forever.
And will you hit him back?

Will you crack the globe around his head
and watch his face turn blue?

My child, whatever it is you do,
you'll wipe up your life as you spill it.

for Nadira

Naomi Wallace

Let the Right One In: On Resistance, Hospitality and New Writing for the American Stage

This essay, reprinted with permission, first appeared in the January 2013 edition of American Theatre *magazine. It reflects, among other things, a creative imperative that had been shaping her work for a decade: "to write against my grain and a mind stewed since birth in racism" (Gardner 2007). Since* Things of Dry Hours *(2004), the majority of her characters have been nonwhite, non-Anglo-American figures. Here, she recommends that practice to others as a form of resistance and hospitality.*

* * *

All writing for the theatre is in some sense an act of violation. By this I mean that when we enter into the lives of others and try to imagine a perspective that is not our own, we have to push through what we know, what we are sure of, what we value—push into the very skin of another life and vision. Sure, that's common sense for a writer, but mainstream theatre does not generally enter into the lives and bodies of those we consider "strangers"; more often than not it bounces off the barriers, contenting itself with the safe and recycled materials of stereotype (albeit refreshed for the present moment), cliché, and hearsay. Writing that does not actually violate boundaries, that does not enter into the process of trespass, is often a writing that is safe, consumable, and shallow. A theatre that does not challenge its own assumptions, its own ignorance, with curiosity and humility is a contracted theatre, a diminished theatre.

And in these harsh and difficult days, when we are afraid of losing what we have, afraid of losing what we almost had, afraid of getting what we've always feared, we make choices. Playwrights make choices. About who enters their stages. Who gets the light and who gets only a glancing view. Who stays around and has the last word, the best word, and who is at the center of the joke. The center of love or humiliation. We are encouraged to fear the outsider, the one at the edge of our stage, the In/spectre at the door.

And here, I am not summoning the overly esoteric otherness in the philosophy of Emmanuel Levinas, the stranger who shatters and consumes us, but rather noting the ones who enter the landscapes of our stage, and the ones who are refused its geography. If, as Terry Eagleton says, "Neighborhood is a practice rather than a locality," we must investigate the neighborhoods of our theatre and highlight what is rendered invisible: Who is missing, who is spoken for, and who is unmentionable. How does the policing of these "neighborhoods on stage," through our selves and/or our institutions, perpetuate a retracted, redacted, and inhospitable theatre?

Coming into stories that we are not familiar with, entering into bodies and genders that are not our own, is a risk and a responsibility that I believe is often taken too lightly, if taken at all. For example, white playwrights, over many decades, have rarely given a second thought to creating characters for black Americans. Our conscious and unconscious sense of entitlement, our skin privilege, our general and often nursed ignorance, have created a legacy of demeaning, shallow, and stereotypical portraits of African Americans and other people of color on stage. Considering the damage that white writers have done, one might come to the conclusion that it's best for white writers to stick to writing for white folks. Too much damage otherwise. And yet I believe that all of us must take the risk to represent anyone and everyone.

But why focus on imagination and its power to violate and trespass? Am I not in danger of advocating a sort of colonization, given that violation also signifies the oppression of one by another? Why not stick with what we know? Write about what we know? Well, certainly there is a place for that. Especially for the stories of those artists and their communities who have not been welcomed onto the American stage but have had to forge a space for themselves there: black artists, Asian American, Latino, Native American, Arab American, and others. However, mainstream American theatre is still largely a white, middle-class endeavor—and, in being so, is not really an "American" theatre, but a specialized, illusionary theatre.

So how do we pillage the material of our own lives to find our connection to the larger historical and social forces swirling around our heads, if not inside them? The important word here is *find* rather than create. Because these connections already exist. The goal is to uncover these live wires, no matter how buried or twisted. The trick is to tap into these lines and charge up our imaginations.

Hospitality plays an important role in Shakespeare. One of drama's worst hosts, Macbeth, is thus because of his appetite for self-serving power. While a victim of inhospitable forces, King Lear comes to disregard power and embrace the out/cast as well as a more egalitarian world:

> Expose thyself to feel what wretches feel,
> That thou mayst shake the superflux to them
> And show the heavens more just.

In thinking about hospitality, we'll need to consider not only whom we welcome onto the stage but how in our writing we might cross the divide between our own personal experiences and that of others; from our own sexuality to that of another sexuality; our own race to that of another race; our own class and gender to that of another class or gender.

First, let us recall that hospitality derives from the Latin *hospitare*—to entertain. This neatly encapsulates the type of theatre I believe we strive for: one that gives, that offers pleasure and nourishment; but it is also a theatre of consideration that is open to ideas, others, dissident selves. The tradition of the unexpected guest who provokes a revelation, if not a reconfiguration of the familiar, is well worn. But as in J. B. Priestley's *The Inspector Calls*, I would like to take this tradition a step further: The Other and ourselves should not be seen as the foreign facing off against the familiar. As the inspector shows, we already know the unknown even if we didn't know we knew it (shades of Donald Rumsfeld there—apologies). My point is this: We are already and always complicit, interconnected, and related to the stranger, the Other, the unfamiliar.

I grew up in Kentucky. Unlike most Kentuckians, I grew up with privilege. My father, Henry, was a journalist and, as he liked to refer to himself, a "gentleman-farmer." I was raised on a small cattle farm, which, while rarely breaking even, was kept going by the sizeable inheritance bestowed on my father. Even though my mother, Sonia, was Dutch working class and educated me in class consciousness, I grew up in an idyllic pastoral landscape.

But over the hill and not so far away, there lived two different communities. One was white working class, the other black working class. They were my neighbors. I slept in their houses. I ran with their children. I kissed their boys. I fell in love with their girls. But the most fruitful thing I did was shut my mouth in the presence of the adults of these families. And I listened. I listened to their dinner chat, their courtesies, their hopes, the vulnerability of their fears that they exposed to me because as long as I was a child, I was still harmless. I hadn't yet stepped into my full privilege of class and skin.

And it was here that I learned most intimately about the magic and seduction of the American dream. In one of these communities over the hill, I found a pickup-truck-driving boyfriend named Jay. Jay's father had fought in Korea and he'd been poisoned by the tin food rations that were distributed to troops by the US government. The poison had corroded his lungs. He had one lung removed, then another half. But this man, Mr. Aldridge, continued to work. I remember a few years later—when I'd lost contact with both Jay and his family—stopping by the local restaurant. There I saw Mr. Aldridge sitting in the corner with a paper cup of coffee and a cigarette. I was taught to be a polite young woman, so I sat with him some moments to say hello. Already he was dying, though he did his best to ignore it. But he asked me a question that I have never forgotten. He said, "How is it that I have worked hard all my life and still I have nothing?" I didn't have an answer. My own father had two lungs. And we didn't have "nothing." We had a lot of things.

I can recall that moment easily and yet still not without unease. Mr. Aldridge must have been in his forties when he started his dying. He was a handsome man. Years later he suffocated to death on what was left of his lung. Jay found him and tried to resuscitate his father with mouth to mouth—for three hours, long after he was dead. Jay never got over his father's death, which was both an economic and physical suffocation. I have not seen Jay for decades. I hear he speaks to invisible beings and lives on the streets.

Mr. Aldridge worked for his family all his life. He died broke and left a broken family behind him because of it. To this day our government continues to deny its culpability for the poisoning of its own troops.

Of course, when Mr. Aldridge asked me that question in the restaurant, I was still only a teenager. I was interested in Bacardi and boys, fishing in Harrod's creek, and field parties where we danced on the hoods of banged-up trucks. While some sense of discomfort lived within me, I thought neither long nor hard on Mr. Aldridge's question. Not until many years later.

We are responsible for the education of our imaginations, for its focus and direction. We must ask ourselves: Whom and what does my imagination serve? Where will I urge my mind to venture and roam, and to what purpose? As Edward Bond, in his *Theatre Poems and Songs*, puts it:

> How is society organized?
> For the happiness of the people?
> Or so that profit can be drawn
> At as many points as possible?

What childhood experiences like knowing Mr. Aldridge relayed to me is that there is something seriously and morally wrong with an economic system that nurtures the few rich and powerful, and diminishes and devours the rest. It is not for lack of effort, will power, or moral fiber that so many have been left broken, impoverished, and afraid, but the fault of a racist and classist social system designed to have the majority struggling and a minority living in the lap of luxury.

Again, I come back to the question: How do we resist the temptation to write it safe? How do we as artists engage with the most urgent questions of our time? With oppression and injustice here within our turbulent home? How do we engage with war without fetishizing it?

As playwrights we need, I would suggest, to become detectives, inspectors, and investigators into our own privilege and power, our culpability, our closing of the door. When we write, we can investigate the unseen, the disremembered. We can cultivate a hospitality toward dissent rather than a nurtured contempt for truth. We can do the hard work of inquiring into history, both immediate and past, both near and remote, with seriousness, imaginative thinking, playfulness, curiosity, and a ruthless, carnivalesque sense of hope. We must do research. If possible, we should travel and talk to others. We read and reread and digest and consider. We imagine. We imagine some more. We listen. And then, if we're lucky, we write something that "entertains."

To go beyond ourselves, to imagine the worlds of others, is always a worthwhile endeavor. With all the obvious and discomforting flaws, we are still grateful for Othello, Lady Macbeth, and Shylock. As we are grateful for the engaged, radical stages created by such a wealth of writers as Kia Corthron, Tanya Barfield, Young Jean Lee, Richard Montoya, Caridad Svich, Ismail Khalidi, Roger Guenveur

Smith, Basil Kreimendahl, Yussef El Guindi, Quiara Alegría Hudes, Mike Geither, Betty Shamieh, and Kwame Kwei-Armah, to name just a few. And to keep hope alive, we have the Oregon Shakespeare Festival's courageous American Revolutions: The United States History Cycle, a ten-year program commissioning up to 37 new plays sprung from moments of change in US history; New York Theatre Workshop and its continuing creative interaction with its associate company, The Freedom Theater of Jenin; Center Stage of Baltimore's daring social media project, My America; and Michael Dixon's New Play Project at Minneapolis's Guthrie Theater, which encouraged playwrights to explore a wider cultural representation in their plays and to travel to Liberia, Cambodia, Turkey, Korea, the Occupied Palestinian Territories, and other neighborhoods coming to a city near you.

Let me be clear here: There are a thousand ways we can trip and flounder when as playwrights we need to become detectives, inspectors, and investigators into our own privilege and power. We enter into writing about experiences far from our own. We might fail to honor the complicated humanity of another. We might find that cliché sneaks into our path and we stand on it and build from there. We might, simply, miss the boat. To aid us in this challenge, we might stay alert to the corrective that Edward Said suggests in his *Humanism and Democratic Criticism* (and here I will substitute the word "playwright" for "intellectual," for we are both): The playwright should be "a kind of counter memory" with his or her "own counter-discourse that will not allow conscience to look away or fall asleep. The best corrective…is to imagine the person you are discussing"—or writing about—"in this case the person on whom the bombs will fall—reading you in your presence."

We live in increasingly inhospitable times. Fanning anti-immigrant hysteria, racism, and increasing attacks on the poor, unions, and women's health are part and parcel of the voracious and reactionary program which distorts our understanding of the world and our place in it, and is rapidly dismantling civic society: undermining our libraries, disappearing our public spaces, threatening our schools, and the right to free education. All the necessary public places where we fall in love with the world, and one another, free from the fundamentalism of the profit-motive.

Inhospitality is about tending one's own garden and locking the gate; it's about greed and fear. NIMBYism as a life philosophy. Mainstream culture suffocates our awareness of the inherent connection, however tenuous, between you and me. Between LA and

Afghanistan. Between Kentucky and Sudan. Between Jenin and New York. Between Pakistan and Cleveland. Between you and you and you.

Randall Jarrell, in his poem "Losses," sums up this notion:

In bombers named for girls, we burned—
The cities we had learned about in school
Till our lives wore out; our bodies lay among
The people we had killed and never seen.

The pilot knows that there is a thread, a wire, connecting his experience to those beneath his bomber. This was exactly the coming to consciousness that turned the late Howard Zinn into both a pacifist and groundbreaking historian-activist. The pilot and the bomb. But what does this have to do with those of us who are neither the pilot nor the bombed? Our connection is actually terribly intimate, and we might begin our investigation of this link, for instance, with a bodily fluid: sweat.

Produced by labor—a good day's labor. We work. All of us. We care about our work. We are citizens. We pay taxes. So I speak to you because I want to be of use—we all want to be of use, and the fruit of our labor is to see our loved ones bloom.

But the fruit of our labor also goes to kill others like us. The bombs we have paid for, the aircraft we have assembled, the napalm we have sweated for. This is the painful and heart-breaking contradiction of living in this culture, this society. How do we open out these contradictions so that they inspire us rather than cripple us?

We might begin with curiosity. For example, in this country, our labor is harnessed in the manufacturing of the near-lethal tear gas, created in Pennsylvania, courtesy of Combined Systems, and used in Egypt, in other Middle Eastern countries, and the illegally occupied Palestinian Territories. Our toil and grind is exploited to build F-16s, drones, Apache helicopters, depleted uranium, and cluster munitions. Curiosity. What is our part in the brutal and lawless killing in 2009 of more than 1,200 Gazan civilians, more than three hundred of whom were children, trapped in the largest open-air prison in the world? How might we begin to imagine the ongoing, relentless violence of an occupation bankrolled by our government and nurtured by our toil? To envision the lives of civilians who live in fear and under the shadow of the fruits of a fruitless Middle East peace plan that has to be, in the words of Sara Roy, one of the most "spectacular deceptions of modern history"?

We must, I believe, disrupt the lie with an imagination that is fierce, demystifying, and persistent. We must meet the perversion of human intellect for the benefit of war and oppression with a creative force, a theatrical force that challenges, interrogates, and disorientates. Or, in more poetic terms, do as Keats suggests, and be "awake for ever in a sweet unrest." Unrest. Yes, that's where the sweetness, the sexiness, the seriousness makes things happen on stage by speaking truth to that most inhospitable terrain of human thriving: global capitalism.

That is all to say that we should aspire to be interested writers. Interest: a word too often hijacked by finance. The Latin prefix *inter* means between or among; also mutually, together. Thus interact, interrelate, and international. Wonderful injunctions for writers. As if describing engaged and challenging writing, the Latin word *interresse* means "to concern, be of importance," and, here's the kicker, "to make a difference." Break interest down, it means basically *inter*— "between" and *esse*—"to be." To live between. To live between self and world, self and others, ourselves, our others, our histories, their histories. Sure, our own stories are occasionally interesting, but what I am talking about is connecting our everyday experiences to a world view, the *longue durée*, the grand narrative, the big picture.

The myth of free enterprise is that we are independent of one another, that we flourish in the me, mine, and myself. But ultimately we are social beings and we need each other to understand ourselves and history. The stranger at the door is there so that we may realize that the stranger is also us. That hospitality, on the stage and off the stage, is what enriches, challenges, haunts, and articulates our lives.

When we cross boundaries, when we violate our own skin to know the heartbreak or hope or resistance of another, what we come closer to, surprisingly, is ourselves. Because through imaginative empathy, we revive our own humanity. So, to put it simply, we must be where we are not, because if we look down we will see that we are already there, here, among those we are encouraged to believe are strangers. Who suddenly are no longer strangers.

Naomi Wallace

Manifesto

Manifesto *was written in 1999 for the Actors Theatre of Louisville's twenty-third Humana Festival of New American Plays as part of a novelty experiment called the T(ext) Shirt Project. Six American playwrights—David Henry Hwang, Tony Kushner, Jane Martin, Wendy Wasserstein, Mac Wellman, and Wallace—were commissioned to write plays "short enough to be printed on the back of a T-shirt yet complex enough to communicate the self-reflective irony" of the T-shirt as a popular form of self-branding (Koger 1999, 296). T(ext) shirts of various colors were sold in the lobby as festival souvenirs.* Manifesto *was silkscreened in white letters on a black cotton tee.*

* * *

Manifesto

Two figures speak to each other. It is almost dark.

RUINED BODY: Look at me. A piece of work. My throat's closed. Legs gone from standing. Arms I can't raise. God damn you.

SPECTRE: A spectre is haunting—

RUINED BODY: Stop playing the ghost. Show me your face.

SPECTRE: The history of all hitherto existing societies—

RUINED BODY: Come near to me. That's right. I can smell you now: the inside of a bird's nest, oranges, gasoline.

SPECTRE: —is the history of class struggle.

RUINED BODY: Stop talking. Shut your mouth.

SPECTRE: Two great classes directly facing each other.

RUINED BODY: Eye to eye. In yours I see myself awake. Listen.

SPECTRE: Abolition of property. Equal liability of all to labor.

RUINED BODY: Listen. Don't fucking move. You must kiss me where no one has ever kissed me. I'm still alive in that place. Put your hand inside me. We're awake now. Work with me.

SPECTRE: Overthrow of all existing social conditions.

RUINED BODY: Work with me. When my tongue moves across the roof of your mouth, I taste the smoke from the chimney.

SPECTRE: All that is solid melts into air. Work with me.

RUINED BODY: We're not abandoned. Someone is still at home.

RUINED BODY AND SPECTRE: And the face by the fire

RUINED BODY: It's still a good world

SPECTRE: to win. And the face by the fire, looks like

RUINED BODY AND SPECTRE: you, looks like me.

THE END

Naomi Wallace

We Are Also Each Other

In August 2002, Naomi Wallace led a delegation of six American playwrights—including Kia Corthron, Tony Kushner, Robert O'Hara, Betty Shamieh, and Lisa Schlesinger—on a seven-day visit to the Occupied Territories. Their mission was, in short, "to break down some of the barriers dividing us from the Palestinian people"—to make contact, to begin a dialogue, to gather ideas and inspiration, to witness for themselves the harsh conditions faced by Palestinian theatre artists. From their base in East Jerusalem, they made day trips to Ramallah, Al Maghar, Hebron, Bethlehem, the Aida Refugee Camp, Gaza City, and to Tel Aviv. In the July/August 2003 edition of American Theatre, *they reported on their trip collectively and in six individual short essays. This is what Naomi Wallace wrote in hers.*

* * *

"Politics is not separate from lived experience or the imaginary world of what is possible," writes historian Robin D. G. Kelley in his book *Race Rebels*. And it was this very idea of interconnectedness and imagination that led me to envision making a trip to visit the Occupied Territories, the West Bank, and Gaza.

A few months since our return, two things especially have stayed hard in my mind. One of these is our trip to the Aida Refugee Camp outside Bethlehem, where our visit interrupted a dancing lesson in progress. The children, aged eight to fourteen, were training in traditional Palestinian dance, the *debka*.

I had never before encountered such an informed and politically mature group of young folks, children who could make the distinction between the actions of a government and its people. The miracle was that these children did not spit at us for the three billion dollars a year in US military aid that supports their occupation. They did not shout at us for the American-made Black Hawk helicopters, F-16s and Cobras that terrify them, even in their sleep, day in and day out. They did not say, "Yankee, go home." They did not hold us accountable, as citizens, for the deaths of their friends at the hands of Israeli soldiers firing American bullets. One could not have blamed them if they had.

Instead, for half an hour in the tiny, hot room of their refugee camp, these children danced for us. Afterward, a boy of ten said to us, "Yes, I throw stones at the tanks. But I would rather play." A 12-year-old girl with her arm in a cast said, "When I grow up, I want to be a doctor." I pray that she will. On both accounts.

Another piece that stays with me is also a memory of children: the almost-still-children of the Israeli army, the shock-troops for a colonial settler state. Along the roads and at each town, we were stopped, our identification was checked and we were questioned. When approached by an armed soldier, one looks first at the gun and only afterward at the face. From the face, one's focus goes quickly back to the gun, then to the hand that holds it and the finger, almost always on the trigger. I was disturbed and moved by the beauty of these young soldiers' hands, the fine hair on their forearms, and simultaneously appalled by the monstrous obscenity of these almost-still-children of Israel sent out for decades to brutalize and subdue an entire people. These young men should have been out kicking a soccer ball, shouting with the excitement of play, not war.

To visit the Occupied Territories, the West Bank, and Gaza as theatre writers is not simply an exercise in forging links between ourselves and the Palestinians. Rather, it is to realize that we, as Americans, are, on an intensely intimate level, already fused, through the overt involvement of our government, with the history of these people. The challenge, then, is to recognize this, and ultimately to do something about it that makes a motion in the direction of that long, hard struggle for peace. As Mahmoud Darwish says in his poem "Psalm 11," "Nothing remains for me / but to inhabit your voice that is my voice." We are not, I thank the gods, only ourselves and our own personal experience. We are also what happens to one another.

And so? In a way, it's a simple aspiration: So we can all meet in the morning on the soccer field, our weapons stacked to make the goal posts, our children dancing with their wild feet, the ball going up, up, somewhere in the big sky, then coming slowly down; and then that enormous, ecstatic, thrilling cheer, because all of us at the end of the day are safe, and we will eat together at dusk, after the sweat and play of the game; and we will sit at the same gigantic table, cooling our hot arms in the bowls of fruit.

And look! Those who want to, even with their shoes still on and muddy, even in the midst of the meal—they can get up on the table, among the vegetables and water, and begin to shout and cry and argue and laugh and forge an uncontrollable, dream-worthy theatre that inscribes every one of our names in the footlights, that changes us all in mid-sentence, exactly in mid-flight.

Naomi Wallace

The Fish Story

This monologue was written while Naomi Wallace was a graduate student at the University of Iowa in the early 1990s. It was included in the 1994 Heinemann collection Monologues for Women by Women *edited by Tori Haring-Smith and was presented by Rogue Planet and Horizon Theatre Company as part of the 2001 Naomi Wallace Festival in Atlanta. It also appears on lists of pieces for oral interpretation in high school forensics competitions. It provides an early indication of Wallace's abiding concern with the body (and particularly the wounded body and sexual contact). And its focus on worms-as-food makes for an interesting comparison with* The Tal Pidae Lehrstücke, *an altogether different monologue written 20 years later for an altogether different character.*

* * *

The Fish Story

(A young woman is telling a story. She has a lure box with her.)

It was almost like they knew they were going to be crucified. First they would lie still on your palm, as though dead. Only a slight tremor, at one end or the other, gave their trick away. It was this moment. This moment of calm right before it happened, that I liked most, when their tender, fleshy bodies, studded with black dirt, would lay in my hand like the trust of an old friend. At seven years old, that glistening body of plumped worminess was more beautiful to me than any... *(Breaks off.)*

But when the hook came up close, the thing would start to writhe like all hell-fire was upon it. *(Beat)* It isn't true that worms wriggle when they're threaded on the hook. Those who say they do never hooked a worm in their life. No, worms don't wriggle, they writhe.

It didn't bother my father. He'd just pluck the worm from the jar and thread it on the hook without blinking an eye. When he wasn't looking, I'd whisper "hush, hush" to the worm and when it turned its stomach to me, that pink band that circles its body like a wedding ring, I'd strike fast, straight through the center. *(She opens the box and carefully lays out some lures.)*

No one made me do it but myself and for a while I felt sorry for the worms. I loved hauling in the bass. And me and my father would stand side by side, casting the deep stream pools. We'd bet on who would holler first "I got one!"

Daddy was my friend. He liked fishing the way I liked it. When he cast a good one, his lips would go white and his chin would tremble just a little as he waited for a strike. Sometimes one of his ears would go red with all that waiting. Not both of them, just the left one. Red as a worm.

(Singing) Oh my love is like a red, red worm.

Once I hooked that red ear. I was fly fishing and I hauled back to snap the line and toss it on a new patch of water and *(Beat. She screams as though she were her father.)* That's how he sounded. *(She polishes some lures.)*

I didn't know at first what had happened so I kept jerking at the rod until my Daddy caught hold of my line with his free hand and jerked back; the rod flew out of my hands and snapped in two on the ground between us. And there hung my fly with three hooks, one hook embedded in that red ear which was redder than I'd ever seen it. He made me get it out. He didn't say a word, just opened his lure box, took out a pair of pliers, and handed them to me. *(Beat)* When a bluegill swallows an artificial fly or a spinner, it usually hooks down into its lungs. You see, bluegills have small mouths and what goes in doesn't come out. If it isn't your favorite lure, you can cut the line and throw the fish back in. They say the creek water will rust a hook out of a fish's mouth in forty-eight hours. If it's your favorite lure, and one time it was my favorite, you just have to pull. That's when a piece of the lung will come out with the hook. *(Beat)* But an ear isn't a fish.

And yet my father's ear was tougher than a catfish lip. I had to twist and pull. Twist and pull. The ear fought me. It wouldn't let go. It held on tight. My father just sat there and I knew if I didn't get it out, if he had to do it himself, then...well, twist and pull. Twist and pull. Finally it tore. The ear. And out the hook came.

He let me choose. My father was good about that. He said I could have a spanking, without my shorts on, or eat a worm as my punishment for not looking behind me when I'd swung the rod. So I dug down into the jar and pulled one out, praying I'd grab a dead one. But that worm must have been sleeping 'cause the moment it got near my mouth it sparked like a firecracker trying to let loose. *(Beat)* Well, I looked at the worm and if a worm can look, it did so at me. I'd never had one before, though once my Daddy let me choose between biting the tail off a grasshopper or not watching television for two whole weeks when I spilled a can of paint in the garage. I went for the grasshopper. Like a saltine cracker, almost exactly, when I ate it. *(She hangs the lures on her outstretched arm as she speaks until they hang like decorations in a row.)*

They say a worm has seven hearts and that if you cut it in the right places, two or three of the pieces will live. The problem was, I didn't know where the hearts were or where to bite. I held it up to the light but I couldn't see anything but red worm. I put it halfway into my mouth. I figured biting it halfway was a choice. Random would kill it for sure. I closed my eyes but I couldn't bite down. The half of the worm that was inside started tickling the roof of my mouth like how the dentist does. I started to laugh but then Daddy started shouting for me to do it. He was saying "Now, now, now." *(Beat.)*

Then Daddy slapped me on the back of the head and I bit down.

I only use artificials now. I like the sound of their names: Switchback, Rapala, Zarco spinner, Bass magnet, Zephyr Puppy, Double-headed jig, and Jitterbug. Twelve-pound line. Eight-pound line. Six-pound line. I was using four-pound line later that day. I cast my line right between a fallen tree and rock ledge. It fell on the water with hardly a splash. I twitched the line once. Twice. Just before the third twitch and reel, the bass struck it.

There must have been some magic to the flesh of that worm I ate because that afternoon I landed a four-pound small-mouthed bass. Almost snapped my line. It took me fifteen minutes to bring that monster close enough to the bank so my father could scoop it up in the net. Daddy and I skinned it right there and cooked it over the fire. I can tell you I was proud that day. And Daddy was proud of me too. He kissed me on the mouth four times, one kiss for each pound of that bass. Have you ever made your father that proud of you? I mean, that proud? Four times. He kissed me four times. On the mouth. Have you ever? Four times? On the mouth? *(Beat)* I can show you. It's hard to tell you just how it went unless I show you. That's how proud he was. That's how. Yes. And I closed my eyes because I had to. Because if a worm has seven hearts it could have eight and I wanted him to know I could take it. And I took it. On the mouth. But once it's cut. The worm. You never can tell just which parts have been killed and which parts will crawl away and start over because all the parts are moving. All of the parts are trying to live. But only one or two of them do. Live.

I'll tell you a secret: I'm not a very good daughter. It was worse. His pride in me. Worse. Than eating that worm. Silly, isn't it? Know what I mean? Do you? Four times. On the mouth. That's how it started. Then we went home to tell Mother about my bass.

You wouldn't know it, would you? To look at me. Some of this, here *(Motions to parts of her body, slowly)* isn't really alive anymore. Deceptive, isn't it? How can one look at the body and see nothing but the whole of it. But I know. I know which parts went on and lived and which parts gave up and died. I can tell them apart just by touching them. *(She gently touches herself in different places, not necessarily sexual parts of her body.)* Can you tell them apart? If you touch yourself, here and here, or there and there? Go on. Try it. That's it. Can you tell just which parts of you are dead and which parts of you are still alive? *(Beat.)* Got it? All right then. When you're ready. *(Beat.)* Let's go fishing.

Naomi Wallace

The Tal Pidae Lehrstücke

In July 2011, British director and playwright Kwame Kwei-Armah came to America to assume his new position as Artistic Director of Baltimore's Center Stage, just as the theatre was preparing to celebrate its fiftieth anniversary in 2012. To mark these occasions, the theatre asked 50 American playwrights—one for each state, if not from each state—to write a dramatic monologue in response to the question: "What is your America? Who is your America?" The playwrights who responded to this invitation included such well-known names as Lee Blessing, Christopher Durang, Naomi Iizuka, Neil LaBute, Lynn Nottage, and Anna Deavere Smith as well as dozens of other interesting, if less familiar, writers.

With the help of the playwrights and a casting director, Center Stage recruited one actor for each piece and then turned to independent filmmaker Hal Hartley to make each monologue into a short film. Starting in September 2012, against the backdrop of the Presidential campaign and Barack Obama's re-election, the finished films were screened in the lobby at Center Stage and posted to a new website—myamerica.centerstage.org. Collectively, these state-of-the-nation snapshots constitute what Kwei-Armah called "an archive of a moment in America's history" (Piepenburg 2012).

Wallace's contribution to the My America project is a monologue written for a mole. Inspired by the "learning plays" of Brecht and written as a kind of dramatic sprechstimme, the piece reflects many aspects of her work: the exacting research that goes into a play; a feisty youthful protagonist; a focus on the musicality of language; a wry, subversive sense of humor; a seriousness of purpose leavened by a touch of whimsy. Wallace's interest in moles goes back at least as far as her first play, In the Fields of Aceldama, in which the character Henry digs up moles to keep as pets. For Center Stage's My America, the role of The Mole was performed by Gayle Rankin.

* * *

The Tal Pidae Lehrstücke

(On an almost bare stage. An actor, preferably a child or youth, stands very still, wrapped in a dirt covered, old wool, grey-black blanket. She is The Mole. Only her feet and face are visible. An old, long rusty knife is hidden under the blanket.

Scattered sparingly around her are other small shapes made from similar blankets, balled up, perhaps simply tied up tight into a round shape with twine. These are the bodies of the other moles. At certain moments, the Mole will cut the twine loose from a bundle, until all are cut free. Perhaps at times when she cuts the twine, she gives them a caress or a friendly "pat".)

MOLE

Molars. That's our predicament.

While the upper jaw consists of three small incisors, a large canine and three unicuspid premolars, the lower jaw has three incisors, followed by a very small canine. Tal Pidae. The perfect living machine. Except for the molars.

Flectere si nequeo superos, Acheronta movebo. (beat) And why wouldn't we study Latin? We guzzle, graze, gnaw, nibble, and munch all the other dross that sinks and stinks in the dirt. Scrichity, scratchity, didacticity. Can't you just smell the delectable decay? *Flectere si nequeo superos*: if I cannot bend the higher powers.

Tal Pidae. Deep chest bone, burly, brawny digging organs, with an extra bone—yes, an extra bone!—to increase the surface area of our limbs, thrusting, stroking, sweeping, quarrying, ramming, prodding, grubbing, gnarling in the dirt in our tunnels of scum. And yes, mas-ti-cating. *(shivers with pleasure)*. And twenty-two tentacles on the snout. Our hairless snouts that we are not ashamed of. An antenna for a tail, testing the delicious stank of the wind. And all this in the service of, all this to make clearance for: the somersault, that trickity turning flip. Though many of us have forgotten, we know how to do it; we've a blueprint in our snout because it's too narrow to turn around in our tunnels and we can't back up in a natural way. (Though what happens all the time is not natural). So we must somersault and then we're facing behind and behind becomes in front and in this way we can push out the muck that we've dug, push it up and out of our tunnels. Over accumulation suffocates. Repeat after me: I will not be mummified under surplus value.

(sings) It's a riot down below.
Under your feet.
Careful how you go.
Suck sparingly on the teat.
Bestow, bestow. Bestow, bestow!

But don't forget to find the naps between hard bouts of mining. Hell, yeah we've got unions. One mole united will eat the defeated!

But no heroics, no, no, no. For that is granting forgiveness to ourselves as perpetrators, and redemption (with a little, bashful "r"), redemption only through accountability! Heroic is death without its sweet, sleepy nap, and property never something natural but founded in convention and that's why we must put the earthworm on the block.

Now we're at the heart of the matter... the question of the molar and the matter of an earthworm's heart, which is its grit. And you gotta know how to handle the grit as you feast:

Song of the Endless Earthworm

It's a delicious hook, this intestinal dream,
a slippery crook, this subterranean dream,
It'll pull you deep in, this lone tug-o-war team,
a sublime ambrosial machine of spin,
have you believing you've hit
the cornucopian seam.

Another piece of Latin I tunnelled into: *caro data vermibus*. A dead language; language fit for mastication; a garbled message from another empire. Across history: the rise and fall. Mountain to *(winks)* a molehill.

In other words, I translate, flesh given to worms: Ca-da-ver. Don't become one. I do everyone a service ripping them apart.

But consuming the earthworm can be deadly. Because of the grit. So listen up. The instructions on eating an earthworm are the following:

Firstly: decapitate. Secondly: pull between the claws of the forefeet with repeated upward jerking motions of the head to cleanse the worm's outer skin and squeeze, squeeeeeze out any remaining grit from the gizzard. The worm must be grit-free before consumption.

(says title) **The Decapitation Song**

(sings) Grit in the gizzard
is a hazard, a trick.
It'll wear down your molars
so you'll starve like a flickering wick.

Consuming grit leads to corrosion and ruination. Ruination of the molars is the main natural reason for the death of moles. Hence, the earthworm's grit must perish with the state because the inability to grieve for the bodies of others, withering, putrefying, blasted, incinerated from below and above, wears down the molars until we can no longer eat. And so we begin to starve until there is only a small sack of bones rolling on a little while, unable to somersault, unable to nap, until it tips on its side, one scrawny limb scratching at the air for traction and gives up its miniscule ghost. Like the petal of a flower, a puff of ash.

Only the whole is true. Not the petal or puff by and of itself.

Why such violent cleansing of the worm? Because we are covered in luxurious fur, our moleskin hunted, flayed, and skinned by the worms of capital, appropriation, and distortion. This cannot continue. This caricature of the world wherein paid work has become death. Now, now, now.

Somersault are our rejuvenation, our necessary frolic, our hard look into the front of the behind. For the future is incalculable. Those are the facts.

Topple, unfix, borrow, burrow, mixity, mixity, all of us, all of us, deep in our tunnels. *Acheronta movebo*. Tremble the underground and the curled rinds of oranges: our bodies, our bodies, for the transfiguration of disaster, the "I" decapitated of its capital, the grit squeezed from its gizard. We're re-emerging, reconstructing, reworking the work into a fruit pit of drossy glee. All for the cause. All for the cause of gainful work to wake to work again to play.

Which is all to say: Thank you. For listening to this introduction to our: Chant Of Ten Necessary Words As Instruction for a Long and Happy Life for Moles:

(Chants simply, slowly)

Dig. Gouge. Burrow.
Nap.
Burrow. Gouge. Dig.
Nap.

(The Mole pauses. Thinking. Then remembers.)

Oh. Forgive me. Left out the tenth and most important word: Somersault.

(The Mole bows its head so the face is invisible once more.)

THE END

Naomi Wallace

On Writing as Transgression

In October 2007, Naomi Wallace, along with playwrights Michelene Wandor and Mike Kenny, participated in a daylong workshop on the principles and challenges of teaching playwriting offered by PALATINE (Performing Arts Learning and Teaching Innovation Network) and hosted by the Centre for Excellence in Teaching and Learning at York St. John University in York, England. Wallace's remarks and admonitions that day have been widely disseminated since a written version was published in the January 2008 edition of American Theatre.

* * *

Writing for the theatre is at its best an act of transgression—and as teachers of playwrights, we should encourage our students to step over the line, redraw the line, erase the line, even multiply the lines so that we sit up, step forward, strike out.

If an intellectual or a writer is "a worker in ideas who uses words as the primary means of production," as Ngugi wa Thiong'o has said, the question then becomes how do we encourage our students to appropriate the means of production (to own language, to be responsible for their writing and to be responsive to that of others) and also have them ask: To what ends am I working? Is my writing merely an exercise in accumulating and/or defending private property, as it were, or a collective endeavor (even when pursued in solitude) that draws upon and adds to a community of writers and practitioners?

In other words, to what purpose, in whose interest am I (are you) writing? As teachers, students, and writers, what is our relationship to the status quo, the powers that be and were, to commonly held assumptions and stereotypes? Is it a relationship of confirmation or challenge? Are we polishers or a pain in the ass? (And to be a pain in the ass is, I think, a noble enterprise.)

I believe the job of mainstream culture and mainstream theatre is to keep the peace. Our job, as teachers, is to encourage new writers to break it, to disrupt the lie, to speak truth to power. Think seriously about the word en-courage: What are we giving our students courage to do, exactly? Not just entertain.

Rarely do students of drama enter the classroom with what we might call, for lack of a better term, "original minds." Surely their originality, their agency for questioning and considering, is there, but it has been dominated and subdued by a culture that amplifies individuality over community, profit over peace, property over human need. For we live in a culture that is hostile to creativity and original thought that does not serve capitalism, empire, and the most virulent by-products of those forces: racism, homophobia, classism, and sexism. Young writers very often bring these values, albeit largely unconsciously, into the classroom and into their writing. And these values make for a diminished, shallow, shopworn, and deadening dramatic arts.

As teachers, we can help writers become aware of what products their writing is "selling"—what values, what reflexes, what assumptions lie below the surface, the dead-weight of which will drag the writing into mediocrity. For all theatre, as Brecht reminds us, is political, and by political we mean human and social in its interaction and impact. All theatre deals with questions of power. Who has it? Who doesn't? Who wants to get it and how? Who lost it and why? Who has killed for it? Who has died for it?

Mainstream theatre, embroiled as it is in mainstream cultural and economic pressures, tends to reward and applaud those who ask the questions that allow for its continued existence, albeit with a few adjustments here and there. But overall the status quo stands largely untouched: heterosexuality continues to be foregrounded; white privilege continues to go unquestioned; writing against injustice continues to be sidelined; and to question our most deeply felt assumptions is, finally, deemed unproductive, not to mention impolite.

When I speak of "writing as transgression," I am calling for a teaching of theatre that encourages students to write against their "taught" selves and to engage, as bell hooks puts it, in the kind of "self-transgression" and "critical awareness of self" that will enable them to become, as John Donne suggests, "citizens of the world." Transgression is, among other things, a dissection of one's self and a discovery of larger worlds. Both processes (or perhaps they are one) involve questioning entitlement and empathy.

While Britain is, I believe, more tolerant about transgressive theatre than the United States, students in both countries are often hesitant to write politically. They are afraid of being deemed doctrinaire, boring, uncreative, or PC. (And let me digress here to say that I agree with Marcus Brigstocke that "accusations of 'politically correct thought control' have become a pathetic and transparent excuse for lazy racists, sexists and Islamophobes the land over.") Worse, students may fear that a politically and morally informed writing might ultimately hamper their career prospects.

We must encourage students to realize that engaging with history—engaging with the collective human dramas around us—does not lead to a dead end for writers; and here let me simply cite the examples of Arthur Miller, Tony Kushner, Adrienne Kennedy, August Wilson, Dario Fo, Harold Pinter, Caryl Churchill, Kwame Kwei-Armah, Tracey Scott Wilson, Debbie Tucker Green, Chay Yew, and Robert O'Hara, to name but a few. Historically, theatre has been synonymous with politically challenging and socially pressing subjects. Shakespeare, Sheridan, Shaw, and Storey spring to mind.

But there can never be enough of a good thing: We need more engaged and dissenting writers in theatre. We need more writers who envision theatre as a space for social and imaginative transformation.

I tend to generalize. I like to generalize. But what are some of the specific ways we can move students to think outside their own experience, their own gender, their own race, their own class? Here are six ways (perhaps irresponsibly vague ways, but I hope helpful) in which we can nudge these new writers to transgress:

- Help them to identify their "ways of seeing," to use John Berger's term—the socially and culturally determined choices they make when writing.
- Encourage them to critique these accepted ways of seeing and to write, as Walter Benjamin suggests, against/around and through them—to write against the grain.
- Study the linguistic mechanisms—the lingo, jargon, rhetoric, obfuscations, coinage—through which inhuman systems are maintained.
- Disrupt the cliché and the cluttered mind. By this I mean to work against the grit and garbage that passes for information and that we have been trained to consume hour in and hour out. For example, if we ask ourselves whose husband Brad Pitt used to be, most of us will know, despite ourselves, that it was Jennifer Aniston, and that he is

now partnered with the gorgeous Angelina Jolie. But if we ask ourselves how many tons of radioactive waste were left behind by the British and American forces in the first Gulf War, across a region that was once known as the land of dates, it might take a little more time to come up with the answer (350 tons). One might suspect that our knowledge about Mr. Pitt is nurtured precisely to obscure more pressing issues.

- Encourage this new agency and/or flourishing of the writer with required readings that include not only Euripides, Webster, Behn, Shakespeare, Chekhov, and Brecht, but the more recent transgressive writings of Heiner Müller, Edward Bond, Trevor Griffiths, Wole Soyinka, Georg Büchner, Betty Shamieh, Richard Montoya, Kwame Kwei-Armah (who should be mentioned twice), Ismail Khalidi, and Kia Corthron. And that is an ungratefully small list.
- Encourage students of playwriting to read history, constantly, aggressively—to inform themselves thoroughly of the subject matter about which they write. As Berger wrote at the end of the last century: "In the modern world in which thousands of people are dying every hour as a consequence of politics, no writing anywhere can begin to be credible unless it is informed by political awareness and principles. Writers who have neither produce Utopian trash. The unpardonable perversity of our fin de siècle is that of its innocence." Yes, that's harsh. Perhaps Berger's words even seem inflexible and unforgiving, but the call for informed writing is one of crucial importance. If writers can reimagine language, with an effort that aspires to fluency in history and its myriad forces, then we can reimagine ourselves and our communities—and that, for me as a writer, is the highest aspiration.

Sometimes I am asked about "dryness"—which I think translates for the questioner into writing devoid of passion and complexity and entertainment. The suggestion is that encouraging students to examine, question, and resist mainstream culture and theatre will be "off-putting," will unplug students from their creative juices, as though creative juice is something outside history, outside politics and social cause-and-effect. In fact, I think that a more ferocious creative juice can be found in the veins of history, which, sadly, are too often filled with blood. Not the blood of the few, not the blood of the privileged, but the blood of the many.

If not the question of dryness, I'm confronted with the question of sex, or the lack of it. Intimacy, when writing, is political, and I think we must acknowledge to students that the human dramas of politics and economics are very, very sexy and very, very intimate. As the critic Terry Eagleton writes, our economic world is about "the plundering of the body of its sensuous wealth"—how the body is broken down, used, and abused under capitalism. What could be more intimate and personal than the history of our bodies and their relationship to the world?

History itself is a study in intimacy, or our lack of it, with others. What else is history and politics but the struggle of people to define who they are and what they can and cannot do? In two books that should be required reading, Howard Zinn's *A People's History of the United States* and Robin D. G. Kelley's *Freedom Dreams: The Black Radical Imagination*, there are sex and strikes, intrigues and visions, empire and estrangement, murder and the marvelous. You name it, it's there waiting to be written about.

That millions of innocent women, men, and children in Africa have died because of the rampant greed and criminal price hiking of multinationals is not sexy, but it is intimate. That thousands have died and many thousands more have been maimed in the Middle East by US bullets and shrapnel is again certainly not sexy, but surely very intimate, as is the fact that the bullets that enter the bodies of Palestinian children, fired by Israeli soldiers, are paid for by American taxes earned by American workers who dream of fishing, baseball, and sex. What could be more personal than the names that are given to the bombs used to tear our fellow humans in Iraq and Afghanistan into as many pieces as possible—Fishbeds, Floggers, Fulcrums. Adams, Beehives, and Bouncing Betties. There is even a weapon called Sad Eyes. What could be more intimate or personal than the fact that we get up in the morning, kiss our loved ones, go to work, come home, pay our taxes—and those taxes from our daily labor are used to kill you and you and you, and I never saw your face nor knew your name.

Dramatic, yes. But we are involved in the job of drama—real drama. It is happening all around us, every minute. And the fact is that while we are "all" connected by the Internet, that "all" does not include the eighty percent of the world's population that has never even made a phone call—because the lives we live here, of abundance and so-called choice, are predicated on the impoverishment and suffering of most of the world.

I am not calling for a condescending theatre or a "preach to the converted" theatre but a welcoming, vigorous, inquisitive, and brutal theatre. If we encourage our students to dig, they will find the body, in all its intimacy and vulnerability, under the garbage of mainstream political rhetoric.

Our job as teachers, as writers with something to humbly give those who will replace us, must be to encourage our students to challenge normative ways of seeing, to get uncomfortable, to get unsafe, to get unsure. To be safe and sure and comfortable in this beautiful, brutalized, vandalized, depleted but continuously awe-inspiring world is in fact to turn away from it-to turn one's back in large part on life and that age-old succor that writers need: truth.

Our job as teachers is to help students move out of what I like to call the "wow" state of mind to a "how" mind: How did it come to this? How am I diminished by my own ignorance? How have I been silenced in ways I am not aware of? How do I restore to language, on the stage, an agency, and quality that clarifies rather than colludes, that resists rather than conforms? Our job is to encourage our students to become, through their writing, responsible both morally and sensuously—to become dangerous citizens. This should happen if not for moral reasons then for the simple reason of self-preservation, because if we do not, as writers and citizens, engage in resistance to all that diminishes us, then our humanity suffers-and with it, our sensibility as creative writers.

Martin Luther King, Jr. said, "Our lives begin to end the day we become silent about the things that matter." I continue to believe that envisioning a different world is what makes us half-divine. To live and write in a world of resistance to injustice is what makes our lives worthwhile.

Four lines of a poem by Randall Jarrell sum up for me our interconnectedness:

In bombers named for girls, we burned
The cities we had learned about in school—
Till our lives wore out; our bodies lay among
The people we had killed and never seen.

And as global warming and environmental crises, as well as human migrations, have underlined, we live in an interdependent and unavoidably intimate world: Yorkshire, where I live in England, is closer to Baghdad than we are led to believe. And Kentucky, where I was born, is closer to Gaza or Jerusalem; London closer to Burma (Myanmar) and Jena, LA; New York closer to Colombia and Congo. The distance between us is an ingenious fabrication that it is worth spending our lives, as teachers and writers, tearing down.

Let us transgress together—and by this heat, by the sparks that are generated, make a light to see by, for all of us.

Appendix A: Naomi Wallace Selected Production History

Production histories can be misleading. A new play comes into being over a period of time, often developed in stages through private readings, public readings, staged readings, and workshop productions. A script might be drafted years before its first full production and change considerably in the process. In the case of Naomi Wallace, dating the plays is complicated by the fact that a number of them are commissioned monologues, ten-minute plays, or short one-acts included in a new play festival or presented for a special occasion.

The plays are listed here in the order of their first professional production (not always an easy judgment to make) by year and month of the first performance. Productions at larger, institutional theatres ran for weeks, even months; others were seen only a few times or presented as one-night-only special events. This list is selective, particularly regarding Wallace's two most popular plays, *One Flea Spare* and *The Trestle at Pope Lick Creek*. It does not list college and university productions except in a few rare instances when they are of historical importance; it should be noted that *The Trestle at Pope Lick Creek* has proven especially attractive to campus theatre groups. Early apprentice works, such as *Blackout Frames* and *The Bone Gardens*, are not included here either, although the latter was presented by PushPush Theater as part of the 2001 Naomi Wallace Festival in Atlanta.

War Boys

May 1992. (workshop) Iowa Playwrights Festival, University of Iowa.
Feb. 1993. (premiere) Finborough Theatre, London, England. Dir.: Kate Valentine.
June 1999. East Window Theatre Company, Chicago, IL. Dir.: Adam Joyce.
Sep. 2001. (staged reading) Dad's Garage, Atlanta, GA. Part of 2001 Naomi Wallace Festival.

In the Fields of Aceldama

May 1991. (workshop) Iowa Playwrights Festival, University of Iowa. Dir.: Diana Dawson.
May 1993. (premiere) London New Play Festival at the Old Red Lion Theatre, Islington, London, England. Dir.: Jessica Dromgoole.
Oct. 2001. (staged reading) Horizon Theatre Company and Georgia State University, Atlanta, GA. Part of 2001 Naomi Wallace Festival. Dir.: Gayle Austin.

The Girl Who Fell Through a Hole in Her Jumper (with Bruce McLeod)

July 1994. (premiere) London New Play Festival, at Old Red Lion Theatre, London, England.
Oct. 2001. PushPush Theater, Atlanta, GA. Part of 2001 Naomi Wallace Festival.
June 2009. Haslington Amateur Theatrical Society, Haslington, Cheshire East, England.

In the Heart of America

Aug. 1994. (premiere) Bush Theatre, London, England. Dir.: Dominic Dromgoole.
Nov. 1994. (workshop) Long Wharf Theatre, Stage II, New Haven, CT. Dir.: Tony Kushner.
Jan. 1995. Theater Dortmund, Dortmund, Germany. As *Im Herzen Amerikas*. Dir.: Wolfgang Trautwein.
June 1995. New Image Theatre at Pilgrim Center for the Arts, Seattle, WA. Dir.: Alan DiBona.
Jan. 1998. About Face Theatre at Jane Addams Center, Chicago, IL. Dir.: Eric Rosen.
Nov. 1998. Tracer Productions at the Oedipus Complex, Denver, CO. Dir.: Jeremy Cole.
June 1999. Fritz Theatre, San Diego, CA. Dir.: Bryan Bevell.
Oct. 2001. PushPush Theater, Atlanta, GA. Part of 2001 Naomi Wallace Festival.
Feb. 2004. InterAct Theatre Company, Philadephia, PA. Dir.: Seth Rozin.
Jan. 2007. Knightsbridge Theatre, Los Angeles, CA. Dir.: Jamil Chokachi.
May 2008. Rep Stage at Howard Community College, Columbia, MD. Dir.: Kasi Campbell.
Feb. 2012. Theatre Seven of Chicago at Greenhouse Theater Center, Chicago, IL. Dir.: Brian Golden.

One Flea Spare

Oct. 1995. (premiere) Bush Theatre, London, England. Dir.: Dominic Dromgoole.

Feb. 1996. Actors Theatre of Louisville/Humana Festival of New American Plays, Louisville, KY. Dir.: Dominic Dromgoole.
Feb. 1997. The Public Theater, New York, NY. Dir.: Ron Daniels.
Mar. 1998. Dolphinback Theatre at Live Bait Theatre, Chicago, IL. Dir.: Matt Wallace.
Apr. 1998. Perishable Theatre, Providence, RI. Dir.: Rebecca Patterson.
Oct. 1998. Evidence Room at the Ivy Substation, Culver City, CA. Dir.: Bart DeLorenzo.
Dec. 1998. Nightwood Theatre at Canadian Stage Theatre, Toronto, Canada. Dir.: Alisa Palmer.
July 1999. Naked Eye Theatre at Goodman Studio Theatre, Chicago, IL. Dir.: Jeremy B. Cohen
July 1999. New Theatre, New Gables, FL. Dir.: Rafael de Acha.
Mar. 2000. Kitchen Dog Theatre at The MAC, Dallas, TX. Dir.: Adrian Hall.
Mar. 2001. New Repertory Theatre at Arsenal Center for the Arts, Watertown, MA. Dir: David Wheeler.
Oct. 2001. Synchronicity Performance Group at 7 Stages Back Stage Theatre, Atlanta, GA. Part of 2001 Naomi Wallace Festival. Dir.: Rachel May.
Apr. 2002. Luna Id Production at the Substation's Guinness Theatre, Singapore. Dir.: Christian Huber
Apr. 2004. Belvoir St Theatre, Surry Hills, Sydney, Australia. Dir.: Tanya Denny.
May. 2005. Chance Theater Repertory Company, Anaheim, CA. Dir.: Patricia L. Terry.
Nov. 2005. The Rep at Pittsburgh Playhouse, Pittsburgh, PA. Dir.: John Shepard.
Apr. 2008. Mildred's Umbrella Theater at the Midtown Art Center, Houston, TX. Dir.: Patricia Duran.
Sep. 2008. Sage Theatre at Joyce Doolittle Theatre, Calgary, Alberta, Canada. Dir.: Geoffrey Ewert.
Feb. 2010. Whistler in the Dark at Factory Theatre, Boston, MA. Dir.: Meg Taintor.
Sep. 2010. Red Dog at foyer arts, Stroud, Gloucestershire, England. Followed by regional tour and Apr. 2011 run at Old Red Lion Theatre, Islington, London, England. Dir.: Sue Colverd.
Feb. 2011. Forum Theatre at Round House Theatre, Silver Spring, MD. Dir.: Alexander Strain.
Apr. 2011. Strand Theatre, Baltimore, MD. Dir.: Jayme Kilburn.
Apr. 2011. Eclipse Theatre at Greenhouse Theater Center, Chicago, IL. Dir.: Anish Jethmalani.
Sep. 2011. Balagula Theatre, Lexington, KY. Dir.: Natasha Williams.
Apr. 2012. Comédie-Française, Théâtre-Éphémère, Paris, France. Dir.: Anne-Laure Liégeois. As *Une puce, épargnez-la*. Trans.: Dominique Hollier

Slaughter City

Jan. 1996. (premiere) Royal Shakespeare Company at The Pit, Barbican Centre, London, England. Dir.: Ron Daniels.
Mar. 1996. American Repertory Theatre, Cambridge, MA. Dir.: Ron Daniels.
Jan. 2002. (staged reading) Studio Theatre at The Studio 2ndStage, Washington, DC. Dir.: Jay Stirpe.
Feb. 2003. Theatre Alliance at H Street Playhouse, Washington, DC. Dir.: Jeremy Skidmore.
Apr. 2004. Crowded Fire, San Francisco, CA. Dir.: Rebecca Novick.
Feb. 2010. Son of Semele Ensemble, Los Angeles, CA. Dir.: Barbara Kallir.
May 2011. Jackalope Theatre at Raven Theatre's West Stage. Chicago, IL. Dir.: Kaiser Ahmed.
June 2013. Prop Thtr, Chicago, IL. Dir.: Karen Fort.

Birdy (adaptation of William Wharton novel)

July 1996. (premiere) Drum Theatre, Plymouth and Lyric Hammersmith Studio, London, England. Dir.: Kevin Knight.
Mar. 1997. Comedy Theatre, London, England. Dir.: Kevin Knight.
June 1998. Philadelphia Theatre Company, Philadelphia, PA. Dir.: Kevin Knight.
Feb. 2000. Tesson Theatre, Johannesburg, South Africa. Dir.: Joshua Lindberg.
Mar. 2000. Duke University in association with Spring Sirkin, Raleigh, NC. Dir.: Kevin Knight.
Oct. 2001. (staged reading) Soul-stice Repertory Ensemble, Atlanta, GA. Part of 2001 Naomi Wallace Festival. Dir.: Barbara Cole.
Nov. 2003. Women's Project and Productions at Reynolds Theater, New York, NY. Dir.: Lisa Peterson.
May 2004. Kangaroo Court Theatre Company at Crescent Theatre, Birmingham England. Dir.: Neil McCurley.
Nov. 2007. Needtheater at The Lounge Theatre. Hollywood, CA. Los Angeles Premiere. Dir.: Matt Wells.

In the Sweat (with Bruce McLeod)

July 1997. (premiere) Chichester Festival Youth Theatre at Royal National Theatre, London, England. Commission for BT National Connections (youth theatre scheme). Dir.: David Gothard.
May 2002. PushPush Theatre, Atlanta, GA. Part of 2001 Naomi Wallace Festival.

Appendix A   291

The Trestle at Pope Lick Creek

Mar. 1998. (premiere) Actors Theatre of Louisville Humana Festival of New American Plays, Louisville, KY. Dir.: Adrian Hall.
June 1999. New York Theatre Workshop, New York, NY. Dir.: Lisa Peterson.
Nov. 1999. Theatre Schmeater, Seattle, WA. Dir.: Sheila Daniels.
Jan. 2000. Frank Theatre at Loring Playhouse, Minneapolis, MN. Dir.: Wendy Knox.
Jan. 2001. Traverse Theatre, Edinburgh, Scotland. Dir.: Philip Howard.
Oct. 2001. Theatre Emory, Atlanta, GA. Part of 2001 Naomi Wallace Festival. Dir.: Vincent Murphy.
Jan. 2002. Aurora Theatre Company, Berkeley, CA. Dir.: Søren Oliver.
Mar. 2002. Rivendell Theatre Ensemble at Breadline Theatre, Chicago, IL. Dir.: Karen Kessler.
May 2003. Southwark Playhouse, London, England. Dir.: Raz Shaw.
Mar. 2005. Sage Theatre at Joyce Doolittle Theatre, Calgary, Alberta, Canada. Dir.: Kevin McKendrick.
Oct. 2006. Prime Cut Productions at Old Museum Arts Centre, Belfast, Northern Ireland. Followed by a regional tour. Dir.: Patrick O'Kane.
Nov. 2006. Alchemy Theatre Company at The Lock Up, Surry Hills, Sydney, Australia. Dir.: Penny Lindley.
Feb. 2008. Kitchen Dog Theater at The MAC, Dallas, TX. Dir.: Tim Johnson.
Oct. 2009. Rapscallion Theatre Collective at The Medicine Show Theatre, New York, NY. Dir.: Christopher Anderson.
July 2011. Eclipse Theatre at Greenhouse Theater Center, Chicago IL. Dir.: Jonathan Berry.
Oct. 2012. Moxie Theatre, San Diego, CA. Dir.: Delicia Turner Sonnenberg.
Feb. 2013. Dreamwell Theatre. Iowa City, IA. Dir.: Chuck Dufano.
Nov. 2013. La Compagnie Ariadne, Théâtre Théo Argence, Saint-Priest, France. As *Au Pont de Pope Lick*. Trans.: Dominique Hollier. Dir.: Anne Courel.

Standard Time

Sep. 1999. "Mumia 911" at Public Theater, New York, NY. Part of A National Day of Art to Stop the Execution of Mumia Abu-Jamal.
Apr. 2000. (premiere) Actors Theatre of Louisville/Humana Festival of New American Plays, Louisville, KY. Dir.: Michael Bigelow Dixon.
Oct. 2001. (reading) Out of Hand Theater at PushPush Theatre, Atlanta, GA. Part of 2001 Naomi Wallace Festival.

The Inland Sea (previously titled Fugitive Cant)

Oct. 2001. Georgia Shakespeare Festival at Oglethorpe University, Atlanta, GA. Part of 2001 Naomi Wallace Festival. Dir.: Richard Garner.
Apr. 2002. (premiere) Oxford Stage Company at Wilton's Music Hall, London, England. Dir.: Dominic Dromgoole.
Nov. 2011. Theatre Department, Macalester College, Saint Paul, MN. Dir.: Beth Cleary.

The Retreating World*

Oct. 2000. (reading) McCarter Theatre Center, Princeton, NJ. Dir.: Jeremy Cohen.
Nov. 2001. (reading) "Imagine: Iraq." Eight short plays produced by Naomi Wallace and Artists Network of Refuse & Resist! at Cooper Union, New York, NY.
July 2002. (premiere) Menagerie Theatre Company, Cambridge, England. Part of "Hotbed" (new writing festival). Dir: Patrick Morris.
Mar. 2003. Menagerie Theatre Company and Latchmere Theatre, London, England. Presented with Fraser Grace's *Gifts of War* as "Two Into War". Dir.: Patrick Morris.
June 2010. Paper Crane Theatre at People's Center Theatre, Minneapolis, MN. Dir.: Levi Morris.
Aug. 2010. The Now Theatre and Rogue Theatre at The Historic Y, Tucson, AZ. On a triple bill with *One Short Sleepe* and Nic Adams's *Guajero*.
* see also *The Fever Chart: Three Visions of the Middle East*

Things of Dry Hours

Apr. 2004. (premiere) Pittsburgh Public Theater, Pittsburgh, PA. Dir.: Israel Hicks.
Jan. 2005. Portland Center Stage, Portland, OR. Dir.: Chris Coleman.
Oct. 2006. Center Stage, Baltimore MD. Dir: Kwame Kwei-Armah.
Feb. 2007. The Studio Theatre at Manchester Royal Exchange, Manchester, England. Transferred to Gate Theatre, London. Dir.: Raz Shaw.
May 2009. New York Theatre Workshop, New York, NY. Dir.: Ruben Santiago-Hudson.
Apr. 2010. Cleveland Public Theatre, Cleveland, OH. Dir.: Sarah May.
July 2011. (staged reading) Théâtre Ouvert and Festival d'Avignon at Chapelle des Pénitents blancs, Avignon, France. As *Les heures seches*. Trans.: Dominque Hollier. Dir.: Guillaume Lévêque.

To Perish Twice (originally titled Rawalpindi)

2005. (staged reading) National Theatre Studio, London, England. Dir.: Raz Shaw.

A State of Innocence*

Sep. 2004. (premiere) 7:84 at Traverse Theatre, Edinburgh, Scotland. Commission for "Global Response" (twelve short plays for the third anniversary of 9/11).
Apr. 2005. Theatre 503, London, England. On a double bill with Thomas Crowe's *Photos of Religion*. Dir.: Raz Shaw.
Nov. 2005. Golden Thread Productions at the Magic Theatre, San Francisco, CA. Part of ReOrient 2005. Dir.: Isis Saratial Misdary.
Dec. 2005. STUC Centre, Glasgow, Scotland. On a double bill with Linda McLean's *Cold Cuts*.
Apr. 2008. Women Center Stage at the Culture Project, New York, NY. Dir.: Suzana Berger.
* see also *The Fever Chart: Three Visions of the Middle East*

Between This Breath and You*

July 2006. (premiere) Menagerie Theatre Company, Cambridge, England. Part of "Hotbed" (new writing festival). Dir.: Patrick Morris
May 2007. (reading) New York Theatre Workshop and Nibras at New York University, New York, NY. Part of "Aswat: Voices of Palestine." Dir.: Isis Saratial Misdary.
Jan. 2008. Golden Thread Productions at Magic Theatre, San Francisco, CA. Part of ReOrient 2008. Dir.: Amy Mueller.
* see also *The Fever Chart: Three Visions of the Middle East*

One Short Sleepe

Oct. 2007. International Writing Program, University of Iowa, Iowa City, IA. Part of "All the World's a Page: The Global Play Project" to celebrate fortieth anniversary of IWP.
Mar. 2008. (premiere) Actors Theatre of Louisville Humana Festival of New American Plays, Louisville KY. Dir.: Marc Masterson.
Aug. 2010. The Now Theatre and Rogue Theatre at The Historic Y, Tucson AZ. On a triple bill with *The Retreating World* and Nic Adams's *Guajero*.

The Fever Chart: Three Visions of the Middle East (includes A State of Innocence, Between This Breath and You, and The Retreating World)

Apr. 2007. (workshop) Mill Mountain Theatre's Norfolk Southern Festival of New Works, Roanoke, VA. Dir.: David Gothard.
Mar. 2008. Falaki Mainstage Theatre at The American University in Cairo, Cairo, Egypt. Dir.: Frank Bradley.
Apr. 2008. (premiere) New York Shakespeare Festival/Joseph Papp Public Theater, New York, NY. Dir.: Jo Bonney.

Oct. 2009. Pilot Theatre and York Theatre Royal, York, England. Moved in Mar 2010 to Trafalgar Studios 2, London. Dir.: Katie Posner and Marcus Romer.

Nov. 2010. Underground Railway Theatre at Central Square Theatre, Cambridge, MA. Dir.: Elena Araoz.

Sep. 2011. Eclipse Theater, Chicago, IL. Presented with *No Such Cold Thing* as "Four Visions of the Middle East." Dir.: Steven Fedoruk and Sarah Moeller.

The Hard Weather Boating Party

Nov. 2007. (staged reading) University of Iowa Theatre Department. Part of "Toxic Talk: A Symposium on Disciplinary Rhetorics, Environmental Justice, and Sustainability."

Mar. 2009. (premiere) Actors Theatre of Louisville/Humana Festival of New American Plays, Louisville, KY. Dir.: Jo Bonney.

Mar. 2009. (reading) Wellfleet Harbor Actors Theatre, Wellfleet, MA. Dir.: Jeff Zinn.

Twenty-One Positions: A Cartographic Dream of the Middle East (with Abdelfattah Abusrour and Lisa Schlesinger)

Feb. 2008. (premiere) Fordham University Theatre Company in association with the Public Theater, New York, NY. Dir.: Lisa Peterson.

No Such Cold Thing

Nov. 2009. (premiere) Golden Thread Productions at the Thick House, San Francisco, CA. Part of "ReOrient 2009: The First Ten Years." Dir.: Bella Warda.

And I and Silence

June 2010. (staged reading) Finborough Theatre, London, England. Dir.: Caitlin McLeod. Part of "Vibrant: An Anniversary Festival of Finborough Playwrights."

May 2011. (premiere) Worn Red Theatre and Clean Break in association with Finborough Theatre. London, England. Dir.: Caitlin McLeod.

Aug. 2011. (staged reading) Eclipse Theatre Company, Chicago, IL. Dir.: Beth Cleary.

June 2013. The Marlowe Society at the Corpus Playroom, Cambridge, England. Dir.: Rosie Skan.

City of Grubs

May 2011. (premiere) La Comédie de Valence, Centre Dramatique National Drôme-Ardèche, at the Atrium Hoel, Valence, France. Part of "A Room in Town" (six monologues for six hotel rooms). Trans.: Dominique Hollier with Richard Brunel. Dir.: Olivier Balazuc.

Nov. 2012. Golden Thread Productions at Z Space. San Francisco, CA. Part of ReOrient 2012. Dir.: Desdemona Chiang.

The Tal Pidae Lehrstücke

Oct. 2012. Center Stage, Baltimore, MD. Commission for "My America," 50 short monologues filmed by Hal Hartley for internet broadcast.

The Liquid Plain

July 2013. (premiere) Oregon Shakespeare Festival, Ashland, OR. Commission for "American Revolutions: The United States History Cycle." Dir.: Kwame Kwei-Armah.

Apr. 2014. Center Stage, Baltimore, MD. Dir.: Kwame Kwei-Armah.

Night Is a Room

Production pending

Appendix B: Naomi Wallace Play Titles and Their Sources

Many Naomi Wallace plays borrow a few words or a phrase from a poem that she likes and use them as a title. Here is a list of those plays, the poem that is the source of their title, and a few excerpted lines that contain the title phrase.

* * *

One Flea Spare (1995)
from the poem "The Flea" by John Donne

> O stay, three lives in one flea spare,
> Where we almost, yea, more than married are.
> This flea is you and I, and this
> Our marriage bed, and marriage temple is.

The Retreating World (2003)
from the poem "Strange Meeting" by Wilfred Owen

> Courage was mine, and I had mystery;
> Wisdom was mine, and I had mastery;
> To miss the march of this retreating world
> Into vain citadels that are not walled.

Things of Dry Hours (2004)
from the poem "kitchenette building" by Gwendolyn Brooks

> We are things of dry hours and the involuntary plan,
> Grayed in, and gray. "Dream" mate, a giddy sound, not strong
> Like "rent", "feeding a wife", "satisfying a man".

To Perish Twice (2005)

from the poem "Fire and Ice" by Robert Frost

> Some say the world will end in fire,
> Some say in ice.
> From what I've tasted of desire
> I hold with those who favor fire.
> But if it had to perish twice,
> I think I know enough of hate
> To say that for destruction ice
> Is also great
> And would suffice.

The Fever Chart: Three Visions of the Middle East (2008)

from the poem "East Coker," Number Two of Four Quartets by T.S. Eliot

> The wounded surgeon plies the steel
> That questions the distempered part;
> Beneath the bleeding hands we feel
> The sharp compassion of the healer's art
> Resolving the enigma of the fever chart.

One Short Sleepe (2008)

from the poem "Death Be Not Proud" by John Donne

> Thou art slave to Fate, Chance, kings, and desperate men,
> And dost with poyson, warre, and sicknesse dwell,
> And poppie, or charmes can make us sleepe as well,
> And better then thy stroake; why swell'st thou then?
> One short sleepe past, wee wake eternally,
> And death shall be no more; death, thou shalt die.

No Such Cold Thing (2009)

from the poem "The Flower" by George Herbert

> Grief melts away
> Like snow in May,
> As if there were no such cold thing.

And I and Silence (2011)

from the poem "I Felt a Funeral, in my Brain" by Emily Dickinson

> As all the Heavens were a Bell,
> And Being, but an Ear,
> And I, and Silence, some strange Race,
> Wrecked, solitary, here -

The Liquid Plain (2013)

from the poem "A Farewell to America" (dedicated to Mrs. S.W.) by Phillis Wheatley

> While for Britannia's distant shore
> We weep the liquid plain,
> And with astonish'd eyes explore
> The wide-extended main.

Night is a Room (2014)

from the poem "Complaint" by William Carlos Williams

> Night is a room
> darkened for lovers,
> through the jalousies the sun
> has sent one golden needle!

Bibliography

Abel, Lionel. *Tragedy and Metatheatre—Essays on Dramatic Form.* Teaneck: Holmes and Meier, 2003.
Ahmad, Aijaz. *In Theory: Classes, Nations, Literatures.* New York and London: Verso, 1992.
Ahmed, Sara. *The Cultural Politics of Emotion.* New York: Routledge, 2004.
Amar, Paul. *The Security Archipelago: Human-Security States, Sexuality Politics, and the End of Neoliberalism.* Durham: Duke University Press, 2013.
Aronowitz, Stanley. *False Promises: The Shaping of American Working Class Consciousness.* Durham: Duke University Press, 1991.
Artaud, Antonin. *The Theatre and Its Double.* Translated by Victor Corti. London: Calder Publications, 1993.
Baker, Barbara, ed. "Naomi Wallace." In *The Way We Write: Interviews with Award-Winning Writers,* 199–213. London: Continuum, 2006.
Bakhtin, Mikhail, Osip Brik, Boris Eichenbaum, and Victor Shklovsky. *Russian Formalist Criticism: Four Essays.* Translated by Lee T. Lemon and Marion J. Reis. Lincoln and London: University of Nebraska Press, 1965.
Baldwin, James. *The Price of the Ticket: Collected Nonfiction, 1948–1985.* New York: St. Martin's, 1985.
Baley, Shannon. "Death and Desire, Apocalypse and Utopia: Feminist Gestus and the Utopian Performative in the Plays of Naomi Wallace." *Modern Drama* 47, no. 2 (Summer 2004): 237–50.
Barnett, Claudia. "Dialectic and the Drama of Naomi Wallace." In *Southern Women Playwrights: New Essays in Literary History and Criticism,* 154–68. Edited by Robert L. McDonald and Linda Rohrer Paige. Tuscaloosa: University of Alabama Press, 2002.
———. "Physical Prisons: Naomi Wallace's Drama of Captivity." In *Captive Audience: Prison and Captivity in Contemporary Theater,* 147–65. Edited by Thomas Fahy and Kimball King. New York: Routledge, 2003.
———. "Judith Thompson's Ghosts: The Revenants that Haunt the Plays." In *Judith Thompson: Critical Perspectives on Canadian Theatre in English,*

vol. 3, 92–98. Edited by Rick Knowles. Toronto: Playwrights Canada Press, 2005.

Bechtel, Roger. "'A Kind of Painful Progress': The Benjaminian Dialectics of *Angels in America*." *Journal of Dramatic Theory and Criticism* 16 (2001): 99–121.

Bell, Hilary. "The Landscape Remembers You: A Reflection by Hilary Bell from an Interview with Naomi Wallace." In *Trans-global Readings: Crossing Theatrical Boundaries*, 111–16. Edited by Caridad Svich. Manchester: Manchester University Press.

Benedetti, Jean. "Brecht, Stanislavski, and the Art of Acting." In *Brecht Then and Now/Damals und Heute, Brecht Yearbook* 20. Edited by John Willet. The International Brecht Society, 1995.

Benjamin, Walter. "Theses on the Philosophy of History." *Illuminations: Essays and Reflections*, 253–64. Edited by Hannah Arendt. New York: Schocken Books, 1969.

Bermingham, Ann. *Landscape and Ideology: The English Rustic Tradition, 1740–1860*. University of California Press, 1986.

Bernstein, Iver. *The New York City Draft Riots*. New York: Oxford University Press, 1990.

Bérubé, Allen and Florence Bérubé. "Sunset Trailer Park." In *White Trash: Race and Class in America*, 15–41. Edited by Matt Wray and Annalee Newitz. New York: Routledge, 1997.

Bilderback, Walter. "The Naomi Wallace Festival and 9/11." *Consciousness, Literature and the Arts* 4, no. 3 (December 2003): http://www.aber.ac.uk/cla/archive/bilderback.html.

Blair, Rhonda. "Reconsidering Stanislavsky: Feeling, Feminism and the Actor." *Theatre Topics* 12, no. 2 (September 2002):177–90.

Bluestone, Barry. *The Deindustrialization of America*. New York: Basic Books, 1984

Boal, Augusto. *The Rainbow of Desire*. Translated by Adrian Jackson. London and New York: Routledge, 1995.

Boyer, Paul. *When Time Shall Be No More: Prophecy and Belief in Modern American Culture*. Cambridge: Harvard University Press, 1994.

Brantley, Ben. "Prisoners in Their Home: Facing the Twin Ravages of Plague and Power." *New York Times*. March 10, 1997: C11+.

Brecher, Jeremy. *Strike! The True History of Mass Insurrections in U.S. History*. Boston: South End Press, 1999.

Brecht, Bertolt. *The Messingkauf Dialogues*. Translated by John Willett. London: Methuen and Co., 1965.

Briggs, Asa. *A Social History of England*. 3rd revised edition. London: Penguin, 1999.

———. *Brecht on Theatre, The Development of an Aestethic*. Translated and edited by John Willett. New York: Hill and Wang, 1992.

Brunetti, Barry. "Eroticizing the Body-In-Crisis: Liminalities in *One Flea Spare*." *On-Stage Studies: A Journal of Production Research* 23 (2000): 20–32.

Burke, Edmund. *A Philosophical Enquiry Into the Origin of Our Ideas of the Sublime and Beautiful*. Edited by James T. Boulton. Notre Dame: University of Notre Dame Press, 1968.

Case, Sue-Ellen. *Feminism and Theatre*. New York: Methuen, 1988.

Casteel, Joshua. *Returns*. Unpublished play script. Sent via email to Erica Stevens Abbitt by David Gothard. August 2012.

Cisneros, Lisa. "Whiz Kids: Elizabeth Stenholt Is Making a Name for Herself on the Stage." *Des Plaines Patch*. (February 28, 2011): http://desplaines.patch.com/articles/whiz-kids-elizabeth-stenholt-is-making-a-name-for-herself-on-the-stage. Accessed March 24, 2011.

Cleary, Beth. "Haunting the Social Unconscious: Naomi Wallace's *In the Heart of America*." *Journal of American Drama and Theatre* 14, no. 2 (Spring 2002): 1–11.

Connolly, Kevin. "Spare the Flea, Spoil the Child: Key Youngster Role Paces London Plague Drama." *Spare Eye Weekly* (December 3, 1998). http://contests.eyeweekly.com/eye/issue/issue_12.03.98/art/flea3.php. Accessed April 14, 2012.

Cummings, Scott T. "Naomi Wallace." In *Twentieth-Century American Dramatists, Third Series*, 345–52. Edited by Christopher Wheatley. Detroit: Thomson Gale.

Dawley, Alan. *Class and Community: The Industrial Revolution in Lynn*. Cambridge: Harvard University Press, 1976.

Deleuze, Gilles. "Society of Control," *L'Autre Journal* 1 (May 1990).

Diamond, Elin. *Unmaking Mimesis: Essays on Feminism and Theatre*. New York: Routledge, 1997.

Dipper, Christoph. "Orders and Classes: Eighteenth Century Society Under Pressure." In *The Eighteenth Century: Europe 1688–1815*, 52–90. Edited by T. C. W. Blanning. Oxford: Oxford University Press, 2000.

Dolan, Jill. "Performance, Utopia, and the Utopian Performative." *Theatre Journal* 53, no. 3 (October 2001): 455–79.

———. *Utopia in Performance: Finding Hope at the Theatre*. Ann Arbor: University of Michigan Press, 2005.

Dowd, Douglas. *The Twisted Dream: Capitalist Development in the United States Since 1776*. Cambridge: Winthrop Publishers, 1977.

Dropkin, Nadia. "Skyscapes of Abdeen, Cairo: Pigeons, Men, and Alternate Socialities." Sexual Sovereignties Conference at the American University of Beirut, Beirut, Lebanon, March 14, 2013.

Elam, Harry Jr. *The Past As Present in the Drama of August Wilson*. Ann Arbor: University of Michigan Press, 2004.

Elias, Amy J. *Sublime Desire: History and Post-1960s Fiction*. Baltimore: Johns Hopkins University Press, 2001.

Fine, Michelle. "Sexuality, Schooling and Adolescent Females: The Missing Discourse of Desire." In *Disruptive Voices: The Possibilities of Feminist Research*, 31–59. Ann Arbor: University of Michigan Press, 1992.
Foley, Neil. *The White Scourge: Mexicans, Blacks, and Poor Whites in Texas Cotton Culture*. Berkeley: University of California Press, 1999.
Freidson, Michael. "Mischa Barton Talks: The Beautiful Star Reveals All in a *Time Out New York* Exclusive." *Time Out New York* (August 25, 2005): http://www.timeout.com/newyork/things-to-do/mischa-barton-talks. Accessed March 24, 2011.
Gardiner, Judith Kegan. *Rhys, Stead, Lessing, and the Politics of Empathy*. Bloomington: Indiana University Press, 1989.
Gardner, Lyn. "Labouring under no illusion." *The Guardian* (24 January 1996a): T-11.
———. "The Mythic and the Marxist." *American Theatre* 13, no. 22 (April 1996b): 4–5.
———. "Enemy Within." *The Guardian*, February 6, 2007.
Gates, Anita. "In Dullsville, Playing Chicken with Life." *New York Times* (July 3, 1999): B9.
Gilligan, Carol, Annie G. Rogers, and Deborah L. Tolman, eds. *Women, Girls and Psychotherapy: Re-framing Resistance*. New York, London, and Sydney: Harrington Park Press and Haworth Press, 1991.
Goodrich, Carter L. *The Frontier of Control: A Study in British Workshop Politics*. New York: Harcourt, Brace, and Howe, 1920.
Gordon, Lewis R. "Through the Zone of Nonbeing: A Reading of *Black Skin, White Masks* in Celebration of Fanon's Eightieth Birthday." *CLR James Journal* 11, no. 1 (Summer 2005): 1–43.
Gornick, Vivian. "An American Exile in America." *New York Times Magazine* (March 2, 1997): 27–31.
Greene, Alexis. "Naomi Wallace." In *Women Who Write Plays: Interviews with American Dramatists*, 449–71. Hanover: Smith and Kraus, 2001.
Hale, Gwendolyn N. "Absence in Naomi Wallace's *The Trestle at Pope Lick Creek*." *Journal of Dramatic Theory and Criticism* 21, no. 2 (2007): 153–60.
Hansel, Adrien-Alice and Amy Wegener, eds. *Humana Festival 2009: The Complete Plays*. New York: Playscripts, 2009.
Harris, Cheryl. "Whiteness as Property." In *Critical Race Theory*, 276–91. Edited by Kimberlé Crenshaw et al. New York: The New Press, 1995.
Héliot, Armelie. "Entrée d'une baroque au répertoire de la Comédie-Française." *Le Figaro* Translated by Dominique Hollier. Théâtre-Ephémère, Comédie-Française. May 1, 2012. Accessed May 15, 2012. http://blog.lefigaro.fr/theatre/2012/05/une-bien-etrange-entree-au-rep.html.
Hill, C. P. *British Economic and Social History, 1700–1982*. 5th edition. London: Edward Arnold, 1985.

Hinde, Thomas. *Capability Brown: The Story of a Master Gardener.* London: Hutchinson, 1986.
Hobsbawn, Eric. *Industry and Empire: From 1750 to the Present Day.* London: Penguin, 1999.
Hogarth, William. *The Analysis of Beauty.* New Haven: Yale University Press, 1997.
Huff, Helen. "A Land of Despair and Change: Landscapes of Wealth and Poverty in Selected Plays of Naomi Wallace." *Revista de Estudios Norteamericanos* no. 15 (2011): 51–68.
Hunter, Tera. *To 'joy My Freedom: Southern Black Women's Lives and Labors After the Civil War.* Cambridge: Harvard University Press, 1998.
Hurley, Erin. *Theatre and Feeling.* London and New York: Palgrave Macmillan, 2010.
Husserl, Edmund. *Ideas: General Introduction to Pure Phenomenology.* Translated by W. R. Boyle. London: Allen and Unwin, 1969.
———. *Cartesian Meditations: An Introduction to Phenomenology.* Translated by. Dorian Cairns. The Hague: Martinus Nijhoff, 1977.
Hymas, Edward. *Capability Brown and Humphrey Repton.* Johns Hopkins University Press, 1989.
Inness, Sherrie A. *Tough Girls: Women Warriors and Wonder Women in Popular Culture.* Philadelphia: University of Pennsylvania Press, 1999.
Isherwood, Charles. "Supplying Shelter and the Gospel of Marx." *New York Times* (June 9, 2009): http://theater.nytimes.com/2009/06/09/theater/reviews/09things.html. Accessed January 28, 2013.
Istel, John. "In the Heart of America: Forging Links." *American Theatre* 12 no. 3 (March 1995), 25.
Jahoda, Gustav. "Theodor Lipps and the Shift from 'Sympathy' to 'Empathy.'" *Journal of the History of the Behavioral Sciences* 41, no. 2 (Spring 2005): 151–63.Jameson, Fredric. *Postmodernism, or, the Cultural Logic of Late Capitalism.* Durham: Duke University Press, 1991.
Jenson, Robert. *The Heart of Whiteness: Confronting Race, Racism, and White Privilege.* San Francisco: City Lights, 2005.
Julian, Connie. "Naomi Wallace: Looking for Fire." *Revolutionary Worker* #1232. (March 14, 2004): http://rwor.org/a/1232/naomirwinterview.htm. Accessed January 28, 2013.
Katz, Robert L. *Empathy: Its Nature and Uses.* London: Free Press of Glencoe, 1963.
Kazanjian, David. *The Colonizing Trick: National Culture and Imperial Citizenship.* Minneapolis: University of Minnesota Press, 2003.
Kearney, Mary Celeste. "Producing Girls: Rethinking the Study of Female Youth Cultures." In *Delinquents and Debutantes: Twentieth-Century American Girls' Cultures*, 285–310. Edited by Sherrie A. Innes. New York and London: New York University Press, 1998.

Kelley, Robin D. G. *Hammer and Hoe: Alabama Communists During the Great Depression.* Chapel Hill: University of North Carolina Press, 1990.

——. *Freedom Dreams: The Black Radical Imagination.* Boston: Beacon Press, 2002.

Khalidi, Ismail, Erin B. Mee, and Naomi Wallace. "Creation Under Occupation." *American Theatre* 29, no. 2 (February 2012), 28–31.

Koger, Kae and Adrian-Alice Hansel. "The T(ext) Shirt Project: An Introduction." In *Humana Festival 1999: The Complete Plays,* 294–97. Edited by Michael Bigelow Dixon and Amy Wegener. Smith and Kraus: 1999.

Kushner, Tony. *Tony Kushner in Conversation.* Edited by Robert Vorlicky. Ann Arbor: University of Michigan Press, 1998.

Kushner, Tony and Naomi Wallace. "Grist for a Writers Mill." *American Theatre* 18, no. 8 (October 2001): 37–38.

Lahr, John. "Death-Defying Acts." *New Yorker* (March 24, 1997): 86–87.

Laurie, Bruce. *Artisans into Workers.* Urbana: University of Illinois Press, 1997.

Leder, Drew. *The Absent Body.* Chicago: The University of Chicago Press, 1990.

Lee, Vernon. "Empathy (*Einfühlung*)." In *The Beautiful: An Introduction to Psychological Aesthetics.* Cambridge: Cambridge University Press, 1913.

Linebaugh, Peter and Marcus Rediker. *The Many-Headed Hydra: Sailors, Slaves, Commoners, and the Hidden History of the Revolutionary Atlantic,* 61–69. Boston: Beacon Press, 2000.

Lipsitz, George. *Rainbow at Midnight: Class and Culture in the 1940s.* Urbana: University of Illinois Press, 1994.

——. *The Possessive Investment in Whiteness.* Philadelphia: Temple University Press, 1998.

Lost and Delirious. Directed by Léa Poole. 2001. Santa Monica, CA: Lions Gate Entertainment, 2001. DVD.

Lott, Eric. *Love and Theft: Blackface Minstrelsy and the American Working Class.* New York: Oxford, 1995.

MacDonald, Claire. "Intimate Histories." *Performing Arts Journal* 28, no. 3 (2006): 93–102.

Machon, Josephine. *(Syn)aesthetics: Redefining Visceral Performance.* Basingstoke and New York: Palgrave Macmillan, 2011.

Makdisi, Ussama. *Faith Misplaced: The Broken Promise of US-Arab Relations, 1820–2001.* New York: PublicAffairs, 2010.

Marlowe, Sam. "A Dry Season in Black and White." *The Times* (London) March 12, 2007.

Mee, Erin B. "Juliano Mer Khamis: Murder, Theatre, Freedom, Going Forward." *TDR: The Drama Review* 55, no. 3 (Fall 2011): 9–17.

Mingay, G. E. *Land and Society in England, 1750–1980.* London: Longman, 1994.

Mootz, William. "Theater of Politics: Prospect Writer's Early Activism Inspires Her Plays." *Louisville Courier-Journal* (November 6, 1994): 1-I.
Morley, Michael. "Brecht and Stanislavski: Polarities or Proximities?" In *I'm Still Here/Ich bin noch da, The Brecht Yearbook 22*. Ontario, Canada: The International Brecht Society, 1997.
Naison, Mark. *White Boy: A Memoir*. Philadelphia: Temple University Press, 2002.
Next Stage Resource Guide: *Things of Dry Hours*. Baltimore: Center Stage Associates, 2007.
Nightingale, Benedict. "Sausage and Mishmash." *The Times* (London), January 29, 1996.
Noble, F.David. *Forces of Production: A Social History of Industrial Automation*. New York: Oxford University Press, 1986.
Nussbaum, Martha C. *Upheavals of Thought: The Intelligence of Emotions*. Cambridge: Cambridge University Press, 2001.
Obenzinger, Hilton. *American Palestine: Melville, Twain, and the Holy Land Mania*. Princeton: Princeton University Press, 1999.
Owens, Craig. "The Allegorical Impulse: Toward a Theory of Postmodernism." In *Beyond Recognition: Representation, Power, and Culture*, 52–69. Edited by Scott Bryson, Barbara Kruger, Lynne Tillman, and Jane Weinstock. Berkeley: University of California Press, 1992.
Ozieblo, Barbara. "Pornography of Violence: Strategies of Representation in Plays by Naomi Wallace, Stefanie Zadravec, and Lynn Nottage." *The Journal of American Drama and Theatre* 23, no. 1 (Winter 2011): 67–80.
Painter, Nell. *The Narrative of Hosea Hudson: The Life and Times of a Black Radical*. New York: W. W. Norton, 2002.
Phelan, Peggy and Jill Lane, ed. Introduction to *The Ends of Performance*. New York: New York University Press, 1998.
Piepenburg, Erik. "A Theater Celebrates 50 Years With 50 New Films." *New York Times*. (September 27, 2012): artsbeat.blogs.nytimes. Accessed June 2, 2013.
Pipher, Mary Bray. *Reviving Ophelia: Saving the Selves of Adolescent Girls*. New York: Ballantine Books, 1994.
Poland, Warren S. "The Limits of Empathy." *American Imago* 64, no. 1 (2007): 87–93.
Porter, Roy. *English Society in the Eighteenth Century*. London: Allen Lane, 1982.
Povinelli, Elizabeth A. *Economies of Abandonment: Social Belonging and Endurance in Late Liberalism*. Durham: Duke University Press, 2011.
———. "Sovereign Disciplines, Queer Objects." Keynote Address at the Sexual Sovereignties Conference at the American University of Beirut, Beirut, Lebanon, March 14, 2013.

Puar, Jasbir K. "I Would Rather Be a Cyborg Than a Goddess: Becoming-Intersectional in Assemblage Theory." *philoSOPHIA* 2, no. 1 (2012): 49–66.

———. "Disabled Diaspora, Rehabilitating State: The Queer Politics of Reproduction in Israel/Palestine." Presentation at the American University of Beirut, Beirut, Lebanon, March 7, 2013.

Rachleff, Peter. *Hard-Pressed in the Heartland: The Hormel Strike and the Future of the Labor Movement.* Boston: South End Press, 1993.

Repton, Humphry. "An Inquiry Into the Changes of Taste in Landscape Gardening." In *The Landscape Gardening and Landscape Architecture of the Late Humphry Repton, Esq*, 325–60. Edited by J. C. Loudon. London: Longman, 1840.

Ridout, Nicholas. *Stage Fright, Animals and Other Theatrical Problems.* Cambridge: Cambridge University Press, 2006.

Robb, J. Cooper. "Gulf Bore." *Philadelphia Weekly* (February 25, 2004): http://pwblogger.com/articles/6895/a-e-stage. Accessed November 27, 2006.

Roediger, David. *The Wages of Whiteness: Race and the Making of the American Working Class.* New York and London: Verso, 1991.

———. *Black on White: Black Writers on What It Means to Be White.* New York: Schocken, 1999.

Rogers, Carl R. "Empathic: An Unappreciated Way of Being." *The Counseling Psychologist* 5, no. 2 (1975): 2–10.

Rosengarten, Theodore. *All God's Dangers: The Life of Nate Shaw.* Chicago: University of Chicago Press, 2000.

Rotbard, Sharon. "Homa Umigdal (Wall and Tower): The Mold of Israeli Architecture." In *A Civilian Occupation: The Politics of Israeli Architecture*, 39–56. Edited by Rafi Segal and Eyal Weizman, London: Verso, 2003.

Saxton, Alexander. *Indispensable Enemy: Labor and the Anti-Chinese Movement in California.* Berkeley: University of California Press, 1975.

———. *The Rise and Fall of the White Republic.* New York: Verso, 2003.

Scarry, Elaine. *The Body in Pain: The Making and Unmaking of the World.* New York and Oxford: Oxford University Press, 1985.

———. *On Beauty and Being Just.* Princeton: Princeton University Press, 2001.

Schechner, Richard. *Between Theatre and Anthropology.* Philadelphia: University of Pennsylvania Press, 1985.

Simon, John. "Up a Creek." *New York* (July 19, 1999): 74–75.

Smith, Anna Deavere. Introduction to *Fires in the Mirror: Crown Heights, Brooklyn and Other Identities.* New York: Anchor, 1993.

Soccio, Lisa. "From Girl to Woman to Grrrl: (Sub)Cultural Intervention and Political Activism in the Time of Post-Feminism." *In[]visible Culture: An*

Electronic Journal for Visual Studies no. 2 (1999): http://www.rochester.edu/in_visible_culture/issue2/soccio.htm. Accessed March 19, 2002.

Solga, Kim. "The Line, the Crack, and the Possibility of Architecture: Future, Ground, Feminist Performance." *Theatre Research in Canada* 29, no. 1 (2008): 1–28.

Solomon, Alisa. *Re-Dressing the Canon: Essays on Theater and Gender*. London and New York: Routledge, 1997.

Stanislavski, Konstantin. *An Actor's Work*. Translated and edited by Jean Benedetti. London and New York: Routledge, 2008.

Steiger, Amy. "Re-Membering Our Selves: Acting, Critical Pedagogy, and the Plays of Naomi Wallace." *Theatre Topics* 21, no. 1 (March 2011): 21–32.

Stein, Edith. *On the Problem of Empathy*. 3rd revised edition. Translated by Waltraut Stein. Washington DC: ICS Publications, 1989.

Stephensen, Heidi, and Natasha Langridge. "Naomi Wallace." In *Rage and Reason: Women Playwrights on Playwriting*, 163–72. London: Methuen, 1997.

Stevens Abbitt, Erica. "Performance Review: *The Trestle at Pope Lick Creek*." *Theatre Journal* 54, no. 3 (October 2002): 498–500.

———. "Resisting Bodies: Promise and Change in the Feminist Representation of Girls in the Performative Arena." Ph.D. dissertation, University of California—Los Angeles, UMI, 2003.

———. "Getting Out, Flying and Returning from the Dead: Girl Ghosts in Live Performance." *Journal of Dramatic Theory and Criticism* 21, no. 2 (2007): 143–51.

———. "Performance Review: *Une puce, épargnez-la (One Flea Spare)*" *Theatre Journal* 65, no. 2 (May 2013): 275–77.

Stroud, Dorothy. *Capability Brown*. London: Faber and Faber, 1975.

Sutherland, Douglas. *The Landowners*. London: Muller, 1988.

Svich, Caridad. "American Playwrights on Language and the War in Iraq: A Virtual Roundtable." *Theater* 39, no. 3 (2009): 90–105.

Thandeka. *Learning to Be White: Money, Race, and God in America*. New York: Continuum, 1999.

Trotter W. Joe Jr. *Black Milwaukee: The Making of an Industrial Proletariat*. Urbana: University of Illinois Press, 1985.

Trouillot, Michel-Rolph. *Silencing the Past: Power and the Production of History*. Boston: Beacon Press, 1997.

Vischer, Robert. "On the Optical Sense of Form: A Contribution to Aesthetics." In *Empathy, Form, and Space: Problems in German Aesthetics, 1873–1893*. Edited and translated by Harry Francis Mallgrave and Eleftherios Ikonomou. Santa Monica: The Getty Center, 1994.

Wallace, Naomi. *To Dance a Stony Field: Poems by Naomi Wallace*. Norfolk: Peterloo Poets, 1995a.

Wallace, Naomi. "In the Heart of America." *American Theatre* 12 no. 3 (March 1995b): 25–41.

———. "In the Heart of America." In *Staging Gay Lives: An Anthology of Contemporary Gay Theater*, 525–70. Edited by John M. Clum. Boulder: Westview Press, 1996a.

———. "One Flea Spare." In *Humana Festival 1996: The Complete Plays*. Edited by Michael Bigelow Dixon and Liz Engelman. Hanover: Smith and Kraus, 1996b.

———. *Slaughter City*. London: Faber and Faber, 1996c.

———. "The Trestle at Pope Lick Creek: A Drama by Naomi Wallace." *TheatreForum – International Theatre Journal* 13 (Summer-Fall 1998): 56–75.

———. "Standard Time." In *Humana Festival 2000: The Complete Plays*, 343–49. Edited by Michael Bigelow Dixon and Amy Wegener. Hanover: Smith and Kraus, 2000.

———. *In the Heart of America and Other Plays*. New York: Theatre Communications Group, 2001.

———. *The Inland Sea*. London: Faber and Faber, 2002.

———. *Birdy*. New York: Broadway Play Publishing, 2003a.

———. "On the Road to Palestine: We Are Also Each Other." *American Theatre* 20 no. 6 (July-August 2003b): 71.

———. "The Retreating World." *American Theatre* 20, no. 6 (July-August 2003c): 37–40.

———. "Strange Times." *The Guardian* (London, England), March 29, 2003d.

———. *The War Boys*. New York: Broadway Play Publishing, 2004.

———. *Things of Dry Hours*. London: Faber and Faber 2007a.

———. "On Writing as Transgression: Teachers of Young Playwrights Need to Turn Them Into Dangerous Citizens." *American Theatre* 25 no. 1 (January 2008): 98–102.

———. *The Fever Chart: Three Visions of the Middle East*. New York: Theatre Communications Group, 2009a.

———. *The Hard Weather Boating Party* in *Humana Festival 2009: The Complete Plays*. Edited by Adrien-Alice Hansel and Amy Wegener. New York: Playscripts, 2009b.

———. "The Ethics of Ethnic." *The Dramatist* (September 2010).

———. *And I and Silence*. London: Faber and Faber, 2011a.

———. "Comment: A Radical's Radical." *TDR – The Drama Review* (Fall 2011b).

———. "A State of Innocence." *PAJ: A Journal of Performance and Art* 84 (September—"No Such Cold Thing." In *Acts of War: Iraq and Afghanistan In Seven Plays*, 317–42. Edited by Karen Malpede, Michael Messina, and Bob Shuman. Evanston: Northwestern University Press, 2011c.

———. *Fousdethéâtre.* Interview by Thomas Baudeau. YouTube. May 2, 2012. Accessed May 12, 2012. http://www.youtube.com/watch?v=8XmHQD2u1v4.

———. "Let the Right One In." *American Theatre* 30.1 (January 2013): 88, 90–94.

Wallace, Naomi and Kwame Kwei-Armah. "Kwame and Naomi Dream of a Different America." In Next Stage Resource Guide: *Things of Dry Hours*, 6–7. Baltimore: Center Stage Associates, 2007b.

Wallace, Naomi and Bruce McLeod. "*In the Sweat.*" *New Connections 1997: New Plays for Young People*, 333–76. Edited by Suzy Graham-Adriani, Nick Drake, and Jim Milligan. London: Faber and Faber, 1997.

———. *The Girl Who Fell Through the Hole in Her Sweater*. New York: Broadway Play Publishing, 2003.

Warner, Michael. *Publics and Counterpublics*. New York: Zone, 2002.

Wise, Tim. *White Like Me: Reflections on Race from a Privileged Son*. New York: Soft Skull, 2011.

Wisner, Buell. "Waiting in the Angel's Wings: Marxist Fantasia in Naomi Wallace's *Slaughter City*." *Journal of American Drama and Theatre* 18 no. 1 (Winter 2006): 54–70.

Wolfe, Patrick. *Settler Colonialism and the Transformation of Anthropology: The Politics and Poetics of an Ethnographic Event*. London and New York: Cassell, 1999.

Contributors

Shannon Baley teaches with University Programs and the School of Humanities at St. Edward's University in Austin, Texas. Her poetry and essays have appeared in *Modern Drama, Experiments in a Jazz Aesthetic, Texas International Law Journal, Texas Borderlands Poetry Review,* and *Farfelu Literary Magazine.*

Walter Bilderback is Dramaturg/Literary Manager at the Wilma Theater in Philadelphia. From 1998 to 2003, he was Director of Theatre at Georgia College & State University. He has worked at numerous regional theaters around the United States as both a resident and freelance dramaturg, as well as on the Broadway production of Lee Blessing's *A Walk in the Woods.*

Art Borreca is Associate Professor of Dramatic Literature and Dramaturgy and Co-Head of the MFA Playwriting and Dramaturgy Programs at the University of Iowa. He has worked as a production dramaturg at the Yale Repertory Theatre, New York Theatre Workshop, LaMama ETC, Oxford Stage Company, and Theatre Project Tokyo, among other theatres. His articles and reviews have appeared in *TDR (The Drama Review), Modern Drama,* and *Theatre Journal,* as well as in several collections, including *Dramaturgy in American Theatre* and *What is Dramaturgy?.* He is a Contributing Editor of *The Norton Anthology of Drama.*

Neil Chudgar is Assistant Professor of English at Macalester College in Saint Paul, Minnesota. He is finishing a book called *Modern Touch,* which is about object-relations in the eighteenth century; his next project, *The Hazard of Loving the Creatures,* will concern the origins of the cute. His essay "Swift's Gentleness" appeared in *ELH.*

Beth Cleary is a director, playwright, and scholar whose research interests include political and feminist theatre, devised performance, and currently, oral histories with unionized nurses working in managed care. She has directed staged readings of plays by Jerome and McKnight Fellows for the Playwrights Center in Minneapolis and of Naomi Wallace's *And I and Silence* for the Eclipse Theater Company in Chicago. She is Associate Professor and Chair of the Theater and Dance Department at Macalester College, where she has taught since 1993.

Lindsay B. Cummings is Assistant Professor of Theatre Studies at the University of Connecticut. Her research focuses on affect theory, feminist performance, community-based performance, and theatre for social change. She received her PhD from Cornell University and has worked as a dramaturg in the literary and education departments of Portland Stage Company and the Actors Theatre of Louisville.

Scott T. Cummings is Associate Professor of Dramatic Literature and Playwriting and Chair of the Theatre Department at Boston College. He is the author *of Remaking American Theatre: Charles Mee, Anne Bogart and the SITI Company* (Cambridge University Press, 2006), *Maria Irene Fornes* (Routledge, 2012), and numerous performance reviews, essays, and articles on contemporary American theatre and drama.

Vivian Gornick is an American critic, essayist, and memoirist whose works include *Essays in Feminism, The Men in My Life, Women in Science: Then and Now, The Romance of Communism, Fierce Attachments: A Memoir and Approaching Eye Level*. For many years she wrote for the *Village Voice*. She currently teaches writing at The New School.

Josephine Machon is Senior Research Fellow in Contemporary Performance Practice at Middlesex University in London. She is the author of *(Syn)aesthetics: Redefining Visceral Performance* (2009, 2011) and the forthcoming Immersive Theatres: *Intimacy and Immediacy in Contemporary Performance*. With Susan Broadhurst, she is series coeditor for Palgrave Studies in Performance and Technology. Her interests also include theatre and disability, the intersections of theory and practice, and performance as a medium for research into human relationships with the environment.

Peter Rachleff is Professor of History at Macalester College, where he teaches courses and conducts research on US labor history, immigration, and African American History. He is the author of *Hard-Pressed in the Heartland: The Hormel Strike and the Future of the Labor Movement* (1993) and *Black Labor in Richmond, Virginia, 1865–1890* (1989), as well as articles and essays in *Dollars and Sense, Against the Current Dissent, MRZine, South Atlantic Quarterly*, and other publications. He has collaborated with Naomi Wallace on several projects, including *Things of Dry Hours* and *The Liquid Plain*. In 2012 he made his professional acting debut as Joseph McCarthy in the Pillsbury House Theatre/Guthrie Theatre production of Carlyle Brown's *Are You Now or Have You Ever Been?*

Erica Stevens Abbitt is Associate Professor at the School of Dramatic Art at the University of Windsor, Canada, where she teaches courses in theatre history, contemporary theatre, critical and gender studies, and Canadian theatre practice. She has worked as a theatre practitioner in Canada, France, Britain, New Zealand, and the United States. Her writing credits include translations, the book for an opera on Sojourner Truth (with composer Nyna Shannon Anderson), plays for children and *Shelter*, a drama based on her experience with the homeless in Manhattan. Her writings on feminist performance, contemporary theatre, youth culture, critical thinking, and theatre pedagogy have appeared in *Theatre Journal, Theatre Topics, Asian Theatre Journal, SIGNS: A Journal of Women and Culture, Performance Research, The Journal of Dramatic Theory and Criticism*, and *American Theatre* magazine.

Adam John Waterman is Assistant Professor in the Department of English at the American University of Beirut. His research interests include the representation of Islam in American literature and the relationship between US settler colonialism and the formation of American literary culture. He was a Fulbright Scholar-in-Residence in Algeria in 2010–2011 and has taught at Macalester College, University of Virginia, and Massachusetts College of Art and Design.

Buell Wisner is Assistant Professor of English at Georgia Perimeter College in Atlanta. His research interests include the history of the novel, postwar British literature, and historical fiction. Wisner has taught at Gordon College in Barnesville, Georgia and at the University of Tennessee-Knoxville, where he received his PhD.

Index

References in bold refer to photographic illustrations.

Aesthetic Theory, 75, 127–8, 131–2
Ahmed, Sara, 81, 183

Baley, Shannon, 19–34, 82, 155, 186n5
Barnett, Claudia, 13, 46, 173, 186n4
Benjamin, Walter, 47–9, 50–1, 54–5
Between This Breath and You. see *The Fever Chart: Three Visions of the Middle East*
Birdy, 4, 10, 172
Blackness, 129, 137, 144. see also Whiteness *and* Race
Blair, Rhonda, 73, 76–7
Brecht, 4, 14, 22, 24, 30–1, 45–7, 73–8, 80–2, 85, 98, 103, 170, 176
Brechtian theatre and theory, 14, 22, 31, 46, 71, 74, 76–7, 85, 98, 103, 170, 249. see also Gestus
Burke, Edmund, 127, 129–31

Capitalism, 13, 19, 21, 26, 31, 43, 45–6, 48, 61, 104, 116, 119, 137–9, 142. see also Marx and Marxism
Case, Sue-Ellen, 73

Child actors, 4, **4**, 176–82, 170, 175–81, **177**, **179**, 179–85
Child labor, 170, 174, 178, 181–2, 184–5
Class, 21–4, 26–7, 37, 45–6, 47–9, 53, 59, 61–3, 79, 113, 116, 119–20, 122–3, 137–9, 141

Daniels, Ron, 4, 23, **40**, **50**, 61, **62**, 140, **179**, 195–8, 200
Death, 21, 23, 27, 43, 49, 151, 155, 172–3, 178
Dialectic(s), 9, 16, 22, 30, 43, 46–8, 51, 53, 55, 74, 96, 108, 115, 138–9, 143, 152, 156, 163. see also Marx and Marxism
Diamond, Elin, 22–3, 30, 74, 84
Dolan, Jill, 21, 23, 33n2, 81, 82, 183
Dramaturgy, 10, 52, 76, 125n1,184
Dromgoole, Dominic, 3, 4, 6, **25**, 78, **83**, 125, 191–3

Empathy, 72–9, 80–2, 85, 122, 172
Erotics, 3, 10, 16, 19, 25, 39, 41, 43, 61, 68–9, 103, 108, 110, 116, 145, 172, 174, 177–8

Feminist theory and theatre, 19–34, 46, 73–4, 173–4, 177, 186n5
  Feminism and Brecht, 46, 73–4 (*see also* Elin Diamond)
  Feminist critique of Stanislavski, 73, 76–77, 86n4, 87n7 (*see also* Sue-Ellen) Case and Rhonda Blair
  Utopia and feminist performance, 21, 23, 33n3, 81, 82, 183 (*see also* Jill Dolan)
The Fever Chart: Three Visions of the Middle East, 5–6, 8, 45, 133, 155–67, **162**, 228–9
  Between This Breath and You, 5, 159–63, **162**
  The Retreating World, 5, 32–3, 67, 163–6
  A State of Innocence, 5, 11, 13–4, 157–60, **158**, 228
Flying Blind, 8

Garner, Stanton B. Jr. 41–3, 44n2
Gender, 21–2, 27, 30, 37, 51, 73–4, 92, 128–9, 136, 139
Gestus, 21–5, 27, 29, 30–2, 71, 77–8, 82. *see also* Brechtian theory
Ghosts and ghosting, 13–14, 20, 27, 28, 36, 48, 52, 56n7, 83, 123, 159, 172–3, 176–8, 150
The Girl Who Fell Through A Hole in Her Jumper, 15, 66, 171
Gothard, David, 3, 171, 187n7, 207–10

The Hard Weather Boating Party, 4, 11, 45, 146–51, **150**
Hogarth, William, 127–31
Homoeroticism, 24, 41, 111, 147
Homophobia, 3, 43, 45, 68, 84, 151, 169
Hurley, Erin, 183–4

Husserl, Edmund, 75, 86–7n6

And I and Silence, 7, 13, 91–6, **97**, 98–9, 237
In the Fields of Aceldama, 3, 13, 203–6
In the Heart of America, 3–4, 10–3, 14, 37–43, 67, 71–86, 109–12, 191, 216
In the Sweat, 4, 15, 171
The Inland Sea, 6, 66, 112–16, 117–25, 127–34, 173

Kelley, Robin D. G. 6, 11, 52, 143
Kushner, Tony, 3–4, 8, 45, 55, 58, 62, 179, 184
Kwei-Armah, Kwame, 6, 53, 93, 201

Labor, 4, 11, 19, 26, 28, 30, 37, 45, 48–9, 50–4, 105–7, 113, 119, 122, 131–2, 135–9, 170–2, 174, 176, 178, 181–6, 263. *see also* Child labor
Lawn Dogs, 5, 57, 171, 173, 179, 196
The Liquid Plain, 6–7, 10, 238–9

Marx, Karl, 53
  Communism, 52–3, 59, 91–2, 143–4, 236–7
  Marxism and Marxist theory, 45–8, 51–2, 54–6, 58, 185
Materialism
  Dialectical materialism, 47–8, 53, 163
  Historical materialism, 10–12, 48, 53, 74, 96
McLeod, Bruce, 3, 171, 241–3
McLeod, Caitlin, 92, **97**, 93–4, 185

Middle East, 5–6, 12, 133, 155–7, 211–13, 263, 285
Militarism, military and war, 8, 37, 67–8, 71, 83–4, 109–11, 138, 172–3, 187n7, 208–9, 222

Night Is a Room, 8
No Such Cold Thing, 6, 13, 15

One Flea Spare, 3–4, 7, 10, 12–5, 23–7, **25**, 30–1, 37–9, **40**, 43, 45, 55, 57–8, 61–3, 66–8, 115, 122, 171, 173–4, 178, **179**–80
One Short Sleepe, 6, 14

Palestine, 5, 6, 13, 32, 155–6, 158, 212, 231–4, 267–9
Pedagogy and classroom practices, 1, 8, 71, 86, 91, 100, 103–16, 106, 172, 173, 183, 223–5, 201, 202, 282–6
Phenomenology, 41–3, 75, 83, 86–7n6. *see also* Merleau-Ponty, and Stanton Garner, Jr.

Queer theory and theatre, 81, 111, 113, 156, 160, 166,186n1. *see also* Sarah Ahmed

Race, 9, 15, 37, 53, 58, 71, 93, 135–40, 143, 145, 147
Rawalpindi, 6, 221
Realism and anti-realism, 22, 32, 47, 48, 52, 175–6, 181, 184, 213
  Magic realism, 13, 52, 135, 228
  Social realism, 48, 58, 63
The Retreating World see *The Fever Chart*
Ridout, Nicholas, 174–6, 182–4

Scenography and design, 12, 21, **62**, 83, 91, 98, 100, 106, 108, 169, 204, 199–201
Sex, 11, 14, 19, 20–4, 26–7, 30, 38–40, 43, 46, 55, 58, 61, 65, 68, 73, 93, 96, 98, 103–5, 107, 110–5, 117, 123–4, 128–9, 135, 144–5, 147, 151, 172–3, 176–9
Shaw, Raz, 6, 92, 219–22
Slaughter City, 4, 12–3, 15, 23, 37–, 41, 43, 46, 48–9, **50**–2, 55–6, 58, 63, 89, 105–9, 139–42, **140**
Springsteen, Bruce, 220
Stanislavski, Konstantin, 71, 73–4, 76–7, 86n2–4, 87n7
A State of Innocence see *The Fever Chart*
(Syn)aesthetics, 89, 90–1, 94, 99

The Tal Pidae Lehrstücke, 11, 275–9
Things of Dry Hours, 6, 10, 14, 36, 45, 47, 52, 54–6, 91–4, 98–100, 143–6, 151, 236–8
To Perish Twice, 6
Transgression, 8, 26, 90, 91, 93,108, 169–82, 281–6
The Trestle at Pope Lick Creek, 4, 12, 15, 19–20, 21, 27–30, **29**, 45, 65, 100, 172–4, 176–7, **177**, 200, 220, 236
Twenty One Positions, 5, 211, 224–5, 233–4, 294

Utopianism, 20–3, 25, 27–8, 30–3, 47–8, 51, 53, 55–6, 81–2, 84, 86, 125, 155–6, 158, 160

Verfremdungseffekt, 46, 75, 81–2. *see also* Brechtian theory

Wallace, Naomi
  Activism, 3, 5, 6, 59, 84, 175, 182–3, 209, 223, 232, 249, 261–2, 267–9, 282–6
  Biography, 1–8
  Characters, 9–13, 15, 23, 36–9, 41–4, 55, 72, 81–2, 85, 96, 98–9, 100, 103–6, 117–8, 139, 151, 170–4, 184–5
  Plays (*see* individual listings by title)
  Poetry and poetics, 3, 4, 16, 33, 36, 57, 66, 90, 91, 96–8, 100, 101n4, 106, 135, 181, 196, 205, 207–8, 209, 211, 212, 213, 216, 236
  Screenwriting (*see* individual films by title) 5, 8, 57, 173, 195, 197, 220, 241, 242
  Use of language, 5, 16, 58–9, 61–3, 93, 109, 135, 163–5, 170, 177, 184, 215–17, 227–8
War Boys, 3, 7, 12, 45, 58, 68, 94, 197
Whiteness, 135–49, 151. *see also* Race
Word's A Slave, 221

Youth, 15, 104, 170–4, 177, 183–6, 271–4

Zionism, 11, 13, 155, 158–60

GPSR Compliance

The European Union's (EU) General Product Safety Regulation (GPSR) is a set of rules that requires consumer products to be safe and our obligations to ensure this.

If you have any concerns about our products, you can contact us on

ProductSafety@springernature.com

In case Publisher is established outside the EU, the EU authorized representative is:

Springer Nature Customer Service Center GmbH
Europaplatz 3
69115 Heidelberg, Germany

www.ingramcontent.com/pod-product-compliance
Lightning Source LLC
LaVergne TN
LVHW011007250326
834688LV00004B/119